Anarchy
and
Cooperation

Anarchy
and
Cooperation

Michael Taylor
University of Essex

JOHN WILEY & SONS
London · New York · Sydney · Toronto

Library of Congress Cataloging in Publication Data:

Taylor, Michael.
    Anarchy and cooperation.

    Bibliography: p.
    Includes index.
    1. Anarchism and anarchists.   2. Public interest. I. Title.
HX833.T38   1976   335′.83   75–12589

ISBN 0 471 84647 3

Photosetting by Thomson Press (India) Ltd.,
New Delhi and Printed in Great Britain by
The Pitman Press Ltd., Bath, Avon.

Preface

'Anarchy' being such a misused and abusive word, I had better make it clear
at the outset that *Anarchy and Cooperation* is about cooperation *in the absence
of government*. It is in fact a critique of what I believe to be the most persuasive—
and in the West probably the most popular—justification of the state. At the
heart of this justification is the argument that, without the state, people would
not act so as to realize their common interests; more specifically, they would
not voluntarily cooperate to provide themselves with certain public goods:
goods, that is to say, which any member of the public may benefit from, whether
or not he contributes in any way to their provision. Hobbes's *Leviathan* was
the first full expression of this way of justifying the state. The public goods with
which he was principally concerned were 'order'—domestic peace and security—and defence against foreign aggression. In our own time, his theory, or
something very like it, finds fresh support amongst those who are concerned
with the environmental crisis. For these environmentalists, such things as
cleaner air and waterways, control of population growth and protection of
endangered species must be provided by the state, or the state must somehow
ensure that people will cooperate to provide them.

Of course, many people believe that the state can be justified on further
grounds and that it has functions other than that of providing public goods.
Certainly, modern states do more than provide such goods. However, the
justification I wish to criticize here is common to the arguments of nearly all
those, in the West at least, who believe that the state is necessary. Its persua-
siveness lies in the fact that the state, on this view, exists to further *common*
interests, to do what *everybody* wants done. Other arguments for the state, for
example, that income redistribution and 'fairer' distributions generally, are
desirable and can be obtained only through the intervention of the state, do
not appeal to common interests, not, at any rate, in an obvious or uncontro-
versial way.

I have found it necessary (and I think profitable) to use some elementary
mathematics in parts of my argument. The mathematics are mainly confined

to Chapters 3 and 4. Although these chapters are about 'games' and 'super-games' they can be read by someone ignorant of game theory and only a little algebra is required. For those who cannot or will not read any mathematics at all, I have given (in Chapter 5) an informal summary of the two mathematical chapters, and it should be possible for the non-mathematical reader to follow the argument of the whole book by omitting these two chapters in favour of a careful reading of Chapter 5. Those who read Chapters 3 and 4 might neverthe-less find Chapter 5 useful as a recapitulation and will, in any case, find some material there which is not in the earlier chapters, namely a brief attempt to interpret and evaluate the mathematical results and (in Section 5.3) a consi-deration of some ways in which the supergame model might be modified or extended so as to provide a more realistic picture of the process of public goods provision.

Of the two mathematical chapters, the main one deals with the Prisoners' Dilemma supergame (the ordinary Prisoners' Dilemma game played an in-definite number of times), in both its two-person and N-person forms. Very little has been written about the N-person Prisoners' Dilemma game and even less about its supergame: all the attention has been directed towards the two-person (non-iterated) ordinary game, which, needless to say, has little to do with anything of importance in the real world.

I owe much to the kind help of Brian Barry, Alan Carling, Ian Grant and Michael Nicholson, who commented extensively on the manuscript. The book was written during 1973–74 when I was a Fellow at the Netherlands Institute for Advanced Study in the Humanities and Social Sciences, and I am grateful to the Institute and its staff for their hospitality and help.

Wivenhoe, Essex   MICHAEL TAYLOR
January 1975

Contents

viii

CHAPTER 1

Introduction

1.1. SURVIVAL, SECURITY AND THE STATE

In recent years, an old argument about the necessity of strong and centralized states has found new supporters. Their common concern is the environmental crisis: the combined effects of rapid population growth, depletion of non-renewable resources and environmental deterioration. They believe that only through powerful state action can the crisis be either averted or survived.[1]

There have of course been other responses to the environmental crisis. In particular, some writers, who probably did not think of themselves as anarchists, have come to embrace essentially communitarian anarchist ideas. However, of those who desire on ecological grounds the goal of a social organization along communitarian anarchist lines, there are very few who believe that a transition to such a society can be made without extensive state activity.[2]

As for the members of governments themselves, and indeed of most political parties, especially in industrialized countries, they generally do not recognize that there is or will be an environmental crisis and they believe, not unnaturally, that pollution and resource depletion are problems which can be adequately dealt with by minor modifications within the present institutional framework of whatever country they happen to live in.[3] Generally speaking, the proposed modifications involve an extension of state activity, in the form of state-enforced pollution standards and resource depletion quotas, taxes on industrial pollution, government subsidies and tax credits for the development of pollution control technology, and so on. Most economists who have written on problems of pollution and resource depletion have also confined their discussions to 'solutions' of this sort.

At the heart of most of the environmentalist justifications of the state or of extensions of the scope of state power is the argument that people will not *voluntarily* restrain themselves from doing those things of which the environmental crisis is the aggregate effect. They will not voluntarily refrain from hunting whales and other species threatened with extinction, from having 'too many' children, from discharging untreated wastes into rivers and lakes, and so on. The argument has two parts. The first part has been set out most explicitly in connection with environmental problems by Garrett Hardin.[4] (The second part will be introduced in Section 1.3 below.) Hardin asks us to imagine a commons, a pasture open to all. The village herdsmen keep animals on the commons. Each herdsman is assumed to seek to maximize his own gain. As long as the total number of animals is below the carrying capacity of the commons, a herdsman can add an animal to his herd without affecting the amount of grazing of any of the animals, including his own. But beyond this point, the 'tragedy of the commons' is set in motion. Asking himself now whether he should add another animal to his herd, he sees that this entails for him a gain and a loss: on the one hand, he obtains the benefit from this animal's yield (milk, meat, or whatever); on the other hand, the yield of each of his animals is reduced because there is now overgrazing. The benefit obtained from the additional animal accrues entirely to the herdsman. The effect of overgrazing, on the other hand, is shared by all the herdsmen; every one of them suffers a slight loss. Thus, says Hardin, the benefit to the herdsman who adds the animal is greater than *his* loss. He therefore adds an animal to the commons. For the same reason, he finds that it pays him to add a second animal, and a third, a fourth, and so on. The same is true for each of the other herdsmen. The result is that the herdsmen collectively bring about a situation in which each of them derives less benefit from his herd than he did before the carrying capacity of the commons was exceeded. The process of adding animals may indeed continue until the ability of the commons to support livestock collapses entirely.

For similar reasons, many species of fish and whales are hunted without limit and in some cases brought close to extinction: the oceans are like a great commons. For similar reasons, too, lakes and rivers are polluted, since each polluter finds that the costs of treating his wastes before discharging them or of modifying his product are too great in comparison with what he suffers from the decline in the quality of the air or water caused by his effluent.

In all these situations, we can say that it is in every individual's interest not to restrain himself (from adding animals to the commons, polluting the lake, etc.) but the result of everyone acting without restraint is a state of affairs in which every individual is less well off than he would be if everybody restrained themselves.

In such situations, we might expect people to make an agreement in which they all promised to restrain themselves. However, no individual has any greater incentive to abide by the agreement than he had to restrain himself voluntarily before the agreement was made.

The recent history of the whale fisheries provides a sad example. During the 1950s and 1960s, unlimited killing of blue and finback whales, which are the biggest, brought these two species close to extinction. When stocks of blues and finbacks became very low, the other large species were hunted without limit. In each case the annual harvest far exceeded the maximum sustainable yield, i.e. the maximum number which can be replaced each year through reproduction (and the whale hunters knew this). The profitability of whaling declined, and most of the former whaling countries were obliged one by one to leave the industry (so that, by 1968, there were only two countries, Japan and the U.S.S.R., left in the field). It seems fairly certain that if it were not for the diminished profits from hunting a sparse population, the blue whale and other species would in fact have been hunted to extinction. After the Second World War, the International Whaling Commission was set up by the seventeen countries who were then interested in whaling and was charged with regulating harvests and ensuring the survival of threatened species. Until very recently, this Commission, which has no powers of enforcement, has not been very successful. Its members were often unable to agree to impose the quotas recommended by biologists, or else they could agree only to limits in excess of these recommendations; and when the Commission did decide either to limit harvests or to protect a species completely, the agreement was not always observed by every country.[5]

This, then, is the first step in the environmentalist justification of the state: people will not voluntarily restrain themselves from killing whales, polluting the lake, and so on; and they will not voluntarily abide by agreements to do so. The second step is to infer from this that coercion is necessary (or that people will agree to be coerced), and that the only effective means of coercion is a strong, centralized state.

Now this, as I have said, is an old argument. It is essentially the argument made by Thomas Hobbes in *Leviathan*. He was concerned, not with environmental problems, but above all with domestic peace and security and also with national defence. If each individual pursues his own interest without restraint (that is to say, in the absence of government), then in the resulting state of affairs (which is a 'war of all against all') each individual is less happy than he would be if everyone restrained themselves (which is a condition of peace and security). It is therefore rational, says Hobbes, for men to institute a government with sufficient power to ensure that everybody keeps the peace.[6]

The 'war of all against all' and the 'tragedy of the commons' are both characterized by the failure of people to provide themselves with *public goods*.

A public good can be defined (for the time being) as a good which has the property that, if any amount of the good is provided, any member of the public in question can benefit from it whether or not he contributed to its provision; it cannot be appropriated by a particular individual and enjoyed exclusively by him. Hardin's commons is a public good for the village herdsmen. A lake or river is a public good for those who may use it freely to swim or fish in, to cool their reactors, or as a receptacle for their sewage and industrial wastes. A wilderness area is a public good. So are whales, in at least two different ways: the mere knowledge of their existence is a source of pleasure to many people (for ecological, 'humanitarian' or even aesthetic reasons); and as long as there is not an effectively enforced ban against any individual or country killing them, they are a public good to the whale hunters, for the hunter may exploit them, if he wishes, whether or not he has contributed to their preservation (by not exceeding his quota, for example). Peace and security are public goods, too: a man benefits whether or not he is doing his part in preserving them, whether or not he contributes taxes for the maintenance of police forces and law courts, and so on.

Now we can restate Hardin's argument in this way: it is in no individual's private interest to contribute to the provision of a public good (by treating his sewage, not exceeding his quota of whales, or whatever) because the cost to him of doing so is greater than the benefit *to him* of the additional amount of the public good (an improvement in water quality, etc.) which would result from his contribution. Thus the public good will not be provided or else an insufficient amount will be provided. Every individual will try to be a 'free rider', hoping to benefit, without making a contribution, from the public good provided by others.

The issue is much more complicated than this, as we shall see (mainly in the next chapter). In the first place, no reference has been made to the *size* of the group for which the good is public, and this would seem to have an important effect on the ability of the group's members to provide themselves voluntarily with a public good. The connection between group size and the provision of public goods has been analysed in some detail by Mancur Olson in his well-known study, *The Logic of Collective Action*. Olson's main conclusion is that 'the larger a group is, the farther it will fall short of providing an optimal supply of any collective (public) good, and the less likely that it will act to obtain even a minimal amount of such a good. In short, the larger the group, the less likely it will further its common interests'.[7] The chief reason for this is that the larger the group, the smaller is the benefit which accrues to any individual member from the additional amount of the public good provided out of his contribution; thus, in a relatively large group this benefit is likely to be less than the cost to him of making the contribution, whereas in a relatively small group this may not be the case. The large group will provide itself with the public good only if there is a *selective* incentive for an individual to contribute, a private benefit which the individual can enjoy *only if* he contributes. Thus, a trade union is primarily formed in order to provide for its members certain public goods, such as higher wages and better working conditions. But no individual, though he desires these things, would pay his dues; he would hope to be a 'free rider'. Hence, says Olson, the 'closed shop' is operated (employment is conditional upon membership), members enjoy sickness benefits, and so on. These are selective benefits.

1.2. THE PRISONERS' DILEMMA

The preferences of individuals involved in the 'tragedy of the commons' and, more generally, of members of a group who fail to provide themselves voluntarily with a public good, would appear to be those of a game known as the Prisoners' Dilemma.[8] This game is defined as follows.

Suppose first that there are just two individuals (or *players*) and that each of them may choose between two courses of action (or *strategies*). The players are labelled 1 and 2 and the strategies C and D. The two players must choose strategies simultaneously, or, equivalently, each player must choose a strategy in ignorance of the other player's choice. A pair of strategies, one for each player, is called a *strategy vector*. Associated with each strategy vector is a *payoff* for each player. The payoffs can be arranged in the form of a *payoff matrix*. The payoff matrix for the two-person Prisoners' Dilemma which will be studied in this book is:

player 2

		C	D
	C	x, x	z, y
player 1			
	D	y, z	w, w

where $y > x > w > z$. Throughout the book, the usual convention is adopted that rows are chosen by player 1, columns by player 2, and that the first entry in each cell of the matrix is the payoff to player 1 and the second entry is 2's payoff.

Notice first that, since we have assumed $y > x$ and $w > z$, each player obtains a higher payoff if he chooses D than if he chooses C, *no matter what strategy the other player chooses*. Thus, it is in each player's interest to choose D, no matter what he expects the other player to do. D is said to *dominate* C for each player.

However, notice now that, if each player chooses his dominant strategy, the outcome of the game is that each player obtains a payoff w, whereas there is another outcome (C, C), which yields a higher payoff to both players, since we have assumed $x > w$.

Let us say that an outcome (Q) is *Pareto-optimal* if there is no other outcome which is not less preferred than Q by any player and is strictly preferred to Q by at least one player. An outcome which is not Pareto-optimal is said to be *Pareto-inferior*. Thus, in the two-person Prisoners' Dilemma, the outcome (D, D) is Pareto-inferior.

If the players could communicate and make agreements, they would presumably both agree to choose strategy C. But this would not resolve the 'dilemma', since neither has an incentive to keep the agreement: whether or not he thinks the other player will keep his part of the agreement, it pays him to defect from the agreement and choose D.

C and D are the conventional labels for the two strategies in the Prisoners' Dilemma. They stand for Cooperate and Defect. I use them throughout this book, though they are not entirely appropriate: one player may 'Cooperate' (choose C) by himself, and he may 'Defect' (choose D) even though no agreement has been made from which to defect. In this book, Cooperation and Defection (with capital initials) will always refer to strategies in a Prisoners' Dilemma.

If communication between the players is impossible or prohibited, or if communication may take place but agreements are not binding on the players, then the game is said to be *non-cooperative*. The Prisoners' Dilemma is defined to be a non-cooperative game. If it were not, there would be no 'dilemma': the players would obtain (C, C) as the outcome, rather than the Pareto-inferior outcome (D, D). In the situations of interest in this book, communication is generally possible but the players are not constrained to keep any agreements that may be made. It is the possibility of Cooperation (to achieve the outcome (C, C)) in the *absence* of such constraint that will be of interest.

As a generalization of this two-person game, an N-person Prisoners' Dilemma can be defined as follows. Each of the N players has two strategies, C and D, available to him. For each player, D dominates C; that is, each player obtains a higher payoff if he chooses D than if he chooses C, no matter what strategies the other players choose. However, every player prefers the outcome $(C, C, ..., C)$ at which everybody Cooperates to the outcome $(D, D, ..., D)$ at which everybody Defects. Thus, as in the two-person game, every player has a dominant strategy but if every player uses his dominant strategy the outcome is Pareto-inferior.

Two-person and N-person Prisoners' Dilemmas can both be defined in the more general case when any finite number of strategies is available to each player. The generalization, which could be made in several ways, must at least have the characteristic that the predicted outcome is Pareto-inferior. In particular, it could again be stipulated that every player has a strategy which dominates each of the others, and if every player uses his dominant strategy the outcome is Pareto-inferior. I shall not elaborate on this here, as my discussion in this book will be confined to the two-strategy games, apart from occasional brief references.

There is, however, an additional difficulty in the multi-strategy Prisoners' Dilemma, which is not present in the two-strategy game. In the latter, there is only one outcome which everyone prefers to (D, D); in the multi-strategy case, there may be several, and several of these in turn may be Pareto-optimal. In this case, it may be difficult for the players to agree on one of the Pareto-optimal outcomes. I shall not treat this additional problem. The Prisoners' Dilemma element is the fundamental problem of concern here, for it is this element which provides the foundation for the argument I am interested in. By concentrating on the simplest two-strategy Prisoners' Dilemmas, this element is kept in focus.

Let us go back now to the 'tragedy of the commons' and, more generally, to the problems of the voluntary provision of public goods. In Garrett Hardin's account, each individual has in effect a dominant strategy: to add an animal to his herd on the commons, to discharge his sewage untreated, to kill as many whales as possible, and so on. Each of these corresponds to strategy D. The alternative, strategy C, is to refrain from doing these things. Hardin assumes, in effect, that D yields the highest payoff to each individual, no matter what strategies the other individuals choose (that is, no matter how many of them Cooperate); and he assumes that every individual prefers the mutual Cooperation outcome $(C, C, \ldots, C)$, to the mutual Defection outcome, $(D, D, \ldots, D)$. In other words, individual preferences are assumed to be those of an N-person Prisoners' Dilemma.

Russell Hardin has made this argument more explicitly, in connection with the provision of any public good.[9] Strategy C corresponds to contributing a unit of the costs of providing the public good and D corresponds to contributing nothing. Hardin's argument, which he puts forward as a restatement of Olson's central argument, is that if the group is sufficiently large, the individual preferences are those of an N-person Prisoners' Dilemma. In this case, each individual chooses D and the public good is not provided.

This argument, if correct, would apply also to the public goods with which Hobbes was chiefly concerned, namely domestic peace and security and national defence. I shall indeed show (in Chapter 6) that Hobbes assumed men's preferences in the absence of the state to be those of a Prisoners' Dilemma game. The remainder of Hobbes's theory can then be summarized, somewhat crudely, as follows: (a) in the absence of any coercion, it is in each individual's interest to choose strategy D; the outcome of the game is therefore mutual Defection; but every individual prefers the mutual Cooperation outcome; (b) the only way to ensure that the preferred outcome is obtained is to establish a government with sufficient power to ensure that it is in every man's interest to choose C.

This is the argument which I wish to criticize in this book. It is this argument, or something very like it, which is now being used (though sometimes not very explicitly) by those who believe that only by means of a strong, centralized state can we avert or survive the environmental crisis.

There is one element of the argument which I shall not quarrel with, namely, the analysis of the Prisoners' Dilemma given above. If individual preferences in the provision of a public good are in fact those of a Prisoners' Dilemma, then it is quite correct to conclude that the players will not voluntarily Cooperate. To avoid any misunderstanding, I emphasize that the conclusion is correct no matter what the entries in the payoff matrix (which is assumed to be a Prisoners' Dilemma) actually represent, just as long as it is assumed that each player is concerned only to maximize his own payoff. Of course, the payoffs may not reflect *all* the incentives affecting the individuals in the situation in question. The conclusion still follows logically; but it is possible to argue that the payoff matrix is a poor description of the relevant real world situation and that in reality the players *do* Cooperate, because the omitted incentives are more important than those reflected in the payoff matrix.

In the next two chapters, the payoffs are assumed *not* to reflect two kinds of incentives: on the one hand, those due to internal norms and values and the informal sanctions sometimes used to secure conformity to them; and on the other, those due to external coercion, especially that applied or threatened by the state. The first class is a broad one. It includes such things as an internalized sense of duty or obligation to act altruistically or cooperatively. In such cases, an individual who does not perform his duty or act cooperatively may be subject to the 'internal sanctions' of guilt, loss of self-respect, and so on, even if he is not detected, and he may also be subject to sanctions like public ridicule and ostracism if he is detected.[10]

In Chapter 4, I shall begin with a matrix of payoffs which again do not reflect these two classes of incentives, but then I shall consider the effects of assuming that individuals are 'altruistic' (that is, they take account of other players' payoffs as well as their own in choosing strategies), and this altruism *may* be the result of internalized norms and values.

The expression, 'voluntary' Cooperation, used occasionally throughout the book, refers to Cooperation (in a Prisoners' Dilemma game) chosen only on the basis of the matrix of payoffs (or utilities, where the individual is in some way altruistic); thus, 'voluntary' Cooperation is Cooperation which is *not* the result of external coercion, including that applied or threatened by the state.

1.3. TIME

The explanation given by Garrett Hardin for the 'tragedy of the commons' can be restated, as we have seen, in terms of the Prisoners' Dilemma game. The 'tragedy' arises because, at any point in time, each individual finds it in his interest to exploit the commons (choose strategy *D*) no matter what the others do. The 'tragedy' does *not* arise, as some people have written, because each man reasons that '*since* the others are going to ruin the commons anyway, I may as well exploit it too'. (In fact, if the others do *not* exploit the commons, if they restrain themselves and choose strategy *C*, then each individual will find it even more profitable to exploit it than if they do.) It cannot be said, then, that the commons would not be ruined if only *one* individual had access to it; that if a lake and all its lakeside factories were owned by one man, he would treat his wastes before discharging them into the lake; that if one man had an exclusive right to kill whales, he would see that they did not become extinct.

But surely, it may be said, the sole hunter of whales would not kill them all off, for his whole future livelihood, or at least all his future profits, depends on their survival. Unfortunately, this may not be the case.

Consider a commons which one man has exclusive rights to exploit without restraint, and suppose now that at some point in time he is contemplating his whole future course of action with respect to this commons. Let us suppose that he divides the future into equal time periods (months, years, or whatever) and that in each time period he will receive a payoff. The sequence of payoffs he will receive depends on the course of action he chooses (for example, how many whales he kills in each period). Clearly, what he chooses to do will depend on the *present* value to him of future payoffs. At one extreme he may place no value whatever on any payoff except the one in the time period immediately before him. In this case, the prospect of zero payoffs from some point in the future onwards (as a result of the extinction of the whales, for example) does not trouble him at all. He will act in each time period so as to maximize his payoff in the current time period, and the result may be the ruin of the commons.

It is generally assumed that future payoffs are exponentially *discounted* to obtain their present values. In the case when future time is divided into discrete periods, this means that the present value of a payoff X_t to be made t time periods from the present is $X_t a^t$, where a is a number such that $0 < a < 1$ and $1 - a$ is called the *discount rate*. The higher the discount rate, the lower the present value of future payoffs. If, for example, the individual's discount rate is 0.1 (that is, $a = 0.9$), then a payoff worth 100 units if received now would have a present value of 90 if it were to be received one period hence, 81 if it were to be received two periods hence, and so on. In certain cases, an individual's discount rate will be closely related to the current marginal opportunity cost of his capital in alternative investments.

Intuitively, we should expect that if the discount rate is sufficiently high, then an exploiter who is seeking to maximize present value may eventually and quite 'rationally' ruin the commons, even in the absence of other exploiters. This is confirmed by Colin Clark in his mathematical study of the exploitation of renewable resources (which, it should be remembered, include atmospheric, soil and water resources as well as such things as whales, fish and bison).[11] In the case when the resource of the commons is a biological population, the discount rate which is sufficiently high to result in the extinction of the population will depend above all on the reproductive capacity of the population. (In Clark's model, this is *all* it depends on.)

The ruin of the commons by a single individual, though it may be unfortunate, is not a 'tragedy' in Hardin's sense. (In the 'tragedy of the commons', the tragedy resides in the fact that 'rational' action on the part of each individual brings about a state of affairs which nobody wants.) Nor would it be a 'tragedy' if several individuals with similar preferences, including a shared high discount rate, ruined the commons together, for this outcome would not be Pareto-inferior for them.

I have briefly considered this case of the lone exploiter in order to underline a shortcoming of the Prisoners' Dilemma model of behaviour on the commons considered in the preceding two sections: it is a *static* model, containing no reference to time; players make one choice (to contribute or not to contribute) once and for all; and there is no discounting of future payoffs, or any other form of intertemporal preferences. Whether or not it is true that in the problem of the commons (or more generally of the provision of public goods) individual preferences *at any point in time* have the structure of a Prisoners' Dilemma, it clearly is the case that there are sequences of choices and that time and the individual's valuation of future payoffs play an important role.

1.4. THE SCOPE OF THE BOOK

The strongest case which can be made for the desirability of the state is that, without it, people would not realize their common interests, and, in particular, would not provide themselves with public goods or at any rate with Pareto-optimal amounts of these goods. The case can be made even stronger, perhaps, by restricting this argument to those public goods whose provision is thought to be essential to the preservation of social order or even to the preservation of human life. The argument that people will not voluntarily provide themselves with public goods rests in turn on the argument or assumption (usually only tacit) that the relevant individual preferences are those of a Prisoners' Dilemma, at least where relatively large numbers of individuals are involved.

Now I believe that very many people accept or have accepted this justification of the state, or something very like it. Amongst political theorists, the argument was set out most explicitly by Hobbes and Hume. Many writers who came after them, including some who professed no sympathy with what they took to be Hobbes's ideas, have taken over the core of his case for the state. Most economists who nowadays write about public goods believe that the failure of people to provide themselves voluntarily with these goods constitutes at least a *prima facie* case for state activity, and most of them presume that the state is the *only* means of remedying this failure.[12]

My purpose in this book is to challenge this argument: to indicate where the reasoning is faulty and what is missing from the argument and above all to call into question the very formulation of the problem and the framework within which it is treated. I shall try to do this in three stages, as follows.

(1) In Chapter 2, I shall briefly show that the connections between public goods provision, the size of the 'public' and the Prisoners' Dilemma are not as simple as Olson and others have argued (and as they have been presented in this Introduction). In particular, I shall show that the Prisoners' Dilemma does not necessarily arise in connection with the provision of public goods even in relatively large groups: that *static* individual preferences—the preferences at any point in time—are not necessarily those of a Prisoners' Dilemma.

(2) Assuming, however, that the 'game' at any point in time *is* a Prisoners' Dilemma, I shall go on to show (in Chapter 3) that if *time* is introduced and the problem is treated more dynamically, then under certain circumstances voluntary Cooperation is rational for each player, even assuming that he seeks to maximize only his own (discounted) payoff.

My argument here will be cased in terms of the Prisoners' Dilemma *supergame*. This is the game consisting of an indefinite number of iterations of one of the Prisoners' Dilemma games (two-person and *N*-person) which were defined earlier. In each *ordinary game* (as the repeated game is now called), players choose strategies simultaneously, as before, but they know the strategies chosen by all other players in previous games. Each player discounts future payoffs; his discount rate does not change with time, but discount rates may differ between players. The ordinary game is assumed not to change with time. (It would be desirable to relax this last assumption in a more general treatment, and permit the payoff matrix to change with time. See Section 5.3 below.)

The really important difference between the single ordinary game and the supergame is that players' strategies can be made interdependent in the supergame but not, of course, in the ordinary game since players must choose strategies simultaneously or in ignorance of each others' choices. In the supergame, a player can, for example, decide to Cooperate in each ordinary game *if and only if* the other player(s) Cooperated in the previous ordinary game. It is on this possibility, the possibility of using *conditional* strategies, that the voluntary Cooperation of all the players turns.

(3) Finally, in Chapter 7, I shall raise doubts about the way in which this justification of the state is approached. It is an essential and fundamental feature of the theory I am criticizing that it takes individual preferences as given and fixed. In particular, it is assumed that the state itself has no effect on these preferences. This rules out *ab initio* the possibility, amongst many others, that the state may exacerbate an already existing Prisoners' Dilemma or create a Prisoners' Dilemma where none existed before: that the state may affect, in other words, the very conditions which are supposed to make it necessary. If preferences may change, especially as a result of the activities of the state itself, it is not at all clear what is *meant* by the desirability of the state.

Criticisms of this sort can of course be levelled against any theory which is founded on assumptions about fixed individual preferences (as most of economic theory and much political theory is); but they are especially important, it seems to me, when the theory purports to justify an institution (like the state) and when the theory is to apply to a very long period of time (as a theory used to justify the state or to explain its origin must do).

I have said that the arguments which are the object of my criticisms in this book have been set out most explicitly by Thomas Hobbes and David Hume. I shall therefore give (in Chapter 6) an exposition of their political theories. My chief reason for devoting to this exposition a rather long chapter later in the book, rather than a short summary at the start of the book where it would otherwise belong, and for making what would otherwise be an unpardonable addition to the considerable critical literature on Hobbes, is that I think it is illuminating to look at these theories in terms of some of the ideas presented in the earlier chapters (1, 3 and 4) on the Prisoners' Dilemma and its supergame. I have asserted rather baldly in this informal Introduction that Hobbes's theory is about non-Cooperation in Prisoners' Dilemma games (other writers have made similar assertions, equating Hobbes's theory with, for example, Hardin's analysis of the 'tragedy of the commons'); but the story is more complicated and more interesting than this and deserves a fuller account.

Hume's political theory is very similar to Hobbes's, in spite of his objections to what he took to be a fundamental element of Hobbes's theory (the idea of the social contract). Nevertheless, I shall consider them both. For, although Hobbes's version is (in *Leviathan*) generally the more rigorous of the two, it suffers from being too static, whereas this deficiency is partly supplied in Hume's treatment. Hobbes, in effect, treats only a Prisoners' Dilemma *ordinary* game; whereas Hume's treatment is more dynamic, with the discounting of future benefits playing an important role. Also, in Hume, but not in Hobbes, there is explicit recognition of the effects of size, a partial anticipation of Olson's 'logic of collective action'.

Some of the ideas I am interested in here appeared much earlier than *Leviathan* (above all in the *Book of Lord Shang* and the works of Han Fei Tzu which were written in China in the fourth and third centuries B.C.), but it was Hobbes and Hume who gave the first full, explicit statements of the argument. In later political theorists the argument is not always explicit, does not stand out boldly, and is less precise and less coherent.

In *Leviathan*, Hobbes seems to assume that each man seeks to maximize not merely his own payoff, but also his 'eminence', the difference between his own and other men's payoffs. Hume, on the other hand, assumes that most men are chiefly concerned with their own payoffs but are also possessed of a limited amount of 'benevolence'. In both cases, individuals take *some* account of other individuals' payoffs; I call this 'altruism'. The effects of various sorts of altruism on the outcomes of Prisoners' Dilemma games are treated briefly in Chapter 4. Some of the material in that chapter will be of use in the discussion of Hobbes and Hume and also in the final chapter.

So much for what I propose to do in the following chapters. It should be clear that I shall *not* be providing a positive theory of anarchy or even an indication of how people might best provide themselves with public goods. The title of the book is nevertheless appropriate, for I am concerned throughout with cooperation in the absence of government. My intention is simply to weaken a widespread presumption that the state is necessary by criticizing what I think is the most powerful case for this belief.

1.5. NOTES

1. Two recent examples are William Ophuls, 'Leviathan or Oblivion?', in Herman E. Daly, (Ed.), *Toward a Steady-State Economy* (San Francisco: W. H. Freeman, 1973), and Robert L. Heilbroner, 'The Human Prospect', *The New York Review of Books*, January 24, 1974.

2. An approximate example is *A Blueprint for Survival*, by the editors of *The Ecologist* (Harmondsworth, Middlesex: Penguin Books, 1972; originally published as Vol. 2, No. 1 of *The Ecologist*, 1972). Their goal is not wholly anarchist, but it does include 'decentralisation of polity and economy at all levels, and the formation of communities small enough to be reasonably self-supporting and self-regulating'. For an anarchist's account of the necessity of anarchist society on ecological grounds, see Murray Bookchin, 'Ecology and Revolutionary Thought', in *Post-Scarcity Anarchism* (Berkeley, California: The Ramparts Press, 1971).

3. See, for example, Anthony Crosland, *A Social Democratic Britain* (Fabian Tract no. 404, London, 1971), and Jeremy Bray, *The Politics of the Environment* (Fabian Tract no. 412, London, 1972).

4. Garrett Hardin, 'The Tragedy of the Commons', *Science*, **162**, 1243–8 (1968).

5. For a brief account of the overexploitation of whales and various species of fish, see Paul R. Ehrlich and Anne H. Ehrlich, *Population, Resources, Environment*, second edition (San Francisco: W. H. Freeman, 1972), pp. 125–34. See also Frances T. Christy and Anthony Scott, *The Common Wealth in Ocean Fisheries* (Baltimore: Johns Hopkins Press, 1965).

6. This is a caricature of Hobbes's argument. In Chapter 6, I give a more detailed account, making use of ideas developed in Chapters 3 and 4.

7. Mancur Olson, *The Logic of Collective Action* (Cambridge, Mass: Harvard University Press, 1965), p. 36. The view that a number of people with a common interest (such as providing themselves with a public good) will necessarily cooperate voluntarily to realize it is labelled by Olson 'the anarchistic fallacy' (p. 131). It is very difficult to accuse the anarchists fairly of this. Their analyses are not based on the 'rational man' assumption of Olson's study. Usually, it is only with respect to *small* groups that they speak of voluntary cooperation. And their approach, unlike Olson's, is not static: they believe that cooperation would *grow* over time in the absence of the state. I discuss these things in Chapter 7. It would be fairer to label this view 'the liberal fallacy', as Brian Barry does in *The Liberal Theory of Justice* (Oxford: The Clarendon Press, 1973), p. 118.

8. The story about two prisoners, which gave the game its name, can be found in R. Duncan Luce and Howard Raiffa, *Games and Decisions* (New York: John Wiley, 1957), p. 95.

9. Russell Hardin, 'Collective Action as an Agreeable n-Prisoners' Dilemma', *Behavioural Science*, **16**, 472–81 (1971).

10. These are all 'selective incentives' in Olson's terminology. Olson explicitly makes no use of them in explaining public goods provision. See *The Logic of Collective Action*, p. 61, footnote 17. See also Brian Barry, *Sociologists, Economists and Democracy* (London: Collier-Macmillan, 1970), especially pp. 33 and 77–8.

11. Colin Clark, 'The Economics of Overexploitation', *Science*, **181**, 630–4, (August 17, 1973).

12. Both of these are true of William J. Baumol's *Welfare Economics and the Theory of the State*, second edition (London: G. Bell, 1965). Much of this book is devoted to the failure of individuals to provide themselves voluntarily with public goods, but I think it is fair to say that 'the Theory of the State' is missing. He is careful to say say that, before it is concluded that state action to ensure the supply of public goods is justified, all the *costs* of state action must also be taken into account (p. 22 in the introduction added to the second edition); nevertheless there is a *presumption* that *only* the state could ensure this supply (and the cumulative 'dynamic costs' of the state, which are introduced later in this section and are the subject of Chapter 7, are nowhere considered).

CHAPTER 2

The Provision of Public Goods

My chief purpose in this short chapter is to consider a little more carefully the idea which was introduced in the first chapter: to show how and in what circumstances the Prisoners' Dilemma arises in connection with the provision of public goods. Before doing this, some remarks on the concepts of public good and externality are necessary.

2.1. PUBLIC GOODS

The most basic characteristic of a public good is its indivisibility. A good is said to exhibit *indivisibility* or *jointness of supply* (with respect to a given set of individuals, or public) if, once produced, any given unit of the good can be made available to every member of the public.

There are degrees of indivisibility. The good may be only partially available to some individuals and in varying degrees; and actual consumption of the good may vary between individuals.[1] If every individual's actual consumption of any given unit is the same, then the good is said to be *perfectly* indivisible. This does not imply that every individual's *utility* in consuming the good is the same.

National defence approximates fairly closely to perfect *indivisibility*; so does clean air, for publics in areas in which the air is uniformly clean. On the other hand, a public road, though it may be equally available to all, is not in practice equally consumed (used) by all.

A loaf of bread or pot of honey is an example of a perfectly *divisible* good: it can be divided between individuals, and once any part of it is appropriated by any individual, the same part cannot be made available to others. A good which is perfectly divisible is called a *private good*.[2] A *public good* is then defined as any good which is not private. Thus, in order to be public, a good must exhibit some degree of indivisibility or jointness; but this does not mean that *publicness* is identified with jointness. There are other components of publicness.[3]

A good may exhibit jointness of supply and yet be such that it is possible to prevent particular individuals from consuming it. A road or bridge or park is such a good. Once supplied to one individual, it *can* be made available to others, but it need not, for particular individuals can be excluded. Tolls and admission charges can be imposed, or certain classes of individuals simply banned from entry. If this is not possible, the good is said to exhibit *non-excludability*.

Indivisibility, then, does not imply non-excludability. Furthermore, divisibility does not entail excludability, although important examples of non-excludable, divisible goods are not easy to come by: economists have suggested such examples as a garden of flowers, whose nectar can be appropriated by individual bees but particular bees cannot be excluded from consumption.

Although jointness and non-excludability are logically independent, they are of course frequently associated in practice.[4] Both properties are important for my purposes. If some amount of the good is already in supply, then an individual may take a 'free ride' (may consume the good without contributing to its production costs) only if the good exhibits some degree of jointness *and* the individual in question is not in fact excluded from consumption (whether he contributes or not). If the good is not yet provided in any amount, then an individual can *expect* to be able to take a free ride only if the good will be jointly supplied *and* he expects that he will not be excluded. If exclusion is actually impossible, this second condition obviously obtains; but it may also obtain even when the good is to be excludable.[5]

Most, if not all, jointly supplied goods are characterized by a certain degree of *rivalness*. A good is said to be *rival* to the extent that the *consumption* of a unit of the good by one individual affects the benefits to others who *consume* that same unit. In the polar case of a private good, the consumption of a particular unit prevents any other individual from consuming it at all, and it is said to be *perfectly rival*.

In the very important class of *congested* public goods (such as crowded parks, beaches and roads, and various forms of pollution), consumption by one individual usually *lowers* the utilities of other consumers. However, there are situations in which an individual's utility is *increased* by the consumption of others (even if the cost of his consumption remains unchanged). He may, for example, enjoy watching a film or football match more when the auditorium or stadium is full than when it is almost empty.

2.2. EXTERNALITIES

Related to, but quite distinct from publicness is the phenomenon of externality. I shall use this term in the broadest sense, and say that an *externality* (or external effect) is present whenever an individual's utility is affected by an activity of some other individual.[6] The production of non-excludable indivisible goods always involves externalities, but externalities are involved in interactions other than those associated with the production or consumption of public goods.

A very rough distinction can be made between *tangible* and *psychic* externalities.[7] If a lakeside factory's effluent diminishes a fisherman's catch, a tangible external effect has been exerted on him; if the factory spoils his view then a psychic externality is involved (he may suffer what has been called 'horizon pollution'). If you are distressed or delighted by my reading a certain book, then I am exerting a psychic external effect on you. And so on.

Clearly, most, if not all activities, including the production and consumption of private goods, have external effects of some sort, though often these are only of the psychic kind or affect only a very small number of individuals. The *production* of any jointly supplied good, however, *always* involves tangible externalities, and these affect all the members of the public in question. For as long as a good is jointly supplied, any member who is not in fact excludable benefits from the production of any amount of the good by any other member— whose activity therefore has an external effect.

These effects are in production. Tangible consumption externalities do not necessarily arise (and in practice usually do not arise) if the jointly supplied good exhibits non-rivalness.[8] The shipowner would of course be very happy that others build lighthouses but may be utterly indifferent about their use of them when built. I may be very happy that others act to conserve an uncongested 'wilderness' area, but their use of it probably has no tangible external effect on me whether I use it or not (though it may have psychic effects on me, whether I consume it or not: I may be delighted that others are benefiting from it).

These production externalities are not of course to be confused with those which are caused by the process of production itself, especially in the form of industrial pollution. These are mainly exerted by producers on non-producers and create, as a by-product, a public 'bad'. The removal or amelioration of this public 'bad' is a public good, and production externalities, of the sort mentioned above, are involved in its production.

If the jointly supplied good exhibits some rivalness in consumption, then consumption externalities arise as well as the production externalities: consumption of the good necessarily affects the benefits to other consumers. (The consumption of congested public goods, such as roads, often has tangible external effects on non-consumers too; and psychic effects can of course arise for consumers and non-consumers alike, whether there is rivalness or not.) If the good is perfectly rival, then there are usually no tangible externalities in consumption, though again there may be psychic effects for consumers or non-consumers.

The presence of an externality may, however, entail nothing whatever about the degree of rivalness. Rivalness is to do with the effects of one individual's consumption of a unit of the good on the benefits to others arising from their *consumption* of that same unit; but an externality is present whenever one person's activity (which may or may not be an act of consumption) affects the utility of another person (who may or may not be a consumer).

A number of writers have considered the presence of externalities as a *prima facie* reason for state intervention. As it stands, this position is not a very useful one, in my opinion. Probably every activity has an external effect of some kind. Even tangible external effects are almost universal. Also, very many activities have several different sorts of externalities, and these may affect different groups of people in different ways and in varying degrees. Again, many external effects involve only very small numbers of people. Finally, and most importantly, a state of affairs in which an external effect is being exerted may already be Pareto-optimal: there is no alternative position in which some individuals are better off and nobody is worse off. Buchanan and Stubblebine have called such an externality *Pareto-irrelevant*.[9] Suppose, for example, that an activity of yours creates external costs for me, and that the least you would accept as compensation for any particular modification of your activity is greater than the most that I am able or willing to give you for such a modification; then your activity exerts an externality on me which is Pareto-irrelevant. Or consider the following simple example, in which two individuals are affected by each other's 'pollution'. Each individual has only two alternatives available to him: to pollute or not to pollute. Each individual prefers to pollute whatever the other does, and each prefers the other *not* to pollute, whatever he himself does. So far, these are like the preferences of a Prisoners' Dilemma. But although B would rather neither of them pollute than both of them pollute, A (who suffers less from the aggregate level of pollution than does B) has the opposite preference. The preferences are shown in the matrix below: the entries are ordinal utilities (that is to say, a higher number indicates a more preferred position).

		B	
		not pollute	pollute
A	not pollute	2, 3	1, 4
	pollute	4, 1	3, 2

It can be seen that *every* possible state of affairs is Pareto-optimal and in every one of them externalities are present.

For these reasons, especially the last one, the presence of externalities does not of itself provide a case for state (or any other coercive) action, and therefore my criticisms in this book are not directed against justifications of the state based on the externalities argument. They are directed instead against what I think is the much more plausible justification which is based directly on the supposed inability of individuals to Cooperate voluntarily in Prisoners' Dilemmas—Prisoners' Dilemmas which arise in connection with the provision of public goods. Externalities are necessarily present in these situations; but not all externalities give rise to Prisoners' Dilemmas (for they must, in the first place, be Pareto-relevant).

2.3. PUBLIC GOODS AND THE PRISONERS' DILEMMA

I turn now to consider some connections between public goods provision, the size of the 'public', and the Prisoners' Dilemma, beginning with a very simple example, due to Russell Hardin.[10] Suppose that a good is perfectly indivisible and non-excludable with respect to a public composed of N individuals. If any amount of the good is produced, it is equally available to and is in fact equally consumed by all N individuals. Suppose that each individual has the choice (and only the choice) between contributing or not contributing one unit of the cost of producing the good (one unit of a *numeraire* private good) and that every unit contributed produces an amount of the public good with benefit r. Suppose finally that each individual's utility is nr/N, if he does not contribute, and $nr/N - 1$, if he does, where n is the total number of units contributed. (Notice that this means that the public good exhibits some rivalness: each individual's utility declines with increasing N, which is the number of individuals who actually consume the good, since nobody is excluded.) Then, if m *other* individuals contribute, an individual's utility is mr/N if he does not contribute, and $(m + 1)r/N - 1$ if he does. Thus, the first of these utilities exceeds the second if and only if $N > r$, which is independent of m. In other words, no matter how many other individuals contribute, it does not pay anyone to contribute as long as the size of the public (N) exceeds the ratio of benefits to costs (r). When $N > r$, the game is an N-person Prisoners' Dilemma (as I defined it earlier): each individual has a dominant strategy, and the outcome which results when everyone chooses his dominant strategy is for every individual less preferable than another outcome. But when $N < r$, the dominant strategy for every individual is to contribute and the resulting outcome is the only Pareto-optimal position.

Let us now modify this example by allowing each individual to choose to contribute *any* amount from zero to some personal maximum. Then, if the total contribution of all other individuals is C and his own contribution is c, his utility is $(C + c)r/N - c$, so that his utility is a linear function of c, which increases with increasing c if $N < r$, decreases if $N > r$, and remains at a constant level if $N = r$. Thus, when $N > r$, the game is a Prisoners' Dilemma and each individual's utility is maximized if he chooses to contribute nothing, but when $N < r$ he should contribute the maximum possible.

But this example is perhaps not very typical of public goods interaction. In particular, each individual's utility is a linear function of the total amount (X, say) of public good produced and of the amount of the private good (Y) which he contributes towards the costs of production. Thus, his *indifference curves*, each one a locus of points (X, Y) between which he is indifferent, are linear. The *transformation function*, specifying the quantity of public good which can be produced with a given input of the private good, is also linear.

More generally, we should expect neither of these two functions to be linear. The indifference curves normally will exhibit 'convexity'; that is, as the amount of either one of the goods increases, an additional unit of it requires a smaller sacrifice of the other good in order to maintain utility at the same level. (See, for example, the indifference curves in Figure 1.) Also, the transformation function would more realistically exhibit 'diminishing marginal returns'; that is, as the amount of public good produced increases, the cost of producing an additional unit increases.

Let us go on to consider, then, the more general situation in which the indifference curves have the conventional convexity property.[11] The linearity of the transformation function, which is less unrealistic than that of the utility functions, is retained, to simplify the discussion. To illustrate the ideas involved in the small group case, I consider a public consisting of just two individuals, for whom some good is perfectly indivisible and non-excludable. For every unit of some *numeraire* private good ('money') which either individual sacrifices, an *amount r* (not benefit, as in the discussion of Hardin's example above) of the public good can be produced. Let Y_1 and Y_2 denote the amounts of the private good possessed by the two individuals, and let X denote the amount of the public good (which is consumed in equal amounts by both individuals no matter how much each has contributed to its provision). The amount of the private good which each individual can devote to the production of the public good is subject to some personal maximum, say $\bar{Y}_1$ and $\bar{Y}_2$ for individuals 1 and 2 respectively. Suppose that there are no restrictions on the total amount of the public good which can be produced, within the range from zero to $r(\bar{Y}_1 + \bar{Y}_2)$.

Now, if the amount of the public good produced by one of the individuals (2, say) is *given* and could not subsequently be changed, then the other individual can certainly decide what is his own best course of action. Consider Figure 1. This shows the indifference curves of individual 1. Suppose that the given amount of the public good produced by 2 is X_2. (Since the good is perfectly indivisible and nobody is excludable, individual 1 also consumes X_2.) Then if 1 produces no additional amount of the public good (so that he retains his maximum, $\bar{Y}_1$, of the private good), he is at the point A in the Figure. If he devotes *all* of his $\bar{Y}_1$ to the public good, then he is at point B (at which a total of $X_2 + r\bar{Y}_1$ of the public good is produced). The points on the line AB give the whole range of alternatives available to him, given 2's choice. He will therefore choose the point P at which his utility is greatest, that is, the point on AB

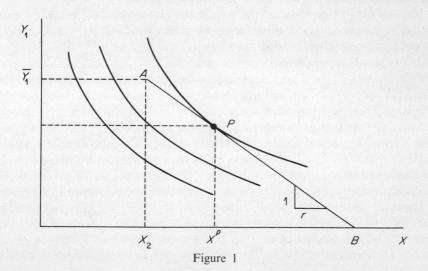

Figure 1

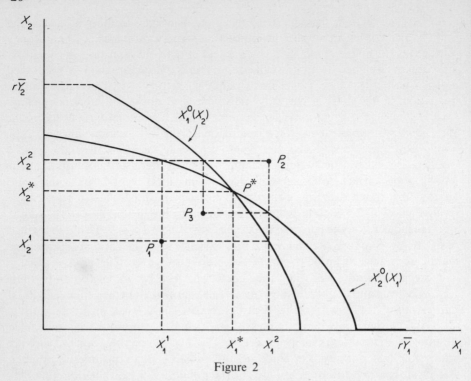

Figure 2

which lies on his highest indifference curve. The total amount of public good produced is thus X^p. (The contrast with the modified example of Hardin can already be seen. In that earlier case, an individual's best reply to any amount of public good production by the other individual is always zero or the maximum possible, according as N is less or greater than r.)

We can see in Figure 1 that the greater the public good return (r) on a unit outlay of the private good, the more of the public good will individual 1 choose to produce, for a given production by individual 2.

Individual 1's optimal response to any choice by 2 can be determined, in the manner indicated in Figure 1. Similarly for individual 2, given 1's choices. Let $X_1^0(X_2)$ denote 1's optimal response for a given value of X_2. Define $X_2^0(X_1)$ similarly. These *response functions* are shown (with typical shapes) in Figure 2.

Suppose first that each individual behaves 'independently' or 'non-strategically', in the sense that he simply reacts to the other person's choices without taking account of the possible effects of his own choices on the other's choices or the expectations which the other may be entertaining of his own choices, and so on. Suppose that initially the two individuals choose to produce amounts X_1^1 and X_2^1 of the public good (the point P_1 in Figure 2). Then each realizes that his own production is not optimal, given the other's choice. Individual 1 will increase his production to $X_1^0(X_2^1) = X_1^2$, and individual 2 will increase his to X_2^2. This brings them to P_2. But here, too, each has an incentive to alter his level of production, and they will move to P_3. This 'process' will converge to the point P^* in Figure 2, the point at which the two response curves intersect, and P^* is the only point at which neither individual has an incentive to change his production level unilaterally. P^* is called an *equilibrium*.[12]

Now P^* is a reasonable prediction of the outcome of interaction in this situation only if the two individuals behave non-strategically in the manner indicated. Suppose instead that individual 1 expects individual 2 to respond non-strategically to his own choices but does not himself respond non-strategically to 2's choices. Then 1 may produce only the amount X_1^1 (for example), in the expectation that 2 will produce X_2^2, which would result in an outcome preferred by 1 to P^* (the total production of the public good, $X_1^1 + X_2^2$, may differ little from and may even exceed the total produced at P^*). Individual 1 might even choose to devote no resources at all to public good production.

Individual 2 may of course behave similarly.

On the other hand, individual 1 might expect 2 to behave strategically and produce less than X_2^*, in which case 1's optimal choice will be to produce *more* than X_1^*.

If the assumption of non-strategic behaviour is abandoned, nothing very general can be said about the outcome. A large number of plausible alternative assumptions can be made and it is difficult to choose between them on *a priori* grounds. In many cases, as in the first example above, the outcome would be less preferred than P^* by both individuals. To such an outcome, the following argument about the equilibrium point P^* applies *a fortiori*.

Let us now see whether P^* is Pareto-optimal. Any unilateral move from P^* by either individual will not, of course, lead to a position preferred to P^* by that individual (because P^* is an equilibrium). Consider Figure 3, in which individual 1's indifference curves are shown again and P^* is the equilibrium point derived above. Clearly, if individual 2 decreases his production of the public good (causing a move to P', say), while 1 increases his production (yielding a net result at P''), the outcome may be preferred by 2 to P^*, but it will necessarily be less preferred than P^* by 1. Similarly, if 1 decreases and 2 increases production, the result will be less preferred than P^* by 2. Thus, both individuals must increase their production if a Pareto-preferred position is to be achieved. Not all such joint increases will yield Pareto-preferred points (P^* may already be Pareto-optimal), but typically very many of them will do so.[13] The point Q in Figure 3 is preferred by individual 1 to P^*, and may also be preferred by 2. Suppose that it is. Then we might expect the two individuals to cooperate to achieve this position (or some other Pareto-optimal point) rather than P^*. Unfortunately, Q is not an equilibrium: we can see in Figure 3 that individual 1 prefers Q_1' (at which his production of the public good is reduced but 2's is not) to Q. The same may be true for the other individual. If it is, we may have here a Prisoners' Dilemma. Clearly, if either individual 'defects' to a preferred position by reducing his production of the public good, the resulting position will be *less* preferred by the other individual than the original position (Q). Thus, if individual 2 defects unilaterally, the result will

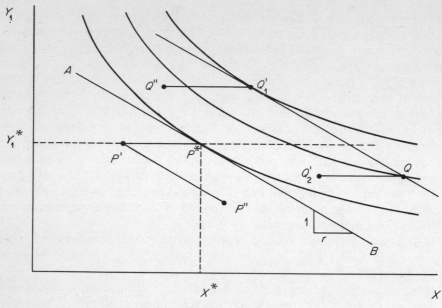

Figure 3

be to move from Q to a point like Q'_2 in Figure 3. Individual 1, then, prefers Q'_1 (where he defects unilaterally) to Q (where neither defects); and he prefers Q'' (where both defect) to Q'_2 (where individual 2 defects unilaterally). Whether he prefers Q to Q'' depends (given everything else) on the amount by which 2 reduces his production when he defects. If this is sufficiently large (as it is for the defections shown in Figure 3), then 1's preferences are those of a Prisoners' Dilemma whose outcomes are Q, Q'_1, Q'_2 and Q'':

	C	D
C	Q	Q'_2
D	Q'_1	Q''

So also are the preferences of individual 2 (he prefers Q'_2 to Q to Q'' to Q'_1).

The outcomes of this Prisoners' Dilemma are, of course, only four of the infinite number of outcomes which are possible if X, Y_1 and Y_2 are continuous variables. Generally, there are many Pareto-optimal positions (each of them preferred by both individuals to P^*) and, for each of them, there are many pairs of defections such that the resulting 2×2 game is a Prisoners' Dilemma. But the larger game in which these 2×2 games are embedded—the game in which all possible combinations of X and Y_1 are feasible outcomes—is obviously never a Prisoners' Dilemma. Even if the possible outcomes are restricted, the game is a Prisoners' Dilemma only under special circumstances. Consider, for example, the game in which each player may choose (or thinks he may choose)

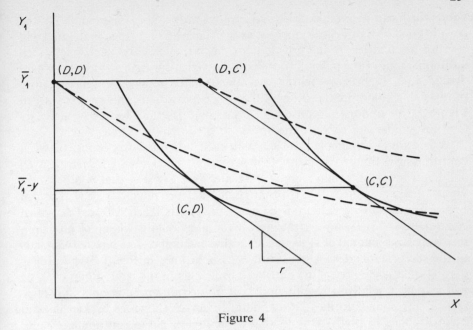

Figure 4

between contributing nothing to the provision of the public good (strategy D) and contributing a certain amount y which is the same for both players (strategy C). The four outcomes are shown in Figure 4 (which shows individual 1's indifference curves). If 1's indifference curves have the shape of the bold curves in Figure 4, then he prefers C to D no matter whether 2 chooses C or D, and he prefers (C, C) to (D, D). If the same is true for individual 2, (C, C) is the only equilibrium and is Pareto-optimal. But if 1's indifference curves have the shape of the broken curves in Figure 4 and 2's curves are similar, then the game is a Prisoners' Dilemma, with (D, D) being the Pareto-inferior equilibrium.

Let us consider now the effects of increasing the number of individuals. It is generally assumed that when the group is sufficiently large, each individual acts independently or non-strategically.[14] But this assumption does not imply that each individual necessarily chooses to contribute nothing to the provision of the public good (as is often concluded). Just as in the two-person case, we can derive a response function for each individual (which specifies his optimal response to the choice of the other individuals) and from the N response functions we can derive an equilibrium (if the functions satisfy certain conditions), and this equilibrium will not necessarily correspond to zero production of the public good (except in very special cases such as the one studied by Hardin).

However, it can be shown that each individual's production at the equilibrium will grow smaller as the size of the group increases, just as long as the public good has the property that the greater the number of people who consume it, the smaller is the *benefit* to any one individual of the given amount of the public good which can be produced with an input unit (his unit, for example) of the private good.[15] If this is true, then, at any given level of X, each individual will give up less and less of the private good, as N increases, in exchange for an additional unit of the public good: his indifference curves become everywhere 'flatter'. Looking back at Figure 1, we can see that for any given total quantity of the public good produced by all the other individuals (this replaces X_2 in Figure 1), his optimal response is to contribute less and less as N increases (and his indifference curves flatten out).[16]

Consider now the simpler case in which each individual may choose between contributing nothing to the costs of the provision of the public good (strategy D) and contributing a certain amount y (strategy C). Suppose that m other individuals make a contribution (so that their total production is mry). Then in Figure 5, individual 1's choice is between the points labelled D and C, which correspond to his D and C strategies. If the individual is willing to give up a relatively large amount of Y_1 to gain an additional unit of X (which corresponds to the 'steep' indifference curves shown as bold lines in Figure 5), he prefers C to D; that is, he prefers to contribute. But it, as in the large group case, he will give up a relatively small amount of Y_1 to gain an additional unit of X (which corresponds to the 'flat' indifference curves shown as broken lines in Figure 5), then he prefers D to C; that is, he prefers *not* to contribute.

The same is true for each individual.

This comparison of the small group and the larger group, with respect to

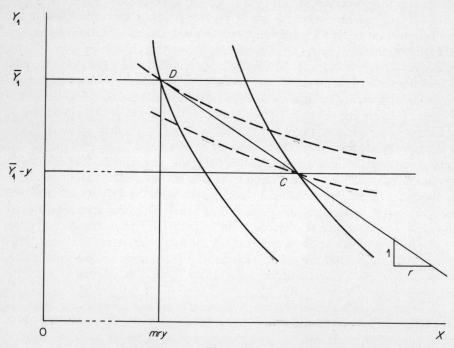

Figure 5

the trade-offs between the private good and the public good, holds no matter what the value of *mry* may be, that is, no matter how many other individuals contribute.

Thus, when the group is 'sufficiently large', strategy D dominates strategy C for each individual. It is not of course possible to specify in general how large is 'sufficiently large'. The threshold depends on the exact shapes of all the individuals' indifference curves and on the transformation function. It also depends on the degree of indivisibility of the good. I have been assuming in this section that the good is perfectly indivisible: every unit produced is fully consumed by all individuals. Generally speaking, the 'sufficiently large' group referred to above will be larger as the good becomes more divisible.[17]

In the 'sufficiently large' group, this two-strategy game is a Prisoners' Dilemma as long as each individual prefers that everybody contributes. This, too, depends on the indifference curves, the transformation function and the degree of divisibility.

These brief remarks on the provision of public goods should suffice to make it clear that it is not possible to make a general, *a priori* statement relating the actual outcome of interaction or the occurrence of a Prisoners' Dilemma to the size of the group. Although the Prisoners' Dilemma does occur in public goods interaction under certain conditions and although it does appear to be more likely to occur in a 'large' group than in a 'small' group, the connections between the optimality of public goods provision, the size of the group and the occurrence of the Prisoners' Dilemma are not as straightforward as Mancur Olson, Russell Hardin and others have supposed. In particular, the Prisoners' Dilemma game does not necessarily characterize public goods interaction, no matter how large the group is.

In the next chapter, however, I shall proceed to assume that individual preferences at each point of time are those of a Prisoners' Dilemma game; for my next object is to show that, when this much is granted, voluntary Cooperation may nevertheless be rational for each individual, if the Prisoners' Dilemma is iterated.

2.4. NOTES

1. See J. G. Head, 'Public Goods and Public Policy', *Public Finance*, **17**, 197–219 (1962), p. 201; and James M. Buchanan, *The Demand and Supply of Public Goods* (Chicago: Rand McNally, 1968), pp. 174–5.

2. The word 'consumption' should perhaps be used only in connection with private goods, where it has a clear meaning. To speak of 'consuming' national defence, wilderness and radio broadcasts is somewhat strained, but for want of a suitable word to cover a variety of applications, I follow the custom of the economists and retain the word. In many cases, 'consume' means 'use'. Cf. Jean-Claude Milleron, 'Theory of Value With Public Goods: A Survey Article', *Journal of Economic Theory*, **5**, 419–77 (1972), pp. 422–3.

3. This follows Samuelson's most recent usage. In his first paper on public goods, Samuelson had defined a *public good* as one which was consumed *equally* by every

individual, so that $x^1 = x^2 = \ldots = x$, where x^i is the ith individual's consumption of the good and x is the total amount available; and he defined a *private good* as one which could be divided amongst individuals so that $x^1 + x^2 + \ldots = x$. See Paul A. Samuelson, 'The Pure Theory of Public Expenditure', *Review of Economics and Statistics*, **36**, 387–9 (1954). In his 1955 paper, he admitted that these were two pure, polar cases; and most recently he has abandoned these two poles in favour of a 'knife-edge pole' of the pure private good and 'all the rest of the world in the public-good domain'. Samuelson, 'Diagrammatic Exposition of a Theory of Public Expenditure', *Review of Economics and Statistics*, **37**, 350–6 (1955); and 'Pure Theory of Public Expenditure and Taxation', in J. Margolis and H. Guitton, (Eds.), *Public Economics* (London: Macmillan, 1969).

4. This independence was emphasized by Head, 'Public Goods and Public Policy'. Note that the Samuelsonian pure public good, which is equally consumed by all individuals, necessarily exhibits non-excludability. See note 3.

5. Here and in what follows, I am speaking only of exclusion from consumption of the good and not of exclusion from consumption of externalities arising from others' consumption of the good. 'Externalities' are discussed below.

6. This is the definition used by James M. Buchanan and Wm. Craig Stubblebine, 'Externality', *Economica*, N.S., **29**, 371–84 (1962). Other writers have insisted on more restrictive definitions; in particular, it is often stipulated that the interdependence between the two or more individuals is 'untraded', that is, no price is paid for the benefit or harm involved in the externality.

7. Cf. E. J. Mishan, 'The Relationship between Joint Products, Collective Goods, and External Effects', *Journal of Political Economy*, **77**, 329–48 (1969).

8. See Buchanan, *The Demand and Supply of Public Goods*, pp. 65 ff. Samuelson (in 'Pure Theory of Public Expenditure and Taxation') says that a public good is one one with the property of involving a 'consumption externality, in the sense of entering two or more persons' preference functions simultaneously'. He is obviously correct if 'consumption' *means* 'enters into a utility function'. Otherwise, I think this usage is confusing: a good can be public even when nobody is consuming it.

9. Buchanan and Stubblebine, 'Externality'.

10. Russell Hardin, 'Collective Action as an Agreeable n-Prisoners' Dilemma', *Behavioral Science*, **16**, 472–81 (1971).

11. My presentation here draws on Buchanan, *The Demand and Supply of Public Goods*; Buchanan, 'Cooperation and Conflict in Public-Goods Interaction', *Western Economic Journal*, **5**, 109–21 (1967); and Gerald H. Kramer and Joseph Hertzberg, 'Formal Theory', in Volume 7 of *The Handbook of Political Science*, F. Greenstein and N. Polsby, (Eds.), (Reading, Mass.: Addison-Wesley, 1975).

12. The 'pseudo-dynamics' in this informal demonstration that P^* is an equilibrium are not intended as a description of an actual *process*. Genuinely dynamic elements are entirely absent from the discussion in this section—and from the accounts of public goods provision in the literature. I return to this omission below.

13. For the derivation of the Pareto-optimal points (in the case of the Samuelsonian pure public good), see Samuelson, 'The Pure Theory of Public Expenditure' and 'Diagrammatic Exposition . . .'

14. See, for example, Buchanan, *The Demand and Supply of Public Goods*, p. 85.

15. This form of rivalness characterizes most public goods. It clearly characterizes, for example, the goods whose provision is supposed to secure domestic peace and

security: police services, courts, etc. It is even true of national defence (though the relation is a weaker one): a given number of divisions, tanks or missiles can generally protect more effectively a smaller group than a larger one. Cf. James M. Buchanan, 'An Economic Theory of Clubs', *Economica*, **32**, 1–14 (1965); and James M. Litvak and Wallace E. Oates, 'Group Size and the Output of Public Goods: Theory and an Application to State–Local Finance in the United States', *Public Finance*, **25**, 42–58 (1970).

16. Note that this does not imply that *total* production of the public good decreases as the size of the group increases. See John Chamberlin, 'Provision of Collective Goods as a Function of Group Size', *American Political Science Review*, **68**, 707–16 (1974). Chamberlin shows that, under certain reasonable assumptions: if the good is perfectly non-rival, then total production *increases* with group size; if the good is perfectly rival (though still non-excludable), then total production decreases with group size; and for intermediate cases exhibiting *some* rivalness, total production may increase or decrease with group size, depending on the individuals' utility functions and the transformation function. This, too, somewhat weakens Olson's conclusions.

17. Cf. Buchanan, *The Demand and Supply of Public Goods*, Chapter 9.

CHAPTER 3

The Prisoners' Dilemma Supergame

3.1. INTRODUCTION

The discussion of the problem of public goods provision in the last chapter was entirely static. It was concerned only with individual preferences at one point in time, and conclusions about public goods provision were derived solely from these static preferences. Individuals were supposed, in effect, to make only one choice, once and for all (a choice of how much to contribute to the provision of the public good). The treatments of this problem by economists, including Olson's *Logic of Collective Action* and the studies referred to in the last chapter, are all static in this way.

Needless to say, it is not always like this in the real world. With respect to most of the public goods of special interest here, the choice of whether to contribute to their provision and of how much to contribute is a recurring choice; in some cases it is a choice which is permanently before the individual. This is true of the choice of how much to exploit the 'commons': how many whales to take in each year or other time period, how much to treat industrial waste before discharging it into the lake, and so on. It is also true of the individual's choice of whether or not to behave peaceably, to refrain from violence, robbery and fraud, and so on.

I propose to consider these recurring choices in the context of a supergame. A *supergame* is simply a sequence of games. The constituent games are called the *ordinary games*. In this chapter, I shall consider only supergames which are iterations of a single ordinary game. The ordinary game will be a Prisoners' Dilemma in which two strategies are available to each player: to Cooperate (*C*) or to Defect (*D*). In each constituent game of this Prisoners' Dilemma supergame, the players make their choices simultaneously (that is, in ignorance of the other players' choices in that game), but they know the strategies chosen by all the players in all previous games.

The Prisoners' Dilemma (ordinary) game was defined in Section 1.2 as a non-cooperative game. The Prisoners' Dilemma supergame is thus also a non-cooperative game. Either agreements may not be made (perhaps because communication is impossible or because the making of agreements is prohibited) or, if agreements may be made, players are not constrained to keep them. It is the possibility of cooperation in the *absence* of such constraint that I am interested in.

The ordinary games of a supergame will be thought of as being played at regular discrete intervals of time, or one in each time period. Each player receives his ordinary game payoff at the end of each time period. The supergame is assumed to 'begin' at time $t = 0$ and the ordinary game payoffs to be made at $t = 1, 2, 3, \ldots$.

It is reasonable to assume that the present worth to a player of a future expected payoff is less the more distant in time the payoff is to be made. Specifically, I make the usual assumption that future payoffs are discounted exponentially. Thus the value at time $t = 0$ of a payoff X_t to be made at time t (at the end of the tth game) is $X_t a_i^t$; a_i is called the *discount parameter* of player i, and $1 - a_i$ is the discount *rate*. It is assumed that $0 < a_i < 1$. Thus the present value of a finite payoff from a game infinitely distant in the future is zero.

The processes in which I am interested are of indefinite length. They are represented here by supergames composed of an infinite number of ordinary games. When future payoffs are discounted back to the present, this representation appears to be a reasonable one.

In any case, if the supergame has only a finite number of states (and the players know this), the 'dilemma' remains, in the sense that Defection in every ordinary game is the only undominated strategy, no matter what the ordinary game payoffs are. For consider a two-person Prisoners' Dilemma game iterated T times. At the start of this supergame, each player knows that in the final game (there being no possibility of reprisals), Defection is his only undominated strategy and he is sure that the other player will choose D. The outcome of the final game is therefore a foregone conclusion. The penultimate, or $(T-1)^{\text{th}}$ game, is now effectively the final game and the same argument applies to it. Each player will choose D and expect the other players to do likewise. Similarly for the $(T-2)^{\text{th}}$ game, and so on, back to the first game.

A *supergame strategy* is a sequence of strategies, one in each ordinary game. In the Prisoners' Dilemma supergame, the strategy in which C is chosen in every ordinary game will be denoted by C^∞; that in which D is chosen in every ordinary game will be denoted by D^∞. Other names for supergame strategies of special interest will be introduced below. A *strategy vector*, in either an ordinary game or a supergame, is a list (an ordered n-tuple) of strategies, one for each player.[1]

The *outcome* of an ordinary game is the actual state of affairs at the end of the game. An outcome of a supergame is a sequence of outcomes, one for each ordinary game. In the ordinary games and supergames considered here, an outcome is uniquely determined by the strategies actually chosen by the players.

Associated with each strategy vector in an ordinary game is a *payoff vector*, which is a list (an ordered n-tuple) of payoffs, one for each player. A payoff is to be thought of as a quantity of some basic private good, such as money, or amounts of several private goods reduced to a single quantity of some *numeraire*, such as money. In this chapter each player is assumed simply to seek to maximize his own payoff, and his payoff scale is assumed to be *cardinal* (that is, it has an arbitrary zero and unit and can be replaced by any positive linear transformation of itself). Here the payoffs may be identified with 'utilities', in the sense that a player (strictly) prefers one outcome to another if and only if the first yields a greater payoff (utility) than does the second and he is indifferent between them if and only if they yield equal payoffs. But in the following chapter on altruism this identification is not made, for here a player's utility is assumed to be a function of the payoffs of other players as well as his own.

A *supergame payoff* to a player is the sum of an infinite series whose terms are his payoffs in the ordinary games. The discounted value of this payoff at $t = 0$ is thus $\sum_{t=1}^{\infty} X_t a_i^t$, where X_t is i's payoff at time t (his payoff from the game in period t). Since $0 < a_i < 1$, this infinite series converges (that is, the supergame payoff is finite) for any sequence of payoffs $\{X_t\}$, just as long as each X_t is finite (as it always will be here). In the two-person case, the supergame payoffs will be exhibited in a payoff matrix, as in the ordinary game.

The concepts of dominance and Pareto-optimality have already been introduced (in Section 1.2). The definitions given there also apply, *mutatis mutandis*, to supergames, but a few more terms are needed. The definitions which follow apply to both ordinary games and supergames.

An outcome is said to be *Pareto-preferred* to another if and only if at least one player (strictly) prefers the first to the second and no player (strictly) prefers the second to the first.

An *equilibrium* is defined as a strategy vector such that no player can obtain a larger payoff using a different strategy while the other players' strategies remain the same. An equilibrium, then, is such that, if each player *expects* it to be the outcome, he has no incentive to use a different strategy. Thus, if indeed every player expects a certain equilibrium to be the outcome, then it is reasonable to suppose that this equilibrium will in fact be the outcome. But a player may have reasons for expecting that a certain equilibrium will not be the outcome. Then he might not use his equilibrium strategy and the equilibrium will not be the outcome.

This possibility is important, as we shall see, in the study of supergames. For whereas in the Prisoners' Dilemma ordinary game there is only one equilibrium and there is no reason for a player not to expect it to be the outcome, in Prisoners' Dilemma supergames there are generally several equilibria and the question arises whether some of them may be eliminated as possible outcomes because at least one of the players does not expect them to occur.

For convenience, the following expressions are sometimes used in this chapter and the next. A strategy vector is said to be *always* an equilibrium if and only if it is an equilibrium no matter what the ordinary game payoffs are (as long as they satisfy the inequality which makes the ordinary game a Prisoners' Dilemma) and no matter what values the discount parameters assume (as long as each a_i satisfies $0 < a_i < 1$). A strategy vector is *sometimes* an equilibrium if and only if it is an equilibrium for some but not all values of the ordinary game payoffs and the discount parameters. If a strategy vector is neither always nor sometimes an equilibrium, then it is said to be *never* an equilibrium.

The remainder of this chapter is devoted chiefly to an equilibrium analysis of the two-person (Section 3.2) and N-person (Section 3.3) Prisoners' Dilemma supergame. The principal object in each section is to determine (for certain sets of available strategies) which strategy vectors are equilibria and under what conditions. A rather lengthy mathematical analysis is required for this, and although the mathematics involved are elementary, some readers may wish at some point to turn to the informal summary and discussion of the results obtained in this chapter (and also in Chapter 4) which is given in Chapter 5.

3.2. THE TWO-PERSON SUPERGAME[2]

Consider first the supergame consisting of iterations of the two-person Prisoners' Dilemma game introduced earlier. The payoff matrix of this ordinary game is:[3]

	C	D
C	x, x	z, y
D	y, z	w, w

where $y > x > w > z$. Rows are chosen by player 1, columns by player 2.

Supergame Strategies

The following strategies in this supergame will be of interest.

C^∞ : C is chosen in every ordinary game.

D^∞ : D is chosen in every ordinary game.

A_k (k is a strictly positive integer): C is chosen in the first game, and it is chosen in each subsequent game as long as the other player chooses C in the previous game; if the other Defects in any game, D is chosen for the next k games; C is then chosen no matter what the other player's last choice is; it continues to be chosen as long as the other player chooses C in the preceding game; when the other player next Defects, D is chosen for $k + 1$ games; and so on; the number of games in which the other player is 'punished' for a Defection increases by one each time; and each time there is a return to C.

A_∞ : C is chosen until the other player Defects, after which D is chosen in all succeeding ordinary games. This is the limiting case of A_k when $k \to \infty$.

B : C is chosen in the first game; thereafter the choice in each game is that of the other player in the preceding game.

B' : D is chosen in the first game; thereafter the choice in each game is that of the other player in the preceding game.

This list of strategies does not of course exhaust the possible strategies.

A_k (including A_∞), B and B' are *conditional strategies* while C^∞ and D^∞ are *unconditional*.

Unless otherwise stated, A_k is assumed throughout this chapter to include A_∞; that is, k need not be finite. It is also assumed that all those players choosing A_k, for finite k, use the same value of k.

When k is finite, A_k embodies an effort to 'teach' the other player to Cooperate. It is a generous effort, for no matter what the other player does he is repeatedly given the opportunity to achieve the state of mutual Cooperation. These offers are made less frequently as the supergame progresses and the 'punishment' for not responding to them becomes more severe.

A_∞ gives the other player at the start of the game an opportunity to Cooperate, but once he has Defected, there is no possibility of mutual Cooperation for the rest of the supergame; he is 'punished' for his Defection forevermore.

B and B' have been called 'tit-for-tat' strategies in the literature on Prisoners' Dilemma experiments. Apart from the choice in the first game in the case of B, no initiative is taken to induce the other player to Cooperate, as it is when A_k is used. The initiative must come from the other player; but when it does, it is responded to immediately.

The three conditional strategies may be interpreted as embodying promises and threats; they may be thought of as taking the form: 'if you Cooperate, then I will too; if not, then I will do …'. Some game theorists have written that a consideration of threats (and presumably also of promises) is out of place in the theory of non-cooperative games. For either the promises and threats cannot be communicated effectively, or, if communication is possible and permitted, they will not be credible since the player in question is not bound to carry them out (or to pursue any particular course of action at all) and it may not be in his best interest to do so. In the applications of the theory in which I am interested, communication takes place. As for the incredibility of promises and threats in all non-cooperative games, a considerable digression would be necessary to defend my belief that this view is mistaken. But we need not involve ourselves in this argument here, since, formally, A_k, B and B' are *strategies* and the analysis which follows is unaffected by whether or not they are interpreted as embodying promises and threats.

The strategies defined above (A_k, B, B' and C^∞ and D^∞) are only five out of an infinite number of possible supergame strategies. I assume in this section that they are the only strategies available to each player. Given this assumption, I shall be able to state necessary and sufficient conditions for each strategy vector to be an equilibrium. I then go on to consider which equilibrium will be the outcome in situations where several equilibria exist simultaneously. Because not all strategies are considered, my analysis is incomplete; but it does illustrate, at least, how mutual Cooperation throughout the supergame can be the outcome under certain conditions. However, it seems to me that the five strategies include those which are most likely to be considered, at least at a conscious level, by real players; inasmuch as this is the case, the analysis given below is complete. When all possible strategies are available to each player, the equilibrium conditions derived below are only *necessary* conditions.

The Supergame Payoffs

The payoffs associated with each of the 25 strategy vectors defined by these five supergame strategies will now be derived. They are assembled in the supergame payoff matrix shown in Table 1.

(i) Suppose that each player chooses C^∞. Then (C, C) is the outcome in every ordinary game, and the total discounted payoff in the supergame to each player $(i = 1, 2)$ is

$$x(a_i + a_i^2 + \ldots + a_i^t + \ldots) = \frac{xa_i}{1 - a_i}$$

the infinite series in the parentheses being convergent since $0 < a_i < 1$ for each i.

(ii) Suppose that each player chooses any one of the strategies A_k (with any value of k), B and C^∞. Then (C, C) is the outcome in every ordinary game and the payoffs are as in (i).

(iii) If both players choose D^∞, then their supergame payoffs are

$$\frac{wa_i}{1 - a_i}, \qquad i = 1, 2$$

(iv) Suppose that one player (labelled i) chooses B, while the other player (labelled j) chooses D^∞. Then player i chooses C in the first game, but, on discovering that player j has chosen D, Defects in all succeeding games. Thus their payoffs are za_i and ya_j, respectively, in the first ordinary game, and w each in all succeeding games. The supergame payoffs are therefore

$$za_i + \frac{wa_i^2}{1 - a_i} \qquad \text{for player } i$$

$$ya_j + \frac{wa_j^2}{1 - a_j} \qquad \text{for player } j$$

(v) Suppose that one player (i) chooses A_k and the other (j) chooses D^∞. This represents, in effect, a failure of player j to respond at any time in the supergame to i's repeated 'invitation' to Cooperate. Each time player i chooses C, his payoff is z. His total payoff in the supergame from the ordinary games in which he chooses C is

$$z(a_i + a_i^{k+2} + a_i^{2k+4} + a_i^{3k+7} + \ldots + a_i^{k(t+1)+t(t+3)/2+2} + \ldots)$$

This series is obviously convergent, since it is less than the convergent series in (i) above. Denote its sum by $S(k, a_i)$:

$$S(k, a_i) = a_i + \sum_{t=0}^{\infty} a_i^{k(t+1)+t(t+3)/2+2}$$

$$= a_i \left\{ 1 + a_i^{k+1} \sum_{t=0}^{\infty} a_i^{t(t/2+k+3/2)} \right\}$$

In each of the remaining ordinary games, in which both players choose D, i's payoff is w; so that his supergame payoff from these games is

$$w \left\{ \frac{a_i}{1 - a_i} - S(k, a_i) \right\}$$

Player i's total supergame payoff is therefore

$$zS(k, a_i) + w \left\{ \frac{a_i}{1 - a_i} - S(k, a_i) \right\} = (z - w) S(k, a_i) + \frac{wa_i}{1 - a_i}$$

Similarly, player j's supergame payoff is

$$(y - w) S(k, a_j) + \frac{wa_j}{1 - a_j}$$

We shall not need to find the sum $S(k, a_i)$ in closed form. We note that $S(k, a_i)$ increases monotically with decreasing k. As $k \to \infty$, $S(k, a_i) \to a_i$. Thus $S(k, a_i) > a_i$ for all permissible values of k and a_i. Henceforth, $S(k, a_i)$ will usually be abbreviated to S_i.

(vi) If one of the players (i) chooses C^∞ and the other (j) chooses D^∞, then their payoffs are z and y, respectively, in each game, so that the supergame payoffs are

$$\frac{za_i}{1 - a_i} \quad \text{and} \quad \frac{ya_j}{1 - a_j}$$

(vii) If both players choose B', or if one player chooses B' while the other chooses D^∞, then (D, D) is the outcome in every ordinary game and the payoffs are as in (iii).

(viii) If one player (i) chooses B while the other player (j) chooses B', then the outcomes permanently *alternate* between (C, D) and (D, C) beginning with (C, D) if player 1 chooses B. Thus,

$$\text{player } i\text{'s payoff} = z(a_i + a_i^3 + a_i^5 + \ldots) + y(a_i^2 + a_i^4 + \ldots)$$

$$= \frac{za_i}{1 - a_i^2} + \frac{ya_i^2}{1 - a_i^2}$$

$$= \frac{(z + ya_i)a_i}{1 - a_i^2}$$

and player j's payoff is similarly

$$\frac{(y + za_j)a_j}{1 - a_j^2}$$

Table 1. Payoff matrix for the two-person Prisoners' Dilemma supergame

	A_k	B	C^∞	B'	D^∞
A_k	$\dfrac{xa_1}{1-a_1},\ \dfrac{xa_2}{1-a_2}$	$\dfrac{xa_1}{1-a_1},\ \dfrac{xa_2}{1-a_2}$	$\dfrac{xa_1}{1-a_1},\ \dfrac{xa_2}{1-a_2}$	Interchange y and z in (B', A_k)	Interchange y and z in (D^∞, A_k)
A_k	$\dfrac{xa_1}{1-a_1},\ \dfrac{xa_2}{1-a_2}$	$\dfrac{xa_1}{1-a_1},\ \dfrac{xa_2}{1-a_2}$	$\dfrac{xa_1}{1-a_1},\ \dfrac{xa_2}{1-a_2}$	Interchange y and z in (B', B)	Interchange y and z in (D^∞, B)
C^∞	$\dfrac{xa_1}{1-a_1},\ \dfrac{xa_2}{1-a_2}$	$\dfrac{xa_1}{1-a_1},\ \dfrac{xa_2}{1-a_2}$	$\dfrac{xa_1}{1-a_1},\ \dfrac{xa_2}{1-a_2}$	Interchange y and z in (B', C^∞)	Interchange y and z in (D^∞, C^∞)
B'	$\{(z-w)+a_2(y-w)\}S_2 + \dfrac{wa_2}{1-a_2}$, $\{(y-w)+a_1(z-w)\}S_1 + \dfrac{wa_1}{1-a_1}$	$\dfrac{(z+ya_2)a_2}{1-a_2^2}$, $\dfrac{(y+za_1)a_1}{1-a_1^2}$	$za_2 + \dfrac{xa_2^2}{1-a_2}$, $ya_1 + \dfrac{xa_1^2}{1-a_1}$	$\dfrac{wa_1}{1-a_1},\ \dfrac{wa_2}{1-a_2}$	$\dfrac{wa_1}{1-a_1},\ \dfrac{wa_2}{1-a_2}$
D^∞	$(z-w)S_2 + \dfrac{wa_2}{1-a_2}$, $(y-w)S_1 + \dfrac{wa_1}{1-a_1}$	$za_2 + \dfrac{wa_2^2}{1-a_2}$, $ya_1 + \dfrac{wa_1^2}{1-a_1}$	$\dfrac{za_2}{1-a_2}$, $\dfrac{ya_1}{1-a_1}$	$\dfrac{wa_1}{1-a_1},\ \dfrac{wa_2}{1-a_2}$	$\dfrac{wa_1}{1-a_1},\ \dfrac{wa_2}{1-a_2}$

(ix) If one player (*i*) chooses C^∞ while the other (*j*) chooses B', then the payoffs are

$$za_i + \frac{xa_i^2}{1 - a_i} \qquad \text{for player } i$$

$$ya_j + \frac{xa_j^2}{1 - a_j} \qquad \text{for player } j$$

(x) Finally, suppose that player (*i*) chooses A_k while the other (*j*) chooses B'. Then the sequence of outcomes, when $k = 2$ for example, looks like:

$$i : C\,D\,D\,C\,D\,D\,D\,C\,D \ldots$$
$$j : D\,C\,D\,D\,C\,D\,D\,D\,C \ldots$$

Player *i*'s payoff $= zS_i + ya_iS_i + w\left\{\dfrac{a_i}{1 - a_i} - S_i - a_iS_i\right\}$

$$= \{(z - w) + a_i(y - w)\}S_i + \frac{wa_i}{1 - a_i}$$

and player *j*'s payoff is similarly

$$(y - w) + a_j(z - w)S_j + \frac{wa_j}{1 - a_j}$$

The supergame payoffs for these five strategies are displayed in Table 1. As usual, rows are chosen by player 1, columns by player 2. The lower or left-most entry in each cell is the payoff to player 1, the upper or right-most entry the payoff to player 2.

Equilibria

Using these supergame payoffs, we can now determine which strategy vectors are equilibria and under what conditions.

In the statements about equilibria made below, 'equilibrium' always means equilibrium *within the set of five strategies* introduced above. However, the statements made in paragraphs (i), (ii) and (iii) would still be true if all possible strategies were available to each player.

(i) It is clear that (D^∞, D^∞) is always an equilibrium. If one player changes from D^∞ to any other strategy, while the other player does not, then in at least one ordinary game he will be playing C instead of D (without having any effect on the other player's future choices) and his payoff in that game will decrease from w to z.

(ii) A strategy vector containing D^∞ and any one of A_k, B and C^∞ is never an equilibrium. The player not using D^∞ always increases his payoff by changing his strategy to D^∞, if the other player does not change.

(iii) Any strategy vector in which either player chooses C^∞ is never an equilibrium. For when one player is using C^∞, the other player always increases his payoff by changing his strategy to D^∞; and if the second player is already using D^∞, then the first player increases his payoff by changing from C^∞ to D^∞ (as in (ii)).

(iv) Consider the strategy vector (A_k, A_k).

A change of strategy of player i to D^∞ does not yield him a greater payoff if and only if

$$\frac{xa_i}{1 - a_i} \geqslant (y - w) S_i + \frac{wa_i}{1 - a_i}$$

that is,

$$\frac{(1 - a_i)S_i}{a_i} \leqslant \frac{x - w}{y - w} \tag{1}$$

A change of strategy of player i to B' does not yield him a greater payoff if and only if

$$\frac{xa_i}{1 - a_i} \geqslant \{(y - w) + a_i(z - w)\} S_i + \frac{wa_i}{1 - a_i}$$

that is,

$$\{(y - w) - a_i(w - z)\} \frac{(1 - a_i)S_i}{a_i} \leqslant x - w \tag{2}$$

Since a change of strategy to B or C^∞ yields the same payoff, we have that (A_k, A_k) is an equilibrium if and only if inequalities (1) and (2) hold for both players. However, (1) implies (2). Thus, (A_k, A_k) is an equilibrium if and only if (1) is true for both players.

This covers the special case of (A_∞, A_∞), but note that when $k \to \infty$ we have $S_i \to a_i$, so that (1) simplifies to:

$$a_i \geqslant \frac{y - x}{y - w} \tag{3}$$

(v) Consider the strategy vector (B, B).

A change of strategy of player i to D^∞ does not yield him a greater payoff if and only if inequality (3) holds. For in reply to D^∞ (and to A_k, B and C^∞) B produces the same supergame outcome as A_∞.

A change of strategy of player i to B' does not yield him a greater payoff if and only if

$$\frac{xa_i}{1 - a_i} \geqslant \frac{(y + za_i)a_i}{1 - a_i^2}$$

that is,

$$a_i \geqslant \frac{y - x}{x - z} \tag{4}$$

A change of strategy to A_k or C^∞ yields the same payoff.

Thus, (B, B) is an equilibrium if and only if (3) and (4) hold for both players.

(vi) Consider the strategy vector (B', B').

A change of strategy of player i to C^∞ does not yield him a greater payoff if and only if

$$\frac{wa_i}{1 - a_i} \geqslant za_i + \frac{xa_i^2}{1 - a_i}$$

that is,

$$a_i \leqslant \frac{w - z}{x - z} \tag{5}$$

A change of strategy of player i to B does not yield him a greater payoff if and only if

$$\frac{wa_i}{1 - a_i} \geqslant \frac{(z + ya_i)a_i}{1 - a_i^2}$$

that is,

$$a_i \leqslant \frac{w - z}{y - w} \tag{6}$$

A change by i to A_k does not yield him a greater payoff if and only if

$$\frac{wa_i}{1 - a_i} \geqslant \{(z - w) + a_i(y - w)\}S_i + \frac{wa_i}{1 - a_i}$$

which simplifies to (6).

A change of strategy to D^∞ yields the same payoff.

Thus (B', B') is an equilibrium if and only if (5) and (6) hold for both players.

(vii) Consider the two strategy vectors in which one player (i) chooses B and the other player (j) chooses B'. The ordinary game outcomes here alternate between (C, D) and (D, C).

It can easily be verified that a change of strategy of player i to A_k or to C^∞ does not yield him a greater payoff if and only if the reverse (not the negation) of inequality (4) obtains and that a change to B' or to D^∞ does not yield a gain if and only if the reverse of (6) obtains.

Similarly, a change of strategy of player j to C^∞, to A_k or to B does not yield him a greater payoff if and only if the reverse of (4) obtains, and a change to D^∞ does not pay if and only if the reverse of (6) obtains.

Thus (B, B') and (B', B) are equilibria if and only if the reverses of (4) and (6) hold for both players. It is easily verified that, for some values of x, y, z, w and a_i, these two conditions cannot hold simultaneously.

(viii) (B', A_k) and (A_k, B') are never equilibria. It is easily checked that it always pays the player using B' to change to D^∞, if the other player is using A_k.

(ix) The equilibrium conditions for the remaining strategy vectors can be obtained immediately from the results already stated. The strategy vector in

Table 2. Summary of conditions for Equilibrium in the two-person
Prisoners' Dilemma supergame

1 \\ 2	A_k	B	C^∞	B'	D^∞
A_k	(1) for $i=1,2$	(3) & (4) for $i=1$; (1) for $i=2$	Never	Never	Never
B	(1) for $i=1$; (3) & (4) for $i=2$	(3) & (4) for $i=1,2$	Never	Reverses of (4) & (6) for $i=1,2$	Never
C^∞	Never	Never	Never	Never	Never
B'	Never	Reverses of (4) & (6) for $i=1,2$	Never	(5) & (6) for $i=1,2$	(5) & (6) for $i=2$
D^∞	Never	Never	Never	(5) & (6) for $i=1$	Always an equilibrium

which player i uses D^∞ and the other player uses B' is an equilibrium if and only if (5) and (6) are true for player i.

The strategy vector in which player i uses B and player j uses A_k is an equilibrium if and only if (1) holds for player i and both (3) and (4) hold for player j.

All these equilibrium conditions are assembled in Table 2. In this Table, 'never' indicates that the strategy vector is never an equilibrium. For a strategy vector which is sometimes an equilibrium the Table gives the necessary and sufficient conditions for equilibrium.

Outcomes

From Table 2 we see that in addition to (D^∞, D^∞), which is always an equilibrium, several other strategy vectors are sometimes equilibria. Four of these (each player selecting one of A_k and B) result in mutual Cooperation in every ordinary game; and four of them (each player selecting one of B' and D^∞) result in mutual Defection in every ordinary game. The remaining two, (B, B') and (B', B), result in the alternation throughout the supergame of (C, D) and (D, C). Are all these equilibria equally plausible outcomes?

We noted earlier that an equilibrium is such that, if every player expects it to be the outcome, then there is no incentive for any player to change his strategy if no other player changes his. But if there are several equilibria, then the fact that a certain strategy vector is an equilibrium is not in itself a sufficient reason for any player to expect it to be the actual outcome. In particular, if one equilibrium is Pareto-preferred to another equilibrium, then each player presumably would expect the first of these to be the outcome rather than the second, and the second would not be the outcome.

Thus when (A_k, A_k) is an equilibrium, since each player prefers (A_k, A_k) to (D^∞, D^∞), neither player will expect (D^∞, D^∞) to be the outcome; therefore it will not be the outcome. The same is true when (B, B) or (A_k, B) or (B, A_k) is an equilibrium.

If all four of these are simultaneously equilibria (which is possible), then each player expects one of them to be the outcome. But it does not matter whether he chooses A_k or B, for the result is the same: mutual Cooperation in every ordinary game. Thus, if the only equilibria are these four together with (D^∞, D^∞), then the outcome is mutual Cooperation throughout the supergame.

If the only equilibria are the four in which each player chooses B' or D^∞, then again it does not matter which strategy each player chooses. The result is the same in all four cases: mutual Defection throughout the supergame.

If the four mutual Cooperation equilibria and the four mutual Defection equilibria co-exist, then, as before, since each of the first four is preferred by both players to each of the last four, one of the first four will be the outcome.

Suppose now that (B, B') and (B', B) are the only equilibria in addition to (D^∞, D^∞). Then it is easily verified that the strategy vector in which player i uses B and player j uses B', is preferred or indifferent to (D^∞, D^∞) by player i if and only if

$$a_i \geqslant \frac{w - z}{y - w}$$

and is strictly preferred by player j if and only if

$$a_i < \frac{y - w}{w - z}$$

The first of these inequalities is the reverse of (6) and is in any case a necessary condition for each of (B, B') and (B', B) to be an equilibrium. Furthermore, if (B, B') or (B', B) is an equilibrium, then, since the reverse of (6) holds for both players, that is

$$a_i \geqslant \frac{w - z}{y - w}, \qquad i = 1, 2$$

and since $a_i < 1$ $(i = 1, 2)$, we have $(w - z)/(y - w) < 1$, and therefore

$$\frac{y - w}{w - z} > 1 > a_i, \qquad i = 1, 2$$

Thus, whenever (B, B') or (B', B) is an equilibrium, it is Pareto-preferred to (D^∞, D^∞).

Suppose next that (B, B') and (B', B) are equilibria simultaneously with (A_k, A_k) and, of course, (D^∞, D^∞). Then (1) and the reverses of (4) and (6) hold for both players. We find that the strategy vector in which i uses B and j uses B' is strictly preferred to (A_k, A_k) by i if and only if

$$a_i > \frac{x-z}{y-x} \tag{7}$$

and is preferred or indifferent to (A_k, A_k) by j if and only if

$$a_j \leqslant \frac{y-x}{x-z}$$

The second of these inequalities is the reverse of (4) and is therefore already satisfied, since it is a necessary condition for (B, B') or (B', B) to be an equilibrium. But inequality (7) cannot be deduced from (1) and the reverses of (4) and (6). A sufficient condition for the truth of (7), given that (1) holds (and therefore also (3), since (1) implies (3)) is:

$$\frac{y-x}{y-w} > \frac{x-z}{y-x}$$

that is,

$$(y-x)^2 > (y-w)(x-z)$$

Put

$$y - w = \gamma(y - x)$$
$$x - z = \delta(y - x)$$

We know that $\gamma > 1$. The sufficient condition becomes

$$\gamma\delta < 1$$

This condition, then, is sufficient for each of (B, B') and (B', B) to be Pareto-preferred to (A_k, A_k), given that these three strategy vectors are equilibria.

Now if (7) and the reverse of (4) hold, then we have:

$$\frac{x-z}{y-x} < a_i \leqslant \frac{y-x}{x-z}$$

which implies that

$$x - z < y - x$$

that is,

$$2x < y + z$$

Thus, $2x < y + z$, which can be written as $\delta < 1$, is a necessary condition for (B, B') and (B', B) to be Pareto-preferred to (A_k, A_k), given that these three strategy vectors are equilibria. But it is not a *sufficient* condition: the sufficient condition is $\gamma\delta < 1$ and this does not necessarily hold whenever $\delta < 1$.

I have derived this particular necessary condition because its reverse ($2x > y + z$) is stipulated by some writers (for example, Rapoport and Chammah, in their book, *Prisoner's Dilemma*)[4] as part of the definition of the Prisoners' Dilemma ordinary game, on the grounds that, if this inequality did not hold, 'tacit collusion' to alternate between (C, D) and (D, C) would be preferable to mutual Cooperation. But this is true in an iterated Prisoners' Dilemma only when there is no discounting; in this case, the condition $2x > y - z$ may play an important role, as it does in the alternative model of the supergame discussed in the first part of the Annex to this chapter. However, in the present analysis of the supergame, in which players discount future payoffs, this condition is not sufficient to make the alternation pattern Pareto-preferred to mutual Cooperation. The important condition in this respect is $\gamma\delta < 1$.

Even if (B, B') and (B', B) are equilibria and each is Pareto-preferred to (A_k, A_k), alternation does not automatically follow. If (B, B') or (B', B) is an equilibrium, then it is Pareto-preferred to (D^∞, D^∞). But if both players eliminate from consideration all strategies except B and B', a problem remains for them. Player 1 prefers (B', B) (in which *he* Defects in the first game) to (B, B') (in which the other player Defects first), whereas player 2 has the opposite preference. Both outcomes, however, are preferred by both players to (B, B)—since they are preferred to (A_k, A_k)—and therefore also to (B', B'). The players have a 'coordination' problem of avoiding (B, B) and (B', B'); but this is not strictly a coordination game,[5] for the two players are antagonistic with respect to (B, B') and (B', B). If mixed strategies are unavailable (as I have been assuming), then the players might use their minimax strategies (minimizing their maximum loss), in which case (B, B) is the outcome.

It is possible, but rather unlikely, that (B, B') and (B', B) are equilibria as well as (B, B) and (B', B'). In this case, (4) and its reverse and (6) and its reverse must hold. Thus we must have

$$a_i = \frac{y - x}{x - z} \quad and \quad a_i = \frac{w - z}{y - w}$$

for *both* players. These can be true simultaneously only if $y(y - w - x) = z(z - w - x)$. In that case both players are indifferent between B and B', for they yield the same payoff no matter whether the other player uses B or B'.

Three outcomes, then, are possible in the two-person Prisoners' Dilemma supergame, when the strategies available to the players are A_k, B, B', C^∞ and D^∞. They are: (i) mutual Cooperation throughout; (ii) mutual Defection throughout; (iii) alternation between (C, D) and (D, C). However, the alternation outcomes occur only if the players do *not* use their minimax strategies (B for each of them) and are unable to 'coordinate' their strategies in the way explained above.

For the mutual Cooperation outcome to occur, one of the four strategy vectors in which each player chooses one of A_k and B must be an equilibrium. Examining the necessary and sufficient conditions for these four equilibria, we see that *if condition* (3) *fails for one of the players, then none of these four strategy vectors is an equilibrium*. For (1) implies (3), so that the negation of (3) implies the negation of (1).

Thus, the negation of (3) plays a crucial role. It can be written in the form:

$$ya_i + \frac{wa_i^2}{1 - a_i} > \frac{xa_i}{1 - a_i}$$

That is, player i's payoff from unilateral Defection in the first game (ya_i) plus his payoff from mutual Defection in all succeeding games $(wa_i/(1 - a_i))$ is greater than his payoff from mutual Cooperation throughout the supergame. In other words, his discount rate is so high that it pays him to 'grab' y in the first game even though this results in his getting only w in all succeeding games.

The negation of (3) is

$$a_i < \frac{y - x}{y - w}$$

Let us call the ratio on the right-hand side of this inequality player i's *temptation* to Defect from mutual Cooperation in the ordinary game. (When he Defects unilaterally, his payoff increases by $y - x$; but this difference should not be used to 'measure' anything, since the payoff scale was assumed to be unique only up to a linear transformation, so has an arbitrary zero and unit.) Notice that the temptation ratio lies between -1 and $+1$.

We can say (informally) that, as the temptation of either of the players increases, mutual Defection throughout the supergame is increasingly likely to be the outcome, other things being equal.

3.3. THE N-PERSON SUPERGAME

I turn now to a consideration of the supergame whose ordinary games are Prisoners' Dilemmas with *any* finite number (N) of players. Very little has been written about such games. In each ordinary game, two strategies (C and D) are again available to each player.

Payoffs in the ordinary game

My analysis of the N-person Prisoners' Dilemma supergame is limited to the case when the ordinary game payoffs associated with a given outcome do not change from game to game. This rules out the important possibility that the payoffs in an ordinary game are functions not only of the players' choices in that game but also of their choices in previous games. (This possibility is discussed in Section 5.3.)

I assume that a player's payoffs in each ordinary game depend upon two things only: his own strategy (C or D) in that ordinary game, and *the number of other players choosing C* in that game. The second part of this assumption is in fact very weak. It is equivalent to assuming that payoffs are independent of the labelling of the players. Its relaxation entails that payoffs depend upon *which* other players choose C.

Denote by $f(v)$ the ordinary game payoff to any player when he chooses C and v other players choose C, and by $g(v)$ the payoff to any player when he chooses D and v others choose C. I assume that $f(v)$ and $g(v)$ are the same for all players.[6]

The following three assumptions about the functions f and g seem to me appropriate for applications of the theory to the class of problems introduced in Chapter 1.

    (i) $g(v) > f(v)$ for each value of $v \geqslant 0$.

    (ii) $f(N-1) > g(0)$.

    (iii) $g(v) > g(0)$ for all $v > 0$.

(i) is true if and only if D dominates C for each player: no matter what strategies the other players use, each player prefers D to C. (ii) is true if and only if each player prefers the outcome which occurs when all the players Cooperate to that which occurs when all the players Defect. Thus (i) and (ii) are necessary and sufficient conditions for the ordinary game to be an N-person Prisoners' Dilemma (according to the definition given in Chapter 1). Assumption (iii) is eminently reasonable; in fact, a much stronger assumption usually holds in practice, namely that both $f(v)$ and $g(v)$ are strictly increasing with v.[7]

Supergame Strategies

In addition to C^∞ and D^∞ I shall consider the following supergame strategies.

$A_{k,n}$: (k is a strictly positive integer): C is chosen in the first game; it continues to be chosen as long as *at least n other players* ($N > n > 0$) also choose C (in the preceding game); if the number of other Cooperators falls below n, then D is chosen for the next k games; C is then chosen in the next game no matter what the other players chose in the preceding game; it continues to be chosen as long as at least n other players choose C in the preceding game; when the number of other Cooperating players next falls below n, D is chosen for $k+1$ games; and so on; the number of games in which the other players are 'punished' for Defection increases by one each time; and each time there is a return to C.

$A_{\infty,n}$: C is chosen in the first game and then for as long as at least n other players choose C in the preceding game; if the number of other Cooperators falls below n, D is chosen in all succeeding games. This is the limiting case of $A_{k,n}$ when $k \to \infty$.

B_n : C is chosen in the first game; thereafter, if the number of other players choosing C in the preceding game is at least n, C is chosen; otherwise D is chosen.

B'_n : D is chosen in the first game, thereafter, if the number of other players choosing C in the preceding game is at least n, C is chosen; otherwise D is chosen.

A_k (including A_∞), B_n and B'_n are called *conditional* strategies.

Unless otherwise stated, $A_{k,n}$ is assumed throughout this chapter to include $A_{\infty,n}$; that is, k need not be finite. When $n = 0$, $A_{k,n}$ and B_n degenerate into C^∞. I assume henceforth that $n > 0$. As in the last section, all players choosing $A_{k,n}$, for finite k, use the same value of k.

Note that when $n = N - 1$, Cooperation in the conditional strategies is contingent upon the Cooperation of *all* the other players.[8] When $N = 2$,

$n = N - 1 = 1$ yields the strategies A_k, B and B' considered in the analysis of the two-person Prisoners' Dilemma.

Player i's discount parameter is a_i as before, with $0 < a_i < 1$.

When players using A_k and both B_n and B'_n are present, the possible patterns of sequences of ordinary game choices are exceedingly diverse, and an exhaustive equilibrium analysis correspondingly complex. I shall not attempt such an analysis here. Instead, I shall consider two important special classes of strategy vectors, and establish necessary and sufficient conditions for them to be equilibria when the available set of strategies is limited. When any of the infinite number of possible strategies is available to each player, then of course these conditions are only necessary. The analysis of these two classes illustrates how rich the N-person game is in possibilities. It also indicates, I think, the broad conclusions which a more complete and general analysis would yield. In particular, I do not think that my general conclusion in this section would be substantially modified: that mutual Cooperation is sometimes rational but depends on precarious arrangements as well as on the sort of conditions encountered in the two-person supergame.

First Class of Strategies: $A_{k,n}$, B_n, C^∞ and D^∞

Consider first the strategy vectors containing some or all of the following

Table 3

	(time) $t =$	1 2 3 . . .
$A_{k,n}\Big\{$	$i = 1$	C
	2	C
	.	.
	.	.
	m_A	C
$B_n\Big\{$	$m_A + 1$	C
	$m_A + 2$	C
	.	.
	.	.
	$m_A + m_B$	C
$C^\infty\Big\{$	$m_A + m_B + 1$	$C\,C\,C . . .$
	$m_A + m_B + 2$	$C\,C\,C . . .$
	.	. . . . . .
	m	$C\,C\,C . . .$
$D^\infty\Big\{$	$j = m + 1$	$D\,D\,D . . .$
	$m + 2$	$D\,D\,D . . .$
	.	. . . . . .
	N	$D\,D\,D . . .$

strategies and no others: $A_{k,n}$, B_n, C^∞ and D^∞. If these are the only strategies available to each player, under what conditions are such strategy vectors equilibria? Suppose that, of the N players, m do *not* choose D^∞. Let these m players be indexed as $i = 1, 2, \ldots,$ and in such a way that the first m_A of them use $A_{k,n}$, the next m_B use B_n, and the last m_C of them use C^∞. Let the remaining $N - m$ players, who use D^∞, be indexed $j = m + 1, m + 2, \ldots, N$. Then $m = m_A + m_B + m_C$. This indexing of the players is shown schematically in Table 3. (The choices of the $A_{k,n}$ and B_n players after the first ordinary game depend of course on the values of n, m_A, m_B and m.)

(0.) First, consider strategy vectors containing only C^∞ and D^∞. (So that $m_A = m_B = 0$.) Two cases are of interest (0.1 and 0.2).

> **(0.1)** Suppose that all players choose D^∞. (So that $m = 0$.) Then each player's payoff is $g(0)a_j/(1 - a_j)$. If any player changes unilaterally from D to C in any one ordinary game, his payoff would be $f(0)$ in that game. Since $f(0) < g(0)$, we see that a change from D^∞ to *any* other supergame strategy would result in a loss. Thus, the strategy vector $(D^\infty, D^\infty, \ldots, D^\infty)$ is always an equilibrium.

> **(0.2)** Suppose now that some players choose C^∞. (So that $m > 0$.) Then the payoff to i is $f(m - 1)a_i/(1 - a_i)$ for all i such that $1 \leqslant i \leqslant m$; and the payoff to j is $g(m)a_j/(1 - a_j)$ for each player j using D^∞. If any of the first m players (i) unilaterally changes his strategy to D^∞, his new payoff is $g(m - 1)a_i/(1 - a_i)$, which always exceeds $f(m - 1)a_i/(1 - a_i)$. Thus, any strategy vector in which some players choose C^∞ and all other players choose D^∞ is never an equilibrium.
>
> A special case occurs when $m = N$; that is, all N players choose C^∞. Thus, $(C^\infty, C^\infty, \ldots, C^\infty)$ is never an equilibrium.

We note before continuing that the presence of players who Defect unconditionally (the $N - m$ players choosing D^∞) does not make an essential difference. The problem in effect reduces to whether Cooperation will occur amongst the remaining players. To avoid possible confusion, I shall not remove the unconditional Defectors from the analysis.

(1.) Now consider strategy vectors in which at least one player chooses one of the two conditional strategies. (In other words, $m_A + m_B > 0$.)

It is assumed in this part (1.) and the next (2.) that every player who uses a strategy which is a function of n selects the same value of n. In section (3.) n is permitted to vary between players.

The payoffs to all players in this case depend upon the values of m_A, m_B, m and n. Three cases have to be considered separately: (1.1) $m - 1 > n$; (1.2) $m - 1 < n$; (1.3) $m - 1 = n$.

> **(1.1)** $m - 1 > n$
>
> In this case, all the first m players choose C in every ordinary game, for

at each stage their Cooperation is conditional upon at least n other players Cooperating, and since there are sufficient Cooperators in the first game, so there are in the second, and therefore also in the third, and so on. Thus, the payoff to each of the first m players is $f(m-1)a_i/(1-a_i)$ and the payoff to each of the players using D^∞ is $g(m)a_j/(1-a_j)$, as in case (0.2). But if any one of the first m players 'defects', that is, unilaterally changes his strategy to D^∞, the remaining $m-1$ conditional Cooperators continue to choose C in every ordinary game, so that the defector's payoff increases, as in case (0.2). Thus, cases where conditional Cooperators are present and $m-1 > n$ are never equilibria.

We might say in this case that, following the lone defection to D^∞ of one of the first m players, the *conditional compact* amongst those using conditional strategies does not 'collapse'. The lone defector benefits from the maintenance of their Cooperation.

A special case of interest is when $m = N$ (so that there are no players choosing D^∞). Then $n < N-1$. Even where *all* players use a conditionally Cooperative strategy, an equilibrium cannot result when $n < N-1$, that is, when Cooperation is *not* conditional upon the Cooperation of *all* other players. We shall see later (case (1.3)) that equilibria can occur only when $N-1 = n$. Thus, when $m = N$, equilibrium requires conditional strategies to depend upon the Cooperation of all other players.

(1.2) $m-1 < n$

All of the first m players choose C in the first ordinary game. Thereafter all conditional Cooperation collapses, for the total number of Cooperators in the first game (m) is too small. The players using B_n and those using $A_{\infty,n}$ choose D in every subsequent game, for there are never enough players using C^∞ to bring them back to C. The players using $A_{k,n}$ (for finite values of k) choose D for k games, then C for one game, then D for $k+1$ games, etc. The payoffs are as follows. The payoff to a player using $A_{k,n}$ is

$$P_1 = f(m-1)a_i + f(m_A + m_C - 1)(S_i - a_i) + g(m_C)\left(\frac{a_i}{1-a_i} - S_i\right)$$

The payoff to a player using B_n is

$$P_2 = f(m-1)a_i + g(m_A + m_C)(S_i - a_i) + g(m_C)\left(\frac{a_i}{1-a_i} - S_i\right)$$

The payoff to a player using C^∞ is

$$P_3 = f(m-1)a_i + f(m_A + m_C - 1)(S_i - a_i) + f(m_C - 1)\left(\frac{a_i}{1-a_i} - S_i\right)$$

The payoff to a player using D^∞ is

$$P_4 = g(m)a_j + g(m_A + m_C)\,(S_j - a_j) + g(m_C)\left(\frac{a_j}{1 - a_j} - S_j\right)$$

If any of the first m players (i) changes his strategy to D^∞, his new payoff is

$$P_5 = g(m - 1)a_i + g(m_A + m_C - \delta)\,(S_i - a_i) + g(m_C - \delta')\left(\frac{a_i}{1 - a_i} - S_i\right)$$

where

$$\delta = \begin{cases} 0 \text{ if player } i \text{ is using } B_n \\ 1 \text{ if player } i \text{ is using } A_{k,n} \text{ or } C^\infty \end{cases}$$

and

$$\delta' = \begin{cases} 0 \text{ if player } i \text{ is using } A_{k,n} \text{ or } B_n \\ 1 \text{ if player } i \text{ is using } C^\infty \end{cases}$$

It can be seen that such a change of strategy always yields a gain, since

$$P_5 > P_1 \text{ for a player } i \text{ using } A_{k,n}$$
$$P_5 > P_2 \text{ for a player } i \text{ using } B_n$$

and

$$P_5 > P_3 \text{ for a player } i \text{ using } C^\infty$$

Since $m_A + m_B > 0$, there must be at least one player in one of these three groups; his defection yields him a gain. Thus, strategy vectors where $m_A + m_B > 0$ and $m - 1 < n$ are never equilibria.

If there are some players using B_n, this result can be seen immediately. For if any one of these B_n players defects to D^∞, his payoff in the first game increases from $f(m - 1)$ to $g(m - 1)$, while his payoffs in all succeeding games are the same.

If there are no players using B_n, then consider a player using $A_{k,n}$. If he defects to D^∞, then in each game the number of *other* players Cooperating is the same as before he defected. Therefore, since he now gets $g(.)$ wherever before he got $f(.)$ in a single game, he gains by defecting.

(1.3) $m - 1 = n$

In this case there are exactly enough players choosing C in each game to maintain throughout the supergame the 'compact' amongst the conditional Cooperators. If nobody changes his strategy, the first m players all choose C in every game and the payoffs are as in case (1.1). In particular, the payoff to any of the first m players is $f(m - 1)a_i/(1 - a_i)$. But if any one of the m players changes strategy, switching to D in any ordinary game, the 'compact' collapses for the rest of the supergame; if any player i switches at the outset (or in any later game, which is then indexed $t = 0$ to D^∞, then his payoff becomes P_5 (as in case 1.2)), and this does not represent a gain if and only if

$$g(m-1)a_i + g(m_A + m_C - \delta)(S_i - a_i) + g(m_C - \delta')\left(\frac{a_i}{1-a_i} - S_i\right)$$

$$\leqslant f(m-1).\frac{a_i}{1-a_i} \quad (8)$$

A change by one of the first m players to any strategy other than D would not yield him a greater gain than D^∞. For as long as $n > 1$ in the conditional strategies $A_{k,n}$ and B_n, then a change to any other strategy such as B_n will not revive the Cooperation of players using these two strategies after the first game.

Thus strategy vectors where $m_A + m_B > 0$ and $m - 1 = n$ are equilibria if and only if inequality (8) holds for each of the first m players.

The following special cases are of interest.

(1.31) Suppose there are no players choosing $A_{k,n}$ or C^∞ (that is, $m_A = m_C = 0$, and therefore $m = m_B$). Then inequality (8) simplifies to:

$$g(m-1)a_i + g(0)\frac{a_i^2}{1-a_i} \leqslant f(m-1).\frac{a_i}{1-a_i}$$

player i being a defector from B_n. Thus, strategy vectors in this category are equilibria only if, for each of the first m players,

$$a_i \geqslant \frac{g(m-1) - f(m-1)}{g(m-1) - g(0)} \quad (9)$$

This inequality can be given an informal interpretation similar to the one which was given in Section 3.2 to the inequality

$$a_i \geqslant \frac{y-x}{y-w}$$

We call the ratio on the right-hand side of inequality (9) a player's *temptation* to defect unilaterally from mutual Cooperation amongst all the players not using D^∞. (The payoff difference $g(m-1) - f(m-1)$ is the increase in a player's payoff when he defects in this way. But since the payoff scales are unique only up to a linear transformation and therefore have arbitrary zeros and units, this payoff difference should not be used alone as a 'measure'.)

(1.32) Suppose there are only two groups, those choosing $A_{k,n}$ and those choosing D^∞ (that is, $m_B = m_C = 0$, and therefore $m = m_A$). Then inequality (8) becomes

$$g(m-1)a_i + g(m-1)(S_i - a_i) + g(0)\left\{\frac{a_i}{1-a_i} - S_i\right\} \leqslant f(m-1)\frac{a_i}{1-a_i}$$

player i being a defector from $A_{k,n}$.

Thus, strategy vectors in this category are equilibria only if, for each of the first m players:

$$\frac{(1 - a_i)S_i}{a_i} \leqslant \frac{f(m - 1) - g(0)}{g(m - 1) - g(0)}$$

This inequality should be compared with (1) in Section 3.2. Note that whenever it holds, so also does the inequality obtained in (1.31) above.

(1.33) Suppose finally that there are no players choosing D^∞ (that is, $m = N$). Then $n = N - 1$, since $m - 1 = n$. Thus, the strategies $A_{k,n}$ and B_n are conditional upon the Cooperation of *every other player*. But inequality (8) cannot be simplified.

Summary

The results obtained so far cover the case when $A_{k,n}$, B_n, C^∞ and D^∞ are the only strategies available to each player and when all players using a conditionally Cooperative strategy depend upon the Cooperation of the same number (n) of other players. They can be summarized as follows.

(i) The strategy vector in which $m = 0$ (that is, all players choose D^∞) is always an equilibrium.

(ii) The strategy vectors in which $m > 0$ but $m_A + m_B = 0$ (that is, no players choose conditionally Cooperative strategies but some choose C^∞) are never equilibria.

(iii) When $m_A + m_B > 0$, a strategy vector in which $m - 1 \neq n$ (that is, the conditional Cooperators do *not* depend on the Cooperation of *all* the other players who are not using D^∞) is never an equilibrium.

(iv) When $m_A + m_B > 0$, a strategy vector in which $m - 1 = n$ is an equilibrium if and only if inequality (8) holds for each of the first m players. This vector, which results in the Cooperation of the first m players throughout the supergame and the Defection of the remainder, is preferred by every player to that in (i). If these two strategy vectors are the only equilibria in the supergame, then the Cooperative one will be the outcome.

The Cooperation of all players is thus possible, but precarious: there must be players whose Cooperation is *conditional* upon the Cooperation of *all* the other players; furthermore, inequality (8) must be true for every one of the Cooperators, conditional or unconditional.

Notice, however, that I have shown that *even when some players insist on using D^∞, Cooperation may still be rational for all the rest*. Here again, though, mutual Cooperation depends on the presence of players whose Cooperation is conditional upon that of all the players who are not using D^∞ and on inequality (8) holding for each of the Cooperators. The value of the right-hand side of this inequality depends of course on the number of players ($N - m$) using D^∞. Generally speaking, the greater the number of players using D^∞

(that is, the smaller the value of m), the smaller must be the discount rate if inequality (8) is to be satisfied. Or, conversely, the greater the discount rate $(1 - a_i)$, the more Cooperators there must be, in order that this strategy vector is an equilibrium. This is illustrated in the following example.

Example

Before continuing with the equilibrium analysis of other types of strategy vectors, I return briefly to Hardin's version of Olson's 'logic of collective action', not to treat it exhaustively but to illustrate and make more concrete the results obtained so far.

There are N players altogether. In the ordinary game, each of them has to choose between contributing a unit of the costs of providing a good which is public for this group of N players (strategy C) or not contributing (strategy D). For each unit contributed, the total benefit to the group is r and the benefit to each player is assumed to be r/N. All players benefit from a contribution by any player.

The payoff functions $f(v)$ and $g(v)$ can be specified as follows:

$$f(v) = \frac{(v + 1)r}{N} - 1$$

$$g(v) = \frac{vr}{N}$$

The ordinary game is a Prisoners' Dilemma if and only if: (i) D dominates C for each player; that is, $g(v) > f(v)$ for all $v \geqslant 0$, which is true if and only if $r < N$; and (ii) the outcome $(C, C, ..., C)$ is preferred by every player to $(D, D, ..., D)$; that is, $f(N - 1) > g(0)$, which is true if and only if $r > 1$.

Thus $1 < r < N$ is a necessary and sufficient condition for the ordinary game to be a Prisoners' Dilemma, with D being each player's rational choice.

Suppose that this condition is met, and consider now the supergame consisting of an infinite number of iterations of this ordinary game. The results just obtained for the N-person Prisoners' Dilemma supergame can be applied, for the functions f and g satisfy the three assumptions on which those results depend. The first two assumptions are simply those which guarantee that the ordinary game is a Prisoners' Dilemma; the third is that $g(v) > g(0)$ for all $v > 0$, which is satisfied here just as long as $r > 0$.

Consider first those strategy vectors in which m players choose B_n and the remaining players choose D^∞. Thus $m_A = m_C = 0$. We know that such strategy vectors are equilibria only if $m - 1 = n$. Let us consider vectors in which this is so. Then the result in case (1.31) is applicable; a strategy vector of this type is an equilibrium only if, for all i such that $1 \leqslant i \leqslant m$,

$$a_i \geqslant \frac{g(m - 1) - f(m - 1)}{g(m - 1) - g(0)}$$

Substituting for f and g, this becomes:

$$a_i \geqslant \frac{N-r}{r(m-1)}$$

Even before assuming a particular value for a_i, a lower bound can be placed on m, the number of individuals choosing B_n, when N and r are given. For a_i must be less than one, so that this inequality can hold only if $m > N/r$. Thus, if there are $N = 100$ players altogether and $r = 5$, then at least 20 players must use the conditionally Cooperative strategy, if the vector is to be an equilibrium.

As the discount rate $(1 - a_i)$ increases, this minimum value of m increases. Thus (assuming again that $N = 100$ and $r = 5$), if $a_i = 0.9$ for every player, we find that $m \geqslant 23$ is required; if $a_i = 0.3$ for every player, $m \geqslant 65$; and so on.

In other words, if, for example, $N = 100$, $r = 5$ and $a_i = 0.9$ (for all i), then a strategy vector in which m players choose B_n and the remainder choose D^∞ can be an equilibrium only if m is at least 23 and the Cooperation of every one of these 23 players is conditional upon the Cooperation of all other players who are not using D^∞ (that is, $n = m - 1$).

The inequality giving the conditions for equilibrium in this special case (1.31) takes a simple form. I consider now the more general case (1.3) of strategy vectors in which the four strategies $A_{k,n}$, B_n, C^∞ and D^∞ appear. Assuming that $m - 1 = n$, a necessary and sufficient condition for such strategy vectors to be equilibria is that inequality (7) holds for each of the first m players. Substituting for f and g, (7) reduces to:

$$m_A \left(\frac{a_i}{1 - a_i} - S_i \right) + m_B \left(\frac{a_i^2}{1 - a_i} \right) \geqslant \frac{N}{r} \cdot \frac{a_i}{1 - a_i} - S_i \text{ for players using } A_{k,n}$$

$$\geqslant \frac{N}{r} \cdot \frac{a_i}{1 - a_i} - a_i \text{ for players using } B_n$$

$$\geqslant \frac{a_i}{1 - a_i} \cdot \left(\frac{N}{r} - 1 \right) \text{ for players using } C^\infty$$

These inequalities being independent of m, equilibrium is dependent only on the number of players using conditional strategies (subject of course to $m_A + m_B < m < N$). Notice, too, that since

$$a_i < S(k, a_i) < \frac{a_i}{1 - a_i}$$

for non-zero finite k, the smallest values of m_A (given m_B) and m_B (given m_A) sufficient for defection to be irrational are greater for players using B_n (or $A_{\infty,n}$) than they are for those using $A_{k,n}$ (for any non-zero finite k), and greater for the latter than for those using C^∞. This is as one would expect.

For the sake of even more concrete illustration, I assume now that in all the strategies of the $A_{k,n}$ type, $k = 3$. (Alternatively, I could seek to determine the values of k which yield equilibria, given the values of n (and therefore m), N, r and a_i.) Suppose again that $a_i = 0.9$, $N = 100$ and $r = 5$.

With this value of k, we have

$$S(k, a_i) = a_i + a_i^5 + a_i^{10} + a_i^{16} + \ldots$$

and with $a_i = 0.9$ this is found to be approximately 2.17. Substituting for S, a_i, N and r, the three inequalities above become:

$$m_A + 1.186\, m_B \geqslant 26.04 \text{ for players using } A_{k,n}$$
$$\geqslant 26.22 \text{ for players using } B_n$$
$$\geqslant 25.04 \text{ for players using } C^\infty$$

Thus, the second of these three inequalities is necessary and sufficient for the strategy vector to be an equilibrium.

We see, for example, that when $m_A = 0$ and $m_B = 20$, the vector is not an equilibrium; but whenever $m_A \geqslant 26$, it certainly is. The general point is that, if the total number $(m_A + m_B)$ of conditional Cooperators is too small, then it pays any of the players not using D^∞ to change to that strategy because such defection leads to the defection of only a few other players and therefore (in view of the assumptions about the payoff functions f and g) to only a small loss of benefits, which is more than compensated by having to pay the cost of Cooperating.

(2.) Second Class of Strategies: B_n and B'_n.

I now consider a second class of strategy vectors: those in which some players use B_n and the others use B'_n. It is assumed that only these two strategies and D^∞ are available to each player. I shall obtain the conditions under which strategy vectors involving only B_n and B'_n are equilibria within this restricted set of three strategies. Let a typical B_n player be labelled i and a typical B'_n player be labelled j. Let the number of players using B_n be m_B, as before. Then there are $N - m_B$ players using B'_n. It is still assumed that the same value of n is used by all N players. The addition of players using C^∞ and D^∞ would make no essential difference (as the analysis in part (1.) should make clear), although of course the actual payoffs and inequalities obtained below would be different.

Three cases have to be considered separately: (2.1) $m_B > n$; (2.2) $m_B < n$; (2.3) $m_B = n$.

(2.1) $m_B > n$

The players using B_n choose C in the first game, while those using B'_n choose D. But there are enough players in the B_n group (since $m_B - 1 \geqslant n$) to guarantee their own continued Cooperation in the second game and also to cause the B'_n players to Cooperate in that game. From the second game onwards, all N players Cooperate.

The payoff to a player using B_n is therefore

$$f(m_B - 1)a_i + f(N - 1)\frac{a_i^2}{1 - a_i}$$

while the payoff to a player using B'_n is

$$g(m_B)a_j + f(N-1)\frac{a_j^2}{1-a_j}$$

When $m_B - 1 > n$ a change by a player using B_N will have no effect on the choices of the other players: all N players will Cooperate from the second game onwards. Thus the defector increases his payoff, for he now receives $g(m_B - 1)$ in the first game whereas before his payoff in that game was $f(m_B - 1)$, and his payoff in all other games is unchanged. A player using B_n will gain even more, of course, if he changes to D^∞.

When $m_B - 1 = n$, there are *exactly* enough players using B_n to maintain their own Cooperation throughout the supergame, so that if one of them changes his strategy to B'_n or D^∞, then the Cooperation of the remaining B_n players collapses in the second game, although the B'_n players Cooperate. What happens thereafter depends on the relation between n and the number of players using B'_n. The defector may or may not gain.

However, a change by one of the B'_n players (whenever $m_B > n$) to D^∞ has no effect on the choices of the other players: they still Cooperate from the second game onwards. Hence, such a change yields a greater payoff for the defector, for while his payoff in the first game is unchanged, his payoff in each succeeding game is increased from $f(N-1)$ to $g(N-1)$.

Thus, strategy vectors of this type, when $m_B > n$, are never equilibria.

(2.2) $m_B < n$

Here, all players Defect from the second game onwards. If a player using B_n changes his strategy to D^∞, his payoff is thereby increased, for in the first game he receives $g(m_B - 1)$ whereas before he received $f(m_B - 1)$, and in all subsequent games his payoff is unchanged. Thus, strategy vectors in this category are never equilibria.

(2.3) $m_B = n$

The B_n players choose C in the first game but Defect in the second. The B'_n players choose D in the first game but Cooperate in the second. What happens in the rest of the supergame depends on the relation between n and the number of players using B'_n. This is examined in the following sub-cases.

(2.31) $N - m_B > n$. (so that $m_B < \frac{1}{2}N$.) Then there are enough B'_n players to bring back the B_n players to Cooperation in the third game and to maintain the Cooperation of the B'_n players themselves. All N players choose C from the third game onwards.

(2.311) $N - m_B > n + 1$. If one of the B'_n players changes his strategy to D^∞, then the choices of the other players are unaffected. He therefore gains by such a change, for though his payoff in the first game is unchanged, his payoff in the second game increases from $f(N - m_B - 1)$ to $g(N - m_B - 1)$ and his payoff in every succeeding game increases from $f(N - 1)$ to $g(N - 1)$. Thus, strategy vectors in this category are never equilibria.

(2.312) $N - m_B = n + 1$. (Thus, $m_B = \frac{1}{2}(N - 1)$, so that N must be odd.) In this case a change of strategy by one of the B'_n players to D^∞ does not leave the other players' choices unaffected. Instead, it results in the B_n players alternating between C and D throughout the supergame, beginning with C in the third game, and the B'_n players alternating similarly but beginning with D in the third game. This does not yield a greater payoff for the defector if and only if

$$f(m_B)(1 - a_j) + f(N - 1)a_j \geqslant g(m_B) \qquad (10)$$

(after simplifying).

If one of the B_n players changes his strategy to D^∞, then all N players Defect from the second game onwards. Such a change does not yield a greater payoff if and only if

$$f(m_B - 1)a_i + g(N - m_B)a_i^2 + f(N - 1)\frac{a_i^3}{1 - a_i}$$
$$\geqslant g(m_B - 1)a_i + g(0)\frac{a_i^2}{1 - a_i} \qquad (11)$$

If one of the B'_n players changes his strategy to B_n, then this results in the B_n players choosing C in the second game but no other choices are changed. Thus, such a change does not yield a greater payoff if and only if

$$f(m_B)(1 - a_j) + f(N - 1)a_j \leqslant g(m_B)$$

but this is the reverse of inequality (10) above. Thus, necessary and sufficient conditions for strategy vectors in this category to be equilibria are the restrictive condition

$$f(m_B)(1 - a_j) + f(N - 1)a_j = g(m_B)$$

(for each of the B'_n players) together with inequality (11) (for each of the B_n players). If $f(N - 1) > f(m_B)$, this equality can be written in the form:

$$a_j = \frac{g(m_B) - f(m_B)}{f(N - 1) - f(m_B)}$$

(2.32) $N - m_B < n$. (So that $m_B > \frac{1}{2}N$.) Then, before any player changes strategy, all N players Defect from the third game onwards. If one of the B'_n players changes his strategy to D^∞, then all N players Defect from the third game onwards. The defector's payoff changes only in the second game: it increases from $f(N - m_B - 1)$ to $g(N - m_B - 1)$. Thus, strategy vectors in this category are never equilibria.

(2.33) $N - m_B = n$. (Thus, $m_B = \frac{1}{2}N$ so that N must be even.) In this case, before any player changes strategy, each player's choices *alternate* between C and D throughout the supergame, the B_n players beginning with C and the B'_n players beginning with D.

If one of the B_n players changes his strategy to D^∞ or B'_n, then all N players Defect from the second game onward. The defector's payoff is not increased if and only if

$$f(m_B - 1)\frac{a_i}{1 - a_i^2} + g(N - m_B)\frac{a_i^2}{1 - a_i^2} \geqslant g(m_B - 1)a_i + g(0)\frac{a_i^2}{1 - a_i}$$

If one of the B'_n players (j) changes his strategy to B_n, then all N players Cooperate from the second game onwards, and j's payoff is not increased if and only if

$$g(m_B)\frac{a_j}{1 - a_j^2} + f(N - m_B - 1)\frac{a_j^2}{1 - a_j^2} \geqslant f(m_B)a_j + f(N - 1)\frac{a_j^2}{1 - a_j}$$

If one of the B'_n players (j) changes his strategy to D^∞, then all N players Defect from the second game onwards, and j's payoff is not increased if and only if

$$g(m_B)\frac{a_j}{1 - a_j^2} + f(N - m_B - 1)\frac{a_j^2}{1 - a_j^2} \geqslant$$

$$g(m_B)a_j + g(N - m_B - 1)a_j^2 + g(0)\frac{a_j^3}{1 - a_j}$$

The three inequalities given above (the first to hold for each of the B_n players, the second and third for the B'_n players) are necessary and sufficient conditions for the strategy vectors in this category to be equilibria.

This completes the equilibrium analysis of strategy vectors containing only B_n and B'_n (with D^∞ also available). It shows that these vectors are equilibria only under very restrictive conditions. For I have shown that equilibrium can occur only when $m_B = n$ *and* $N - m_B = n$ (when N is even) or $n + 1$ (when N is odd); that is, equilibrium can occur only when the two blocs of players using B_n and B'_n are of equal size (N being even) or when the B'_n bloc has one more player than the B_n bloc (N being odd). In the first case, the two blocs alternate between C and D before any player changes strategy; in the second case, the 'pivotal' extra player in the B'_n bloc causes such alternation by defecting to D^∞ (thus making the two blocs equal in size). In addition to this stringent condition, certain conditions relating the ordinary game payoffs to the discount parameters of all the players must be met.

This completes what I have to say about strategy vectors containing only

B_n and B'_n. I return now to the class of strategy vectors considered earlier, those containing some or all of the strategies $A_{k,n}$, B_n, C^∞ and D^∞, to examine briefly the effect of removing the assumption that the same value of n must appear in all conditional strategies.

(3.) Variable n

In part (0.), no player chooses a conditional strategy. In parts (1.) and (2.) some players use conditional strategies (which are functions of n), but the same value of n is selected by all such players. Here in part (3.), n is permitted to vary between the players. Once again, my analysis is not exhaustive; I illustrate the ideas involved by considering only those strategy vectors containing $A_{k,n}$, B_n, C^∞ and D^∞, as in part (1.). It is assumed that $m_A + m_B > 0$; i.e. that at least one player chooses a conditional strategy.

Let the set of values of n used by the players be

$$\{n_{\min}, n_2, n_3, \ldots, n_{\max}\}, \text{ where } n_{\min} < n_2 < \ldots < n_{\max}$$

The set of players using conditional strategies with $n = n_i$ is called the n_i group. (Both conditional strategies may be in use by members of the group simultaneously.) Let the number of players in the n_i group be N_i.

The players are indexed as in part (1.), *disregarding the values of n*, while m_A, m_B, m_C and m are defined as before. Thus, all those using $A_{k,n}$, for any value of n, are indexed $i = 1, 2, \ldots, m_A$, and so on.

The analysis must first be divided into three cases: (3.1) $m - 1 > n_{\max}$; (3.2) $m - 1 < n_{\min}$; (3.3) $n_{\min} \leqslant m - 1 \leqslant n_{\max}$.

(3.1) $m - 1 > n_{\max}$

In this case, as in (1.1), the 'conditional compact' does not collapse following unilateral defection by one of the first m players. All of the first m players choose C in every game. If any one of them defects to D^∞, his payoff increases. Thus a strategy vector in this category is never an equilibrium. The payoffs to each player before and after the defection are the same as in part (1.1).

(3.2) $m - 1 < n_{\min}$

There are insufficient players to maintain the conditional Cooperation of even the 'stalwarts' using $n = n_{\min}$. All of the first m players choose C in the first game. Thereafter, each player using B_n (or $A_{\infty,n}$) chooses D in every game (regardless of the value of n he uses), and each player using $A_{k,n}$ (for finite k) chooses D for k games, then C for one game, etc. (regardless of the value of n he uses). The payoffs are exactly as in case (1.2). As in that section, any one of the first m players increases his payoff by defecting to D^∞, his new payoff being P_5 as before. Thus, a strategy vector of this type is never an equilibrium.

(3.3) $n_{\min} \leqslant m - 1 \leqslant n_{\max}$

(Note that when all players use the same value of n, so that $n_{\min} =$

$n_{max} = n$, this inequality collapses to $m - 1 = n$, which was treated as case (1.3).) The sequence of choices in this case depends upon the value of $m - 1$ and upon the distribution of players over the values of n and, for each n, the distribution between the strategies $A_{k,n}$ and B_n.

In *all* of the possibilities covered by this inequality, there is a collapse, in the second game, of *some but not all* of the mutual support amongst the $m_A + m_B$ players using conditionally Cooperative strategies. In some cases, no further collapse takes place. In other cases, the withdrawal of the conditional Cooperation of some players in the second game leads to a further collapse of Cooperation in the third game. This process may continue until ultimately there is no (conditional) Cooperation at all. Of course, those players using $A_{k,n}$ (if there are any) periodically return to a Cooperative choice; and this may result in a return of some players to conditional Cooperation. *This 'recovery of Cooperation' can only take place when not all players use conditional strategies with the same value of n* (and then only under special conditions).

We note the following:

(i) If $N_i + m_C > n_i$ for any group i, then all of the members of that group will in all circumstances Cooperate in every game.

(ii) Whenever $m - 1 \leqslant n_i$ (for some group i) then once that group's Cooperation has collapsed, it will never be regained (except trivially when all the players in that group are using A_{k,n_i}, in which case, of course, they periodically return to Cooperation regardless of the behaviour of others). In particular, since $m - 1 \leqslant n_{max}$ (throughout part (3.3) and its sub-cases), the n_{max} group's Cooperation can never be recovered, once lost.

I offer some examples of this case, to illustrate the great variety in the patterns of choices which can occur.

(3.31) $m - 1 = n_{max}$. Here, there are exactly enough players choosing C in each game to maintain the conditional Cooperation of the n_{max} group and therefore of all other groups. As in case (1.3), if nobody changes his strategy, the payoff to each of the first m players is $f(m - 1)a_i/(1 - a_i)$. But if any one of the first m players defects to D^∞ unilaterally, the conditional support of the n_{max} group collapses after the first game. If the total number of Cooperators in the second game, following the collapse of the Cooperation of the n_{max} group, is sufficiently large, there will be no subsequent collapse of Cooperation of any other groups. I consider this case first.

(3.311) $m - 1 - N_{max} > n_{max-1}$. In this case, after the withdrawal of Cooperation by the n_{max} group following a defection to D^∞, there is no further collapse, and all other groups choose C in every game. Of course, those in the n_{max} group using $A_{k,n}$ with a finite k (let there be μ of them) will periodically choose C, but this will not result in a return to Cooperation of any other players in the group.

If any of the first m players defects unilaterally to D^∞, his new payoff is:

$$P_6 = g(m-1)a_i + g(m - \{N_{max} - \mu\} - \delta'')(S_i - a_i) +$$

$$g(m - N_{max} - \delta')\left(\frac{a_i}{1-a_i} - S_i\right)$$

where

$\delta'' = 0$ if i is a member of the n_{max} group but is not using A_{k,n_i}
(for finite k),
$= 1$ otherwise,

and

$\delta' = 0$ if i is a member of the n_{max} group,
$= 1$ otherwise.

Under some conditions, $P_6 \leqslant f(m-1)\dfrac{a_i}{1-a_i}$. Thus, acase (3.311) strategy vector is sometimes an equilibrium.

(3.312) $m - 1 - N_{max} \leqslant n_{max-1}$. In this case, the collapse of the Co-operation of the n_{max} group in the second game (following a

Table 4. An illustration of case (3.312). Blank cells represent D choices

$t =$			1	2	3	4	5	6	7	8	9	10	11	12	13	14	15	16	...
$n=8$	$A_{1,8}$	1	C	C	C		C			C	C					C		C		
		2	C	C	C		C			C	C					C		C		
		3	C	C	C		C			C	C					C		C		
	B_8	4	C	C	C		C				C							C		
		5	C	C	C		C				C							C		
$n=12$	$A_{1,12}$	6	C	C		C			C			C				C				
		7	C	C		C			C			C				C				
	B_{12}	8	C	C		C			C			C				C				
		9	C	C																
$n=18$	$A_{1,18}$	10	C			C			C			C								
		11	C			C			C			C								
		12	C			C			C			C								
	B_{18}	13	C																	
		14	C																	
	$A_{\infty,18}$	15	C																	
C^∞		16	C	C	C	C	C	C	C	C	C	C	C		C	C	C	C	C	
		17	C	C	C	C	C	C	C	C	C	C	C		C	C	C	C	C	
		18	C	C	C	C	C	C	C	C	C	C	C		C	C	C	C	C	
D^∞		19																		
		20																		

defection to D^∞) results in the collapse of the $n_{\max-1}$ group in the third game. This may in turn lead to the collapse of the $n_{\max-2}$ group, and so on. If some players are using $A_{k,n}$ (for finite k), then there may be a partial recovery of Cooperation, in the manner outlined above. The resulting payoffs (after the defection of one player to D^∞) are unwieldy and are not displayed here. As in case (3.311) it is found that some strategy vectors are equilibria.

An example of the sequence of choices is shown in Table 4. There are twenty players altogether. Initially, one player uses D^∞ (so that $m = 19$). The payoffs shown (for the first 16 time periods) are those which result from the defection of one player to D^∞. After this defection, the players are distributed between various groups, as indicated. Three values of n are in use (8, 12 and 18). These values are such that, given the value of m, the Cooperation of the $n = 18$ group collapses in the second game, that of the $n = 12$ group in the third, and that of the $n = 8$ group in the fourth. Thereafter, there is a recovery of the $n = 8$ group, followed by its immediate collapse. No other group ever recovers. This pattern—the rise and fall of the first group—recurs *ad infinitum* at ever wider intervals of time.

If in this example no players have been using an $A_{k,n}$ strategy (for finite k) then, after the first collapse of Cooperation in each group, all its members would choose D in all remaining games.

(3.32) $m - 1 < n_{\max}$. Even before the unilateral defection to D^∞ of any player, the Cooperation of the $n_{\max}$ group collapses in the second game.

If $n_{\max-1} \leqslant m - 1$, then no other group's Cooperation collapses *before* a defection, and if $m - 1 - N_{\max} > n_{\max-1}$, then no other group's Cooperation collapses *after* a defection. In this event, the defection of any one of the first m players will always increase his payoff, so that there can be no equilibria.

If $n_{\max-1} \leqslant m - 1$ but $m - 1 - N_{\max} \leqslant n_{\max-1}$, then, after a defection, further collapse takes place, and the strategy vector may or may not be an equilibrium.

Suppose now that $n_{\max-2} \leqslant m - 1 \leqslant n_{\max-1}$. Then, even before a defection, the Cooperation of the $n_{\max}$ and $n_{\max-1}$ groups, and of no others, collapses in the second game. As in the preceding two paragraphs, strategy vectors are never equilibria if no further collapse follows a defection; otherwise, they may or may not be.

Similarly for smaller values of $m - 1$ in the range $n_{\min} \leqslant m - 1 < n_{\max}$.

This completes what I have to say about the *N*-person Prisoners' Dilemma supergame. My account is far from complete, but suffices, I think, to indicate the broad conclusions which a more complete and general analysis would yield. In particular, I doubt whether a comprehensive analysis would substantially modify the general conclusion of the analysis made here, namely, that *conditional* Cooperation throughout an N-person Prisoners' Dilemma supergame, no matter how many players there are, is *sometimes* rational but is somewhat precarious, inasmuch as the Cooperation of each of the conditional Cooperators has to be contingent upon the Cooperation of *all* the other Cooperators (in addition to a requirement that the discount rates of every one of the Cooperators must not be too high).

A short, informal summary and discussion of the results obtained in this section on the N-person supergame is given in Section 5.1 below.

The two-person and N-person Prisoners' Dilemma supergame models considered here are relatively simple ones. In Section 5.3 (to which the mathematical reader who has read this chapter should turn after reading Chapter 4), I indicate some ways in which they might be extended or revised so as to provide a more realistic picture of the dynamics of public goods provision.

3.4. NOTES

1. Mixed strategies are ruled out, chiefly because they do not seem to correspond to any realistic courses of action in the real world problems of public goods provision which are of interest in this book.

2. This section extends, in certain respects, earlier work on the two-person Prisoners' Dilemma supergame in Martin Shubik, *Strategy and Market Structure: Competition, Oligopoly, and the Theory of Games* (New York, Wiley, 1959); Shubik, 'Game Theory, Behavior, and the Paradox of the Prisoner's Dilemma: Three Solutions', *Journal of Conflict Resolution*, **14**, 181–93 (1970); and Michael Nicholson, *Oligopoly and Conflict* (Liverpool: Liverpool University Press, 1972).

3. Observe that the payoff matrix is *symmetric*: it remains unchanged when the players are interchanged (relabelled). Abandoning symmetry would require minor modifications of detail (in the conditions given below for strategy vectors to be equilibria and for equilibria to be outcomes, the payoffs would have to be subscripted as well as the discount parameters); but the argument would not be changed. This applies also to my treatment of the N-person Prisoners' Dilemma supergame in the next section, where I again assume symmetry. Abandoning symmetry would require more modification in the details of the following chapter on Altruism, but the argument would not be substantially changed. In making this assumption, I do not wish to imply that I (or the writers I am criticizing) believe that it is an accurate description of the real world. I do not wish to assert, for example, that in the mutual Cooperation or mutual Defection outcomes, the payoffs to members of different social classes are the same. However, neither the argument for the state which is criticized here nor my arguments against it would be modified essentially if symmetry were abandoned. In some situations, it is true, asymmetry in Prisoners' Dilemmas may make Cooperation even more difficult (there is some experimental evidence for this in J. P. Sheposh and P. S. Gallo, Jr., 'Asymmetry of Payoff Structure and Cooperative Behavior in the Prisoner's Dilemma Game', *Journal of Conflict Resolution*, **17**, 321–33 (1973), and in earlier studies cited there); but here I am concerned only with the Prisoners' Dilemma element.

4. Anatol Rapoport and Albert C. Chammah, *Prisoner's Dilemma* (Ann Arbor: The University of Michigan Press, 1965), p. 34.

5. Coordination games will be defined in Chapter 6, in the section dealing with Hume's political theory.

6. The remarks made in note 3 (at the start of Section 3.2) about the assumption of symmetry apply here as well.

7. A different definition of the N-person Prisoners' Dilemma has been given recently by Thomas C. Schelling ('Hockey Helmets, Concealed Weapons, and Daylight Saving: A Study of Binary Choices with Externalities', *Journal of Conflict Resolution*, **17**, 381–428 (1973). He defines a 'uniform multiperson prisoner's dilemma' (or MPD) as a game such that: (1) each player has just two strategies available to him and the payoffs can be characterized (in effect) by two functions $f(v)$ and $g(v)$, which are the same for every individual; (2) every player has a dominant strategy (D); (3) $f(v)$ and $g(v)$ are monotonically increasing; (4) there is a number $\kappa > 1$, such that, if κ or more players choose C and the rest do not, those who choose C are better off than if they had all chosen D, but if they number less than κ, this is not true. Schelling's (1) and (2) are also part of my definition. His (3) is a much stronger requirement than my (iii). And his (4) is stronger than my (ii). For all I require in (ii) is that the first part of Schelling's (4) holds for $\kappa = N$; and I leave open the question of whether fewer than N individuals obtain a higher payoff when they all Cooperate (and the rest do not) than when they all defect. Schelling's definition is therefore more restrictive than mine. His requirement (4), it seems to me, partly removes the 'dilemma' in the Prisoners' Dilemma.

   Other ways of defining the N-person Prisoners' Dilemma more restrictively than I define it here can be found in Henry Hamburger, 'N-Person Prisoner's Dilemma', *Journal of Mathematical Sociology*, **3**, 27–48 (1973).

8. A generalization of the strategy $A_{\infty, N-1}$ for any non-cooperative game has been considered by James W. Friedman ('A Non-cooperative Equilibrium for Supergames', *The Review of Economic Studies*, **38**, 1–12 (1971).

Annex to Chapter 3

1. AN ALTERNATIVE ANALYSIS OF THE SUPERGAME

In my analysis of the Prisoners' Dilemma supergame in Chapter 3, I assumed throughout that every player *discounts* the payoffs of future ordinary games. If this discounting takes the form specified, then payoffs for the whole supergame are well-defined finite quantities. Without discounting, the supergame payoff, defined as the sum of the ordinary game payoffs, would generally not be finite. An alternative assumption, on which a theory of the supergame could be founded, is that each player seeks to maximize the *average* payoff per ordinary game. Such averages, taken over an indefinitely large number of ordinary games, are called *average long-run payoffs*.

This assumption is used in a recent study of the two-person Prisoners' Dilemma by Harris.[1] In this study, a strategy for player i is a specification of the following four 'state-conditioned propensities':

$$\xi_i = Pr(C_{i,n+1}|C_{i,n}\,C_{j,n}), \qquad \eta_i = Pr(C_{i,n+1}|C_{i,n}\,D_{j,n})$$
$$\zeta_i = Pr(C_{i,n+1}|D_{i,n}\,C_{j,n}), \qquad \omega_i = Pr(C_{i,n+1}|D_{i,n}\,D_{j,n})$$

where ξ_i is the probability that player i chooses C in the $(n+1)^{\text{th}}$ game given that (C, C) was the outcome of the nth game, and so on.

Harris uses two results from an earlier study by Amnon Rapoport: the average long-run payoffs of pairs of players using such strategies are well-defined; and maximizing average long-run payoff requires the use of a strategy in which each of ξ, η, ζ and ω is equal to either zero or unity. Such strategies are called *policies*. Each player thus has 16 policies available to him. Since, however, the average long-run payoffs depend in general on the players' choices in the first ordinary game, the number of strategies available to each player is 32 (assuming that players are restricted to policies).

Of the 32×32 strategy vectors of this supergame, at least 11 are equilibria. Ten of these result in mutual Defection throughout the supergame. The eleventh equilibrium is a choice by each player of '$\{C, (1,0,0,0)\}$', that is, C in the first game, then C if and only if (C, C) was the outcome of the previous game. Under certain conditions, there are other equilibria.

In particular, (B, B) is an equilibrium if and only if $y + z < 2x$. (What I have been calling B corresponds to $\{C,(1,0,1,0)\}$ in Harris's notation.) But if $y + z > 2x$, then (B, B') and (B', B), which result in the ordinary game outcomes alternating between (C, D) and (D, C), are equilibria. Harris notes that, in the case when $y + z > 2x$, the players are in a coordination game, and there is no basis for recommending whether B or B' should be chosen (i.e. whether C or D should be chosen in the first game), unless mixed strategies are available.

Comparing these results of Harris's with those obtained in Section 3.2, we note in particular that: (i) whereas (B, B) is an equilibrium in Harris's model if and only if $y + z < 2x$, this is not the case in my analysis, where the inequalities (3) and (4) involving the discount parameters must be satisfied; (ii) in my analysis $y + z > 2x$ does not imply that the alternation strategy vectors, (B, B') and (B', B), are equilibria as it does in Harris's; conditions involving the discount parameters must be satisfied for these two to be equilibria; and (iii) under certain conditions (when the players' discount rates are sufficiently high), the strategy vector (D^∞, D^∞) is in my analysis the *only* equilibrium, whereas in Harris's it always coexists with at least one equilibrium yielding mutual Co-operation throughout the supergame.

Harris's study provides a valuable alternative model of the two-person Prisoners' Dilemma supergame. It is perhaps the appropriate model for explaining behaviour in experiments with a Prisoners' Dilemma iterated a large but finite number of times, especially if the number of iterations is unknown to the players. These experiments are of very short duration relative to the time-span of the processes in the real world which they are supposed to simulate and, in a relatively brief experiment, discounting is obviously unimportant. (For this reason, the enormous experimental literature on the iterated Prisoners' Dilemma is of rather limited relevance to the problems of interest here.) For the explanation of behaviour in non-experimental Prisoners' Dilemmas, and in particular for applications to problems of the kind described in Chapter 1, I believe that the discounting of future benefits is an important fact which must be taken into account.[2]

2. THE THEORY OF METAGAMES

I am aware of only one attempt to 'rationalize' Cooperation in the *ordinary* Prisoners' Dilemma game. This is the theory of metagames proposed by Nigel Howard in his *Paradoxes of Rationality*.[3] He believes the theory to be predictive: Cooperation in the Prisoners' Dilemma is 'rational' if a player reasons in a certain way, and this mode of reasoning is claimed to be characteristic of real persons.

If Cooperation is 'rational' in the ordinary game, then it should also be 'rational' in the supergame. Our efforts in Chapter 3 were clearly unnecessary if Howard's argument is valid. Anatol Rapoport believes that it is. In an enthusiastic article, he has stated that Howard's theory has 'resolved' the 'paradox' of the Prisoners' Dilemma, reconciling individual and collective rationality.[4]

In this part of the Annex, I state why I believe that Howard and Rapoport are mistaken. The relevant part of Howard's argument as it applies to the Prisoners' Dilemma is first briefly presented with reference to the two-person, two-strategy case which we considered in Chapter 3.

Consider the game with the following payoff matrix:

	C	D
C	x, x	z, y
D	y, z	w, w

where $y > x > w > z$. Call this now the *basic game*.

Suppose now that player 2's choices are not between the *basic strategies* C and D, but between the *conditional strategies* (Howard calls them 'policies') consisting of all the mappings from player 1's basic strategies to his own. Let S_1/S_2 denote the conditional strategy whereby player 2 chooses S_1 if player 1 chooses C and S_2 if he chooses D. Then 2's conditional strategies are:

C/C: to choose C regardless of player 1's choice,
D/D: to choose D regardless of player 1's choice,
C/D: to choose the same strategy as player 1,
D/C: to choose the opposite of player 1's strategy.

If player 2's choices can in fact be made dependent upon player 1's choices in this way, then it is as if the two are playing in a game whose payoff matrix is:

	C/C	D/D	C/D	D/C
C	x, x	z, y	x, x	z, y
D	y, z	$\boxed{w, w}$	w, w	y, z

This is called the *2-metagame*. Its only equilibrium is $(D, D/D)$, corresponding to the only equilibrium (D, D) in the basic game.

Suppose next that player 1's choices are not between the basic strategies C and D but are conditional upon the conditional strategies of player 2 in the 2-metagame. Let $S_1/S_2/S_3/S_4$ denote the conditional strategy whereby player 1 chooses S_1 if player 2 chooses C/C, S_2 if he chooses D/D, S_3 if he chooses C/D, and S_4 if he chooses D/C. If the players' choices can in fact be made interdependent in this way, then it is as if they are playing a game whose payoff matrix is that shown in Table 5.

This game is called the *12-metagame*. It has three equilibria, which are marked in the payoff matrix; but if the two players were indeed playing in this game, they would not expect the uncooperative equilibrium $(D/D/D/D, D/D)$ to occur, for each of them strictly prefers either of the other two equilibria. Both of these two other equilibria are outcomes of a single strategy of player 2, and since $D/D/C/D$ weakly dominates $C/D/C/D$ for player 1, both players should expect

Table 5. Payoff matrix for the 12-metagame

	C/C	D/D	C/D	D/C
$C/C/C/C$	x, x	z, y	x, x	z, y
$D/D/D/D$	y, z	$\boxed{w, w}$	w, w	y, z
$D/D/D/C$	y, z	w, w	w, w	z, y
$D/D/C/D$	y, z	w, w	$\boxed{x, x}$	y, z
$D/D/C/C$	y, z	w, w	x, x	z, y
$D/C/D/D$	y, z	z, y	w, w	y, z
$D/C/D/C$	y, z	z, y	w, w	z, y
$D/C/C/D$	y, z	z, y	x, x	y, z
$D/C/C/C$	y, z	z, y	x, x	z, y
$C/D/D/D$	x, x	w, w	w, w	y, z
$C/D/D/C$	x, x	w, w	w, w	z, y
$C/D/C/D$	x, x	w, w	$\boxed{x, x}$	y, z
$C/D/C/C$	x, x	w, w	x, x	z, y
$C/C/D/D$	x, x	z, y	w, w	y, z
$C/C/D/C$	x, x	z, y	w, w	z, y
$C/C/C/D$	x, x	z, y	x, x	y, z

$(D/D/C/D, C/D)$ to be the outcome. It is therefore the outcome. $(D/D/C/D, C/D)$ corresponds to (C, C) in the basic game. In this way, according to Howard, mutual cooperation is rationalized even in the ordinary game.

A similar outcome occurs in the '21-metagame', where player 1's strategies are conditional upon the choices of player 2, which are in turn conditional upon the basic strategies of player 1. That is to say, the outcome is $(C/D, D/D/C/D)$, corresponding to (C, C) in the basic game.

Conditional strategies of a higher order could be considered. Thus player 2's strategies could be conditional upon those of player 1 in the 12-metagame, whose payoff matrix is exhibited in Table 5. (The resulting game is called the '212-metagame'.) However, neither this nor any higher order metagame would yield new equilibria, for Howard shows that all equilibria corresponding to distinct outcomes in the basic game are revealed in the nth-order metagames in which each of the n players is 'named' once and only once—the 12-metagame and the 21-metagame in this two-person Prisoners' Dilemma instance.

I have two comments to make on this theory of metagames.

1. The first is for me decisive in rejecting the theory as an explanation of behaviour in the ordinary Prisoners' Dilemma in which, as I have assumed, binding agreements are not possible. In this game, the players choose their strategies *independently*; they are in effect chosen simultaneously, with no knowledge of the other's strategy. And no matter how much they may indulge in 'metagame reasoning' they must in fact ultimately choose one of their *basic* strategies.

In metagame theory, on the other hand, the player's strategies are required to be interdependent, even in this *ordinary* Prisoner's Dilemma game.

In the ordinary game, strategies could be made interdependent by use of a 'referee', not in the game theorist's usual sense, but in the sense of a third party who would be notified of the players' strategies, compare them, *and* ensure that a conditional strategy is in fact made dependent upon the specified strategies of others. However, this is equivalent to the user of a conditional strategy making his choice of a basic strategy *after* the choices of those whose strategies his depends upon.

Furthermore, the referee could in general decide a unique outcome only if the conditional strategies were of the appropriate orders of 'sophistication'. The 'resolution' of the two-person Prisoners' Dilemma takes place in the 12- or 21-metagame. Each of these games is asymmetric in the sense that one player's strategies are first-order conditional, while the other's are second-order conditional. This asymmetry is of course essential to the resolution, for if both players use conditional strategies of the same order, then some conditional strategy combinations do not yield determinate outcomes (as when, for example, each player would Cooperate if and only if the other Cooperates). This asymmetry is to some extent arbitrary; or rather, it emphasizes again that one player's choices of basic strategy must in fact follow the other's.

Of course, a player may try to ensure that other players will act Cooperatively, by announcing his intention to use a conditionally Cooperative strategy, and generally by *bargaining* with them. However, such exchanges, supposing them to be possible, would not have the effect of producing mutual Cooperation, unless agreements reached in this way were binding. Such agreements are ruled out in the specification of the game. In any case, if a mechanism for enforcing agreements existed, then the players would presumably have had little difficulty in agreeing on mutual Cooperation in the first place, and there would be no need of a theory of metagames to explain this.

Howard is neither clear nor consistent about the interpretation to be placed upon strategies in metagames. He often suggests that metagame strategies are made interdependent through *actual* bargaining (as on p. 101 of *Paradoxes of Rationality* and in applications of the theory throughout the book) and that a player's choice *follows* certain other players' choices in full knowledge of them (pp. 23, 27, 54 and 61 for example). Elsewhere, however, he seems to say that the choices are not actually sequential; the players behave *as if* they were. Thus (at the first order of sophistication), a player (k, say) 'sees' the other players choosing basic strategies, which he 'correctly predicts', while he himself plays as if he were in the k-metagame, his strategies being conditional on the other players' basic strategies. Metagames of higher order are reached ('subjectively') by similar reasoning.[5]

If the players can negotiate binding agreements or if in some other way their choices are made interdependently, then they are not playing in the Prisoners' Dilemma ordinary game which I have been discussing in this book. Yet Howard clearly assumes that they are. Part of his case for the need for a theory such as his own is based on the 'breakdown of rationality' (as this concept is used in conventional game theory) which is indicated, according to Howard, by the standard analysis of the Prisoners' Dilemma ordinary game.

The conclusions of the standard analysis of this game may be distressing; but they are unaffected by a consideration of metagames.

2. My second comment is that, if bargaining or any other dynamic process is indeed the object of study, then the ordinary game (with or without its metagames) is in any case an inappropriate model. In bargaining, there are *sequences* of choices; there are bluffs, threats and promises; there is learning and adaption of expectations; the value of an outcome is discounted with future time; and so on. These things are not explicitly taken into account in the theory of metagames.

3. NOTES

1. Richard J. Harris, 'Note on "Optimal Policies for the Prisoner's Dilemma"', *Psychological Review*, **76**, 363–75 (1969). Harris's own analysis is preceded by a criticism of an earlier paper by Amnon Rapoport ('Optimal Policies for the Prisoner's Dilemma', *Psychological Review*, **74**, 136–48 (1967)), which also treated the Prisoners' Dilemma supergame with two players who maximize average long-run payoff. Harris rejects Rapoport's model for reasons which I find compelling, and therefore I have not discussed Rapoport's work in this Annex. Neither of these authors considers the N-person game.

2. Harris's study is, I think, the best of the several theoretical studies of the iterated Prisoners' Dilemma which are based on an assumption of rational individual choice but take no account of discounting. It is for this reason that I have singled it out in this Annex. Discounting is not, of course, taken into account in the many models which are not of the rational choice sort, such as the Markov chain and stochastic learning models in Rapoport and Chammah's *Prisoner's Dilemma* and in later studies by Rapoport and others.

3. Nigel Howard, *Paradoxes of Rationality: Theory of Metagames and Political Behavior* (Cambridge, Mass.: The M.I.T. Press, 1971).

4. Anatol Rapoport, 'Escape from Paradox', *Scientific American*, 50–6, July 1967.

5. See, for example, pp. 55 and 62 of *Paradoxes of Rationality*.

CHAPTER 4

Altruism in the Prisoners' Dilemma

In the last chapter, it was assumed that each player seeks to maximize only his own payoff. In this chapter, each player is assumed to maximize a function of both his own payoff and the other players' payoffs. In this case, I shall say that he is acting *altruistically*. I shall also consider briefly what I call 'sophisticated altruism', where a player's utility depends upon the other players' utilities as well as their payoffs.

I emphasize that 'altruism' here is confined to a regard for other persons' payoffs and utilities. A player's utility is not dependent upon anything else to do with the other players—for example, their strategy choices *per se*. (A conformist, for example, might value doing what others do regardless of their payoffs.)

In the last chapter, it sufficed to assume only that each player's payoff scale is unique up to a linear transformation. In this chapter, it must in addition be assumed that each player is able to compare other players' payoffs with his own. He must be able to place the origins and units of the payoff scales of the other players in a one-to-one correspondence with those of his own payoff scale. This is not the same as the usual assumption of 'interpersonal comparisons of utility', or rather of its analogue for payoffs. Here, each player makes his own comparisons.

To make such comparisons, a player must of course *know* the other players' payoffs. This is a rather strong assumption, but I do not see how very much can be said about altruism without it. It is possible that alternative, less extreme assumptions would suffice for my purposes. For example, players might have knowledge only of parts of the payoff scales of other players, or, in the n-person case, of the payoff scales of only some other players; they might have knowledge of the others' scales at only the ordered-metric level; they might have inaccurate estimates of the others' payoffs, and so on. These alternative assumptions are not explored here.

In the course of this chapter, some simple ideas and results are introduced which will be of use in the two final chapters of the book. I have, however, gone a little further than is necessary in this respect and developed these ideas as part of a broader treatment of altruism in the Prisoners' Dilemma. Nevertheless, only a brief introduction to this subject is given. It is mainly confined to the two-person game. In the N-person game, the different forms which altruism can take are almost limitless in number; of these I shall consider only one which is of special interest.

4.1. THE ORDINARY GAME

We consider first the two-person, Prisoners' Dilemma ordinary game. The payoff matrix is, as before,

	C	D
C	x, x	z, y
D	y, z	w, w

with $y > x > w > z$.

The general form of the assumption of altruistic behaviour is that each player i maximizes the following *utility function*:

$$u_i = u_i(p_1, p_2)$$

where p_1 and p_2 are the two players' payoffs.

More specifically, I assume that each player maximizes a *weighted sum* of p_1 and p_2:

$$u_i = \alpha_i p_i + \beta_i p_j \qquad (i, j = 1, 2; i \neq j)$$

where $-1 \leqslant \alpha_i \leqslant 1$ and $-1 \leqslant \beta_i \leqslant 1$ $(i = 1, 2)$

When $\beta_i = 0$ (and $\alpha_i \neq 0$), player i is called a *pure egoist*. In this case the analysis is the same for all positive values of α_i. If $\alpha_i > 0$, then, I choose $\alpha_i = 1$. This is the case we have considered already (in the last chapter). Similarly, for $\alpha_i < 0$, I set $\alpha_i = -1$.

When $\alpha_i = 0$ (and $\beta_i \neq 0$), player i is called a *pure altruist*. When $\beta_i > 0$, the particular value of β_i is irrelevant, so I choose $\beta_i = 1$. Similarly, for $\beta_i < 0$, I choose $\beta_i = -1$.

These are polar cases. In between lie those cases in which egoism and altruism are present together. It is not assumed that an individual can be altruistic only at the expense of being egoistic: α_i and β_i need not, for example, be complements or inverses.

When $\beta_i > 0$, player i's altruism is said to be *positive*. When $\beta_i < 0$, it is called *negative*.

I am aware that 'altruism' is popularly limited to what I call 'positive altruism', but it is convenient here to use the more literal, root meaning. In particular contexts, 'positive altruism' and 'negative altruism' might alternatively be called 'benevolence' and 'malevolence' (or various other pairs of words). These expressions would, however, be quite inappropriate in other contexts, and I therefore use the more neutral terms.

Sometimes, 'egoism' is limited to the case when $\alpha_i > 0$, but again it is convenient here to use the term more literally.

When $\alpha_i < 0$, the player's behaviour might in various contexts be called 'ascetic', 'anticompetitive', 'masochistic', and so on.

The utilities of the players in the two-person Prisoners' Dilemma, based on the payoff matrix shown above, can be displayed in a *utility matrix*, as follows.

	C	D
C	$(\alpha_1 + \beta_1)x, (\alpha_2 + \beta_2)x$	$\alpha_1 z + \beta_1 y, \alpha_2 y + \beta_2 z$
D	$\alpha_1 y + \beta_1 z, \alpha_2 z + \beta_2 y$	$(\alpha_1 + \beta_1)w, (\alpha_2 + \beta_2)w$

For emphasis, I speak of the resulting game as the *transformed game*.

In this transformed game, D dominates C for player i if and only if

$$\alpha_i y + \beta_i z > (\alpha_i + \beta_i)x$$

and

$$(\alpha_i + \beta_i)w > \alpha_i z + \beta_i y$$

that is,

$$\alpha_i > \frac{x - z}{y - x} \cdot \beta_i \tag{12}$$

and

$$\alpha_i > \frac{y - w}{w - z} \cdot \beta_i \tag{13}$$

Outcome (C, C) is (strictly) preferred to (D, D) by player i if and only if

$$(\alpha_i + \beta_i)x > (\alpha_i + \beta_i)w$$

that is,

$$\alpha_i + \beta_i > 0 \tag{14}$$

Thus, the transformed game is a Prisoners' Dilemma, with (D, D), *the only equilibrium, being Pareto-inferior to* (C, C), *if and only if* (12), (13) *and* (14) *are true for both players.*

We see that for given values of x, y, w and z, the inequalities (12) and (13) are 'more readily' satisfied as the ratio α_i/β_i increases, that is, as player i's 'egoism' increases relative to his 'altruism'.

I examine now some cases of special interest—some more so than others.

(1.) $\alpha_i \geqslant 0$, $\beta_i > 0$ ($i = 1, 2$): each player's utility increases as his own payoff increases and as the other player's payoff decreases.

(1.1) **Egoism and Positive Altruism** $(\alpha_i > 0, \beta_i > 0, i = 1, 2)$: each player cares about both his own and the other player's payoff; his utility increases with increases in either of them, other things being equal. For given values of x, y, w and z, the transformed game may or may not be a Prisoners' Dilemma. Inequality (14) is always satisfied, but (12) and (13) may not be. For example, if the original Prisoners' Dilemma is:

	C	D
C	1, 1	$-1, 2$
D	2, -1	0, 0

then the transformed game is still a Prisoners' Dilemma when $\alpha_i = 0.3$ and $\beta_i = 0.1$ (for $i = 1, 2$), but it no longer is when $\alpha_i = 0.5$ and $\beta_i = 1$ (for $i = 1, 2$).

(1.2) **Pure Positive Altruism** $(\alpha_i = 0, \beta_i = 1, i = 1, 2)$: each player desires only to maximize the other player's payoff. This is no longer a Prisoners' Dilemma, for any values of x, y, w and z. Since $y > x > w > z$, the reverses of the inequalities (12) and (13) are true. Thus C dominates D for each player. Since (14) holds, (C, C) is preferred by each player to (D, D). (C, C), then, is always the outcome of this game, but although (C, C) is the only equilibrium, each player's first preference is for the other player to Defect while he Cooperates.

(2.) $\alpha_i \geqslant 0, \beta_i < 0$ $(i = 1, 2)$: each player's utility increases as his own payoff increases and as the other player's payoff decreases.

(2.1) **Pure Negative Altruism** $(\alpha_i = 0, \beta_i = -1, i = 1, 2)$: each player desires only to *minimize* the other player's payoff. The transformed game is:

	C	D
C	$-x, -z$	$-y, -z$
D	$-z, -y$	$-w, -w$

D dominates C for each player (inequalities (12) and (13) hold for each player). (D, D) is thus the only equilibrium; it is preferred by both players to all other outcomes. As in the case of Pure Positive Altruism, then, the transformed game is never a Prisoners' Dilemma; but in this case the outcome is always (D, D).

(2.2) **Egoism and Negative Altruism** $(\alpha_i > 0, \beta_i < 0, i = 1, 2)$. Inequalities (12) and (13) are always satisfied (since $\dfrac{x-z}{y-x} > 0$ and $\dfrac{y-w}{w-z} > 0$), so that D dominates C for each player, and (D, D) is the only equilibrium. But (14) is satisfied if and only if $-\alpha_i/\beta_i > 1$.

The following special case of Egoism and Negative Altruism is important.

(2.21) Games of Difference. Suppose that each player's utility increases both with his own payoff and with the *difference* between his and the other player's payoff. Specifically, suppose that each player seeks to maximize a convex combination of his own payoff and this difference. That is,

$$u_i = \lambda_i p_i + (1 - \lambda_i)(p_i - p_j), \qquad i = 1, 2, i \neq j$$

where $0 \leqslant \lambda_i < 1$ ($i = 1, 2$). (When $\lambda_i = 1$, we have the original Prisoners' Dilemma game.) $\lambda_i/(1 - \lambda_i)$, then, is the weight player i attaches to his payoff relative to the excess of his own payoff over the other player's payoff.

This expression for u_i can be obtained from the general form, $u_i = \alpha_i p_i + \beta_i p_j$, by setting

$$\alpha_i = 1, \ \beta_i = \lambda_i - 1 \ (i = 1, 2)$$

The transformed game, which I call a *Game of Difference*, is:

	C	D
C	$\lambda_1 x, \lambda_2 x$	$z - (1 - \lambda_1)y, \ y - (1 - \lambda_2)z$
D	$y - (1 - \lambda_1)z, \ z - (1 - \lambda_2)y$	$\lambda_1 w, \lambda_2 w$

We have already noted (in paragraph (2.2)) that D dominates C whenever $\alpha_i > 0$ and $\beta_i < 0$ (for $i = 1, 2$), which is the case here.

Thus (D, D) is the only equilibrium. But (C, C) is preferred to (D, D) by player i, if and only if $\lambda_i > 0$. (When $\lambda_i = 0$ he is indifferent between these two outcomes.)

Thus, if and only if $\lambda_i \neq 0$ ($i = 1, 2$), the Game of Difference is always a Prisoners' Dilemma with (D, D) as the only equilibrium.

Each player's *temptation* (to Defect unilaterally from mutual Cooperation) in the original game was defined (at the end of Section 3.2) as $(y - x)/(y - w)$. Player i's temptation in the Game of Difference is therefore

$$\frac{\{y - (1 - \lambda_i)z\} - \lambda_i z}{\{y - (1 - \lambda_i)z\} - \lambda_i w}$$

It is easily shown that this temptation is always greater than the original one. I shall say that a Prisoners' Dilemma becomes 'more severe' if any player's temptation increases, other things being equal. Thus, the Game of Difference is a more severe Prisoners' Dilemma than the original (untransformed) game.

In the special case when $\lambda_i = 0$ ($i = 1, 2$), each player seeks only to maximize the difference between the two payoffs. I call this zero-sum game a *Pure Difference Game*. (D, D) is still the only equilibrium.

But it is no longer Pareto-inferior; for each player is indifferent between (D, D) and (C, C). (D, D), which is the minimax solution, will presumably be the outcome.[1]

(3.) Games of Anti-Difference

A player in a Game of Difference is concerned, to some extent, to raise his own payoff above that of the other player. An *opposite* concern could take several forms. The most extreme of these would presumably be a desire to maximize the excess of the other player's payoff over one's own. Less extreme would be the maximization of a convex combination of this excess and one's own payoff:

$$u_i = \lambda_i p_i - (1 - \lambda_i)(p_i - p_j)$$

with $0 \leqslant \lambda_i < 1$, but I do not think behaviour of this sort is very common.

Of more interest, I think, is a desire to minimize the difference, whether positive or negative, between the other player's payoff and one's own—a desire, that is, for *equality*. More generally, consider the game in which player i seeks to maximize the following utility function:

$$u_i = \lambda_i p_i - (1 - \lambda_i)|p_i - p_j|$$

where $0 \leqslant \lambda_i < 1$. (If $\lambda_i = 1$, we have the original Prisoners' Dilemma game.) This represents a convex combination of 'egoism' (maximizing one's own payoff) and 'equality' (minimizing the absolute value of the difference between the two payoffs). I call this game a *Game of Anti-Difference*. 'Anti-difference' is not a very beautiful expression, but it is sufficiently neutral to cover a number of different interpretations of this game.

We cannot use the earlier general results for Prisoners' Dilemma games with altruism, by substituting for α_i and β_i, since α_i and β_i are unobtainable in this case; but, since $y > x > w > z$ in the original matrix, the utility matrix is easily obtained. It is as follows:

	C	D
C	$\lambda_1 x, \lambda_2 x$	$\lambda_1 z - (1-\lambda_1)(y-z), \lambda_2 y - (1-\lambda_2)(y-z)$
D	$\lambda_1 y - (1-\lambda_1)(y-z), \lambda_2 z - (1-\lambda_2)(y-z)$	$\lambda_1 w, \lambda_2 w$

In this transformed game, D dominates C for player i if and only if:

$$\lambda_i y - (1 - \lambda_i)(y - z) > \lambda_i x$$

and

$$\lambda_i w > \lambda_i z - (1 - \lambda_i)(y - z)$$

The first of these inequalities can be rewritten in the form:

$$\frac{\lambda_i}{1 - \lambda_i} > \frac{y - z}{y - x} \tag{15}$$

$\lambda_i/(1 - \lambda_i)$ is of course the ratio of the weight attached to player i's own payoff to the weight attached to the payoff-difference.

The second inequality can be rewritten as:

$$\lambda_i < \frac{y - z}{y - w} \qquad (16)$$

which is easily seen to be true for all values of λ_i, y, w and z, since the right-hand side exceeds one while $\lambda_i < 1$. Thus, Defection is always the best reply to a choice of D by the other player.

The outcome (C, C) is preferred by player i to (D, D) if and only if $\lambda_i \neq 0$. Thus the transformed game is a Prisoners' Dilemma if and only if (15) holds and $\lambda_i \neq 0$. (Notice that (15) implies that $\lambda_i \neq 0$, but not conversely.)

Since (16) is always true, C can never dominate D. But suppose now that (15) does not hold. In this case the game has two equilibria, (C, C) and (D, D); but player i prefers (C, C) to (D, D) if $\lambda_i \neq 0$ and is indifferent between these two outcomes if $\lambda_i = 0$. Thus, if $\lambda_i \neq 0$ for $i = 1, 2$, neither player will expect (D, D) to be the outcome. (C, C) will therefore be the outcome.

If $\lambda_i = 0$, we have quite a different sort of game, a *coordination game*. The utility matrix simplifies to:

	C	D
C	0, 0	$z - y, z - y$
D	$z - y, z - y$	0, 0

The off-diagonal elements are negative. The players have no reason for expecting either one of the two equilibria, (C, C) and (D, D), to be more likely to be the outcome than the other. Their problem is to 'coordinate' their strategies, so that their payoffs (in the original game) are equal: but they have no reasons for choosing C rather than D or *vice versa*. It is not possible to say which of the four possibilities will be the outcome of this game.

However, coordination games, or rather their supergames, do not present serious problems in practice. In time, a convention to adopt a particular equilibrium grows up, and once it has been adopted, there is no incentive for any player not to conform to it. I shall return to this subject in my discussion of Hume's political theory in the next chapter.

My analysis of Games of Anti-Difference can be summarized as follows:

(i) The Game of Anti-Difference is a Prisoners' Dilemma if and only if inequality (15) holds and $\lambda_i \neq 0$.

(ii) If (15) does not hold and $\lambda_i \neq 0$, then (C, C) is the outcome.

(iii) If (15) does not hold and $\lambda_i = 0$, then the game is one of coordination and no outcome can be indicated.

The conclusion in case (iii) should not distress us too much. $\lambda_i = 0$ is an extreme case. The players are obsessed with achieving equality regardless of their own payoff.

(4.) Egoism and Asymmetric Altruism

In the cases so far considered, the games have been symmetric, in the sense that both players have the same type of utility function. For an asymmetric example, consider the game in which both players are egoists but one ($i = 1$, say) is positively altruistic while the other ($i = 2$) is negatively altruistic. Then in the utility functions we have $\alpha_i > 0$ ($i = 1, 2$), $\beta_1 > 0$ and $\beta_2 < 0$. For player 1, D may or may not dominate C. He always prefers (D, D) to (C, C). For player 2, D always dominates C. He may or may not prefer (D, D) to (C, C), depending on whether $\alpha_2 + \beta_2 < 0$ or not. Thus, the only equilibrium is (D, D) or (C, D), depending on whether D or C is dominant for 1. In the first case, the game is a Prisoners' Dilemma if player 2 prefers (C, C) to (D, D).

Other special cases could be mentioned. I shall not examine them individually, for they involve assumptions (about the values of α_i and β_i) which, though certainly descriptive of some people in some contexts, are generally less plausible than those already considered. I believe that cases (2.21) and (3.), Games of Difference and of Anti-Difference, are the most interesting.

Sophisticated Altruism

Before going on to examine altruism in the supergame, I want briefly to consider what I call 'sophisticated altruism'.[2]

An altruistic player was defined earlier as one whose utility function is of the form:

$$u_i = u_i (p_1, p_2)$$

where p_1 and p_2 are the payoffs to the two players. A player's utility, however, may depend not only directly on the other's payoff but also on his utility. In this case, we have:

$$u_i = u_i (p_1, p_2, u_j), \quad j \neq i$$

Thus, I may derive pleasure directly from the contemplation of your loss of payoff, but if I believe that you derive pleasure from your loss of payoff, then I may cease to be happy (and may cease to act so as to diminish your payoff).

If a player's utility depends in any way on another player's *utility*, I call him a *sophisticated altruist*.

Consider, for example, two pure altruists, one positive (A) and the other negative (B), in a Prisoners' Dilemma. If their utilities are simply of the form $u_i = u_i (p_1, p_2)$, then (C, D) would be the happy outcome (a Pareto-optimal, unique equilibrium): A would be happy because B's payoff is a maximum and B would be happy because A's payoff is a minimum. At the 'first-order of sophistication', A is very happy because B is happy (with A's minimal payoff), but B is now unhappy because A is happy (with B's maximal payoff). At the 'second-order of sophistication', A now becomes unhappy because of B's unhappiness at the first-order level, and B is very unhappy at A's increased happiness at the first-order level. And so on.

In practice, however, the levels of sophistication will not all carry the same weight, and there will be an end to this potentially infinite regress. In particular, it is unlikely that anybody goes beyond the first-order level:

$$u_i = u_i(p_1, p_2, u_j(p_1, p_2)), j \neq i$$

The implications of sophisticated altruism for behaviour in the Prisoners' Dilemma are illustrated in the following example. Consider a Prisoners' Dilemma with these payoffs:

	C	D	
C	1, 1	−1, 2	(Matrix 1)
D	2, −1	0, 0	

Suppose that player 1 is a pure positive altruist while player 2 is a pure negative altruist, with utilities.

$$u_1 = p_2, \quad u_2 = -p_1$$

Then the transformed matrix is:

	C	D	
C	1, −1	2, 1	(Matrix 2)
D	−1, −2	0, 0	

This is no longer a Prisoners' Dilemma. (C, D) is the Pareto-optimal, unique equilibrium.

If the players are 'pure, first-order-sophisticated (positive and negative) altruists', then this matrix in turn becomes:

	C	D	
C	−1, −1	1, −2	(Matrix 3)
D	−2, 1	0, 0	

which is a Prisoners' Dilemma, but with (C, C) as the only equilibrium and (D, D) preferred to (C, C) by both players.

If the players are 'pure', second-order-sophisticated (positive and negative) altruists', this matrix becomes:

	C	D	
C	−1, 1	−2, −1	(Matrix 6)
D	1, 2	0, 0	

which is not a Prisoners' Dilemma, (D, C) being the Pareto-optimal, unique equilibrium. And so on.

More realistically, suppose that both players ignore orders of sophistication beyond the first, and that their utilities are (for the sake of illustration) simply the average of those in Matrix 2 and those at the first level in Matrix 3; that is,

$$u_1 = \tfrac{1}{2}p_2 + \tfrac{1}{2}(-p_1)$$

and

$$u_2 = \tfrac{1}{2}(-p_1) - \tfrac{1}{2}(p_2)$$

Then the game is:

	C	D
C	$0, -1$	$3/2, -1/2$
D	$3/2, -1/2$	$0, 0$

Here, C dominates D for player 1, while D dominates C for player 2 so that (C, D) is the only equilibrium. But the game is not a Prisoners' Dilemma, for this equilibrium is Pareto-optimal.

4.2. THE SUPERGAME

Consider now the supergame consisting of an infinite number of iterations of the transformed Prisoners' Dilemma game (in which the players are unsophisticatedly altruistic). The utility matrix of the ordinary game is shown here again.

	C	D
C	$(\alpha_1 + \beta_1)x, (\alpha_2 + \beta_2)x$	$\alpha_1 z + \beta_1 y, \alpha_2 y + \beta_2 z$
D	$\alpha_1 y + \beta_1 z, \alpha_2 z + \beta_2 y$	$(\alpha_1 + \beta_1)w, (\alpha_2 + \beta_2)w$

Let the discount parameters in the supergame be a_1 and a_2 as before.

The following paragraphs give necessary and sufficient conditions for strategy vectors containing A_k, B_n, C^∞, B' and D^∞ to be equilibria, when these five strategies are the only ones available to each player. The complete derivations of these are not given; they follow straightforwardly, with a little algebraic manipulation, from the utility matrix, which is obtained from the payoff matrix shown in Section 3.2 for the supergame without altruism, by replacing x by $(\alpha_i + \beta_i)x$, y by $\alpha_i y + \beta_i z$, etc.

(i) (D^∞, D^∞) is an equilibrium if and only if

$$\alpha_i \geqslant \frac{y - w}{w - z} \cdot \beta_i \tag{17}$$

for $i = 1, 2$. This is the same as the inequality (13) obtained for the ordinary game. It is a necessary and sufficient condition for a change by player i to A_k, B, C^∞ or B' not to yield him a greater payoff.

(ii) Consider the strategy vector (A_k, A_k).

A change of strategy of player i to D does not yield him a greater payoff if and only if

$$\{\alpha_i(y - w) - \beta_i(w - z)\}\left(\frac{1 - a_i}{a_i}\right)S_i \leqslant (\alpha_i + \beta_i)(x - w) \tag{18}$$

This generalizes inequality (1) in Section 3.2.

A change of strategy of player i to B' does not yield him a greater payoff if and only if

$$(\alpha_i + \beta_i)(x - w) \geqslant \{\alpha_i(y - w) - \beta_i(w - z) - a_i\{\alpha_i(w - z) -$$
$$\beta_i(y - w)\}\}\left(\frac{1 - a_i}{a_i}\right)S_i \tag{19}$$

Note that this is implied by (18) if and only if (17) holds.

(A_k, A_k) is an equilibrium if and only if (18) and (19) hold for both players.

(iii) Consider the strategy vector (B, B).

A change of strategy of player i to D^∞ does not yield him a greater payoff if and only if

$$\{\alpha_i(y - w) - \beta_i(w - z)\}a_i \geqslant \alpha_i(y - x) - \beta_i(x - z) \tag{20}$$

Defection to B' does not yield him a greater payoff if and only if

$$\{\alpha_i(x - z) - \beta_i(y - x)\}a_i \geqslant \alpha_i(y - x) - \beta_i(x - z) \tag{21}$$

A change to A_k or C^∞ yields no change.

Thus, (B, B) is an equilibrium if and only if (20) and (21) hold for both players.

(iv) Consider the strategy vector (B', B').

A change of strategy of player i to B does not yield him a greater payoff if and only if

$$\{\alpha_i(y - w) - \beta_i(w - z)\}a_i \leqslant \alpha_i(w - z) - \beta_i(y - w) \tag{22}$$

A change of strategy to C^∞ does not increase his payoff if and only if

$$\{\alpha_i(x - z) - \beta_i(y - x)\}a_i \leqslant \alpha_i(w - z) - \beta_i(y - w) \tag{23}$$

A change of strategy to A_k does not increase his payoff if and only if (18); and defection to D^∞ does not change his payoff, of course.

Thus (B', B') is an equilibrium if and only if (22) and (23) hold for both players.

(v) Consider the strategy vector (C^∞, C^∞). Without altruism, this is never an equilibrium.

A change of strategy by either player (i) to D^∞ does not yield him a gain if and only if (20) holds.

A change to A_k or B yields no change; while a change to B' does not yield him a greater payoff if and only if

$$\alpha_i \leqslant \frac{x - z}{y - x} \cdot \beta_i \tag{24}$$

Thus (C^∞, C^∞) is an equilibrium if and only if (20) and (24) hold for both players. Notice that (24) is independent of the discount parameter.

(vi) Consider the strategy vector in which player i uses B and player j uses B'. The ordinary game outcomes alternate between (C, D) and (D, C).

A change of strategy of player i to D^∞ or B' does not yield him a greater payoff if and only if the reverse of (22), with y and z interchanged, holds.

A change of strategy of player i to C^∞, or of player j to C^∞ or A_k or B, does not yield a greater payoff if and only if the reverse of (21) holds (with i or j in (21), as appropriate).

A change of i to A_k or of j to D^∞ does not yield a gain if and only if the reverse of (22) holds.

Thus the strategy vector in which player i uses B and j uses B' is an equilibrium if and only if the reverses of (21) and (22), and the reverse of (22) with y and z interchanged, hold for i, and the reverses of (21) and (22) hold for j.

Equilibrium conditions for the remaining asymmetric strategy vectors can be obtained straightforwardly from the results already stated. In contrast with the supergame without altruism, it is found here that *every* strategy vector is an equilibrium for some values of y, x, w, z, a_i, α_i and β_i, and under certain conditions is an outcome. Writing down the general conditions for each strategy vector to be the outcome, or one of several equally likely outcomes, is not very fruitful. As an illustration, let us return to the most important special case, which was introduced in the analysis of the ordinary game.

Games of difference.

In these games, we have $\alpha_i = 1$, $\beta_i = \lambda_i - 1$, $0 \leqslant \lambda_i < 1$, $i = 1, 2$. The strict part of inequality (14) is always satisfied (since $\alpha_i > 0$, $\beta_i < 0$ and $(y - w)/(w - z) > 0$). Thus (D^∞, D^∞) is always an equilibrium (an equilibrium, that is, for all permissible values of y, x, w, z, a_1, a_2, λ_1 and λ_2), while the eight strategy vectors in which D^∞ is paired with one of A_k, B, C^∞ and B' are never equilibria. Inequality (24) is never satisfied, so that (C^∞, C^∞) is never an equilibrium. It is easily verified that the six strategy vectors in which C^∞ is paired with A_k, B or B' are never equilibria. All the remaining strategy vectors are sometimes equilibria.

In any supergame with altruism, each of the mutual conditional Cooperation outcomes in which each player chooses A_k or B is strictly preferred by player i to (D^∞, D^∞) if and only if $\alpha_i + \beta_i > 0$. This condition is met in Games of Difference if and only if $\lambda_i \neq 0$. Thus, if any of these mutual Cooperation strategy vectors is an equilibrium, in addition to (D^∞, D^∞), then (D^∞, D^∞) will not be the outcome. If, as is possible, these four mutual conditional Cooperation strategy vectors are the only equilibria besides (D^∞, D^∞), and $\lambda_i \neq 0$, it will not matter which of A_k and B each player chooses. The result will be the same; the outcome will be mutual cooperation throughout the supergame.

This contrasts with the *ordinary* Game of Difference, where, although (C, C) is preferred by both players to (D, D), (D, D) is the *only* outcome (and the Game is a more severe Prisoners' Dilemma than the original one). *Cooperation is sometimes rational in the Super-Game of Difference; it is never rational in the ordinary Game.*

4.3. AN N-PERSON GAME OF DIFFERENCE

In the general N-person Prisoners' Dilemma game, the number of different forms which altruism can take is very large. I shall consider only one of them. It is one of many possible generalizations of the two-person Game of Difference which I discussed earlier. Of all the transformed Prisoners' Dilemma games involving egoism and some form of altruism, Games of Difference are the most important for my purposes in this book. When we come to consider in the next chapter the political theory of Hobbes, we shall see that the 'game' which Hobbes assumes people to be playing in the absence of government (in 'the state of nature') is in effect a generalized Game of Difference.

In the two-person Game of Difference, each individual's utility is a convex combination of his own payoff (p_i) and the difference ($p_i - p_j$) between his and the other player's payoff. Let us anticipate a Hobbesian term of the next chapter and call this difference the *eminence* of the ith over the jth individual. In a game with more than two players, there are a number of ways in which an individual might be said to seek 'eminence': he might, for example, seek to maximize the number of other individuals with respect to whom he is eminent (his positive eminence); he might seek to maximize the sum of his eminences over each other individual; and so on. The definition which I shall adopt here is that an individual's eminence in the N-person game is the *average* of his eminence over each other individual. I use the same word, eminence, in both the two-person and N-person cases: eminence in the former is a special case of eminence in the latter. Thus, the ith individual's *eminence* is defined as:

$$E_i = \frac{1}{N} \sum_{\substack{\text{all } j=i}} (p_i - p_j)$$

The untransformed game (with payoff p_i to the ith individual) is the N-person Prisoners' Dilemma specified in Section 3.3; that is, the two payoff functions $f(v)$ and $g(v)$ —which are each player's payoffs when he chooses C and D, respectively, and v others choose D—satisfy the three conditions:

(i) $g(v) > f(v)$ for all $v \geqslant 0$
(ii) $f(N - 1) > g(0)$
(iii) $g(v) > g(0)$ for all $v > 0$

The N-person generalization of the two-person Game of Difference which I shall now consider is the game in which each individual is assumed to seek to maximize a convex combination of his own payoff and his eminence. The ith individual's utility, then, is defined as:

$$u_i = \lambda_i p_i + (1 - \lambda_i)E_i$$

where $0 \leqslant \lambda_i \leqslant 1$. When $\lambda_i = 1$ for all i, we have of course the original, untransformed Prisoners' Dilemma in which every player is a pure egoist.

I shall do no more than establish the conditions under which this N-person Game of Difference is a Prisoners' Dilemma game satisfying the three conditions listed above. This is all I require for my purposes in Chapter 6. For when these conditions are met, the general results on the N-person Prisoners' Dilemma apply to the Game of Difference.

If the ith individual and v others Cooperate, then the payoff to i and to each of the v others is $f(v)$ while the payoff to each of the $N - v - 1$ who do not Cooperate is $g(v + 1)$. Thus, individual i's utility is:

$$u_i = \lambda_i f(v) + (1 - v_i) \frac{1}{N} (N - v - 1) \{f(v) - g(v + 1)\}$$

$$= F(v), \text{ say}$$

If individual i does *not* Cooperate, while v others do, then we find that

$$u_i = \lambda_i g(v) + (1 - v_i) \frac{1}{N} (v) \{g(v) - f(v - 1)\} \text{ if } v \neq 0$$

$$= G(v), \text{ say}$$

and

$$u_i = \lambda_i g(0) = G(0) \text{ if } v = 0$$

because

$$f(v - 1) = f(-1) \text{ is undefined}$$

The necessary and sufficient condition for the ith individual to choose not to Cooperate is of course $G(v) > F(v)$. This condition cannot be essentially simplified unless further assumptions are made about $f(v)$ and $g(v)$.

However, we can certainly say that $G(v) > F(v)$ *if* (but not only if)

$$v\{g(v) - f(v - 1)\} > -(N - v - 1)\{g(v + 1) - f(v)\}$$

which in turn is true if $g(v)$ is strictly increasing with v (for we have already assumed that $g(v) > f(v)$ for all v).

Thus, if $g(v)$ is strictly increasing, each player prefers D to C no matter what the other players choose; and therefore the outcome is that every player chooses D. Let us see whether this outcome is Pareto-inferior.

If everybody Cooperates, each player's payoff is $f(N - 1)$ and therefore the ith player's utility is $F(N - 1) = \lambda_i f(N - 1)$.

If nobody Cooperates, each player's payoff is $g(0)$ and therefore the ith player's utility is $G(0) = \lambda_i g(0)$.

As long as $\lambda_i \neq 0$, we have $\lambda_i f(N - 1) > \lambda_i g(0)$, for we have already assumed that $f(N - 1) > g(0)$. Thus, if $\lambda_i \neq 0$ for all i, every individual prefers the outcome when everybody Cooperates to the outcome when everybody Defects.

Finally, observe that $G(v) > G(0)$ *if* (but not only if) $g(v)$ is strictly increasing with v.

Thus, *this N-person Game of Difference is a Prisoners' Dilemma satisfying* *conditions (i), (ii) and (iii) if (but not only if) $\lambda_i \neq 0$, for all i, and g(v) is strictly increasing with v.*

The condition $\lambda_i \neq 0$, for all i, simply requires that the game is not one of *pure* eminence; each individual must attach some weight to his own payoff *per se*. All other convex combinations of his own payoff and his eminence are permitted.

The condition that $g(v)$ is strictly increasing with v requires only that the greater the number of individuals who Cooperate, the greater is the payoff to any individual who does not Cooperate. This condition is always satisfied in the public goods problems discussed in Chapter 1: just as long as each individual's payoff increases with increasing production of the good and the good exhibits jointness of supply and non-excludability.

4.4. NOTES

1. What I have called Games of Difference have been considered by James R. Emshoff ('A Computer Simulation Model of the Prisoner's Dilemma', *Behavioral Science*, **15**, 304–17 (1970). He refers to λ_i as the 'competitiveness parameter'. Pure Difference Games have been studied by Martin Shubik ('Games of Status', *Behavioral Science*, **16**, 117–29 (1971)), who calls them 'difference games'. He considers also a further transformation to what he calls 'games of status', in which there are only three different payoffs: one for winning (when the payoff difference is positive), one for losing (when the difference is negative) and one for drawing.

2. Sophisticated altruism or something like it is discussed under different names by Stefan Valavanis ('The Resolution of Conflict When Utilities Interact', *Journal of Conflict Resolution*, **2**, 156–69 (1958)) and Thomas C. Schelling ('Game Theory and the Study of Ethical Systems', *Journal of Conflict Resolution*, **12**, 34–44 (1968)).

CHAPTER 5

Conditions for Cooperation

Since the analysis in Chapter 3, and to some extent in Chapter 4, was somewhat involved and mathematical, in the present chapter a brief informal summary and discussion is given of the main ideas and conclusions of these two chapters. The conclusions cannot be stated fully or precisely and the details of their derivations must be omitted; nevertheless, it should be possible for the reader with little knowledge of mathematics to follow the thread of the argument of this book by moving from the end of Chapter 2 directly to this chapter. With such a reader in mind, some of the introductory material of Chapters 3 and 4 is repeated here. In addition to these informal summaries of the main results obtained earlier, some effort is also made here to interpret and evaluate them. Section 5.1 is devoted to Chapter 3 and Section 5.2 to Chapter 4. In a final section, some extensions and revisions of the Prisoners' Dilemma supergame model are discussed.

5.1. THE PRISONERS' DILEMMA SUPERGAME

In Chapter 2 it was shown that the structure of individual preferences in public goods interaction is that of a Prisoners' Dilemma game only under certain special conditions. This is true of both small and large publics. Although suboptimal provision of public goods and the occurrence of a Prisoners' Dilemma do seem to be more likely in the case of relatively large groups than in the case of relatively small ones, the connections between the optimality of public goods provision, the size of the group and the occurrence of the Prisoners' Dilemma are not at all straightforward, and it appears that no general, *a priori* statement can be made about these connections.

The analysis of these connections which I presented in Chapter 2 is (like the standard analyses of the economists on which it is based) entirely static; it is concerned with individual preferences at only one point in time, and proceeds as if the individual makes only one choice, once and for all, of the amount of his contribution to the provision of a public good. But in the real world the choice of whether to contribute and of how much to contribute, in the case of the public goods which are of special interest here, is a *recurring* one. In Chapter 3 these recurring choices are treated in the context of a *supergame*, that is, a sequence of games, which are called the *ordinary games*. The principal object of that chapter is to show that even if it is assumed that individual preferences in each ordinary game are those of a Prisoners' Dilemma, individual voluntary Cooperation in every constituent game of the supergame is nevertheless rational under certain conditions.

The supergames considered here consist of an indefinite number of iterations of a single ordinary game. The ordinary game is a Prisoners' Dilemma (as defined in Chapter 1) in which each player must choose between two strategies, Cooperation (C) and Defection (D). In each constituent game of this Prisoners' Dilemma supergame, the players choose their strategies simultaneously (that is, in ignorance of other players' choices in that game), but they know the strategies chosen by all the players in all previous games. The ordinary games of the supergame are thought of as being played at regular discrete intervals of time, or one in each time period, and each player receives his ordinary game payoff at the end of each time period.

It is assumed that the further off in time a future expected payoff is to be received, the smaller is its present worth to a player. More specifically, it is assumed that future payoffs are discounted *exponentially* (in the manner introduced in Section 1.3). Associated with each player (i) is a *discount parameter* (a_i, with $0 < a_i < 1$), whose complement ($1 - a_i$) represents the *rate* at which he discounts future payoffs.

In each ordinary game, a player chooses between C and D. A sequence of such choices, one in each ordinary game, is called a *supergame strategy*. There are of course an infinite number of such strategies, but only a few of them are considered here. The actual choices of all players in any ordinary game determine its *outcome*; and the outcome of a supergame is the sequence of outcomes of its constituent ordinary games. Corresponding to a supergame outcome is a *payoff* for each player, which is the sum of the suitably discounted payoffs he obtains in each of the ordinary games.

We are now in a position to introduce the concept of an equilibrium, which plays an important role in the analysis. An *equilibrium* is a strategy vector (that is, a list of strategies, one for each player) such that no player can obtain a larger payoff by using a different strategy while the other players continue to use the same strategies. The importance of the equilibrium concept is that, if every player *expects* an equilibrium to be the outcome, then he has no incentive to use a different strategy (different from the one he uses in the equilibrium strategy vector); thus, if indeed every player expects a certain equilibrium to be the outcome, then it is reasonable to suppose that it will in fact be the outcome.

The Prisoners' Dilemma ordinary game has only one equilibrium, namely the strategy vector in which every player chooses D, and there is no reason for any player not to expect it to be the outcome. In Prisoners' Dilemma supergames, on the other hand, there may be several equilibria; if so, is it possible

86

to indicate which of them will be the outcome? If a player has a reason for expecting that a certain equilibrium will not be the outcome, then he might not use his equilibrium strategy and the equilibrium would not in fact be the outcome. Suppose, in particular, that, of two equilibria, one is *Pareto-preferred* to the other; that is to say, at least one player strictly prefers the first to the second (his payoff from the first is greater than his payoff from the second) and no player strictly prefers the second to the first. Then presumably no player would expect the second of these two to be the outcome and therefore it would not be the outcome. Thus, in a supergame with several equilibria, if one of the equilibria is Pareto-preferred to each of the others, then it is reasonable to suppose that it will be the outcome.

This is the approach used in the analysis of the Prisoners' Dilemma in Chapter 3. First, it is established which of the strategy vectors are equilibria; and second, an attempt is made to indicate which of the equilibria will be outcomes, by examining the individual preferences amongst the equilibria.

The Two-person Supergame

The two-person supergame examined here consists of an indefinite number of iterations of the two-person, two-strategy Prisoners' Dilemma ordinary game with the payoffs specified in Section 1.2:

	C	D
C	x, x	z, y
D	y, z	w, w

where $y > x > w > z$. Five supergame strategies are considered:
(i) C^∞: strategy C is chosen in every ordinary game.
(ii) D^∞: strategy D is chosen in every ordinary game.
(iii) A_k (where k is a strictly positive integer): C is chosen in the first game and it is chosen in each subsequent game as long as the other player chooses C in the previous game; if the other player Defects in any game, D is chosen for the next k games; C is then chosen no matter what the other player's last choice is; it continues to be chosen as long as the other player chooses C in the preceding game; when the other player next Defects, D is chosen for $k + 1$ games, and so on; the number of games in which the other player is 'punished' for a Defection increases by one each time; and each time there is a return to C. (In the limiting case of A_k when $k \to \infty$, denoted by A_∞, C is chosen until the other player Defects, after which D is chosen in *all* succeeding ordinary games.)
(iv) B: C is chosen in the first game; thereafter the choice in each game is that of the other player in the preceding game.
(v) B': D is chosen in the first game; thereafter the choice in each game is that of the other player in the preceding game.

B and B' have been called 'tit-for-tat' strategies. A_k, B and B' are *conditional strategies* (ordinary game choices are conditional upon the choices of the other player), while C^∞ and D^∞ are *unconditional*.

It is assumed that these five strategies are the only ones available to each player (out of an infinity of possible strategies). The conditions, summarized below, for various strategy vectors to be equilibria and for mutual Cooperation to be the outcome, are necessary and sufficient conditions so long as this assumption is made; if other strategies are available to any player, then these conditions are only necessary.

With each of the two players choosing amongst the five strategies, there are twenty-five possible strategy pairs. It is a straightforward matter to calculate the payoffs to each player associated with each of these possible strategy pairs and, by comparing them, to establish which of them are equilibria and under what conditions. It is found that the strategy pair (D^∞, D^∞) in which each player uses D^∞ is *always* an equilibrium, that is to say, it is an equilibrium for all possible values of the ordinary game payoffs x, y, z, w (as long as they satisfy the inequality which makes the ordinary game a Prisoners' Dilemma) and for all possible values of the two players' discount rates (as long as each a_i satisfies $0 < a_i < 1$). In addition, several other strategy pairs are equilibria *sometimes*, that is, for values of the ordinary game payoffs and discount rates which satisfy certain conditions. These are as follows.

(i) The four pairs in which each player uses either A_k or B. In each of these four cases, the outcome is mutual Cooperation, (C, C), in every ordinary game throughout the supergame.

(ii) The three strategy pairs in which either player chooses B' and the other chooses B' or D^∞. In each case, the outcome is mutual Defection throughout the supergame.

(iii) The two strategy pairs (B, B') and (B', B). Here, the outcome is an *alternation* throughout the supergame of (C, D) in one ordinary game and (C, D) in the next, beginning with (C, D) in the first game in the case of (B, B') and with (D, C) in the case of (B', B).

Each of these nine strategy pairs is an equilibrium if and only if certain conditions are met. In the case of the mutual Cooperation equilibria in group (i), each of the conditions requires that each player's *discount rate* does not *exceed* a certain number, which is a function of the payoffs in the ordinary game. In the case of the mutual Defection equilibria in group (ii), the discount rates of the player or players using the B' strategy must not be *less* than certain functions of the ordinary game payoffs. In the case of the alternation equilibria in group (iii), an inequality of both these types must be satisfied for both players, and hence each player's discount rate must be confined within a certain range (whose end points are functions of the ordinary game payoffs).

The remaining strategy pairs are *never* equilibria, that is to say, they are equilibria for no values of the ordinary game payoffs and the discount rates. (A summary of these equilibrium results is displayed in Table 2 in Section 3.2.)

Having established that, besides (D^∞, D^∞), which is always an equilibrium, other strategy pairs are equilibria under certain conditions, we must ask which of these equilibria will be the actual outcome when several of them exist simultaneously. Clearly, if (A_k, A_k) is an equilibrium, since each player prefers it to (D^∞, D^∞), neither player will expect the latter to be the outcome. Thus, if (A_k, A_k) is the only equilibrium besides (D^∞, D^∞), it is the outcome. The same is true of the other mutual Cooperation equilibria, (B, B), (A_k, B) and (B, A_k). If all four of these are simultaneously equilibria, then each player expects one of them to be the outcome. However, it does not matter whether he chooses A_k or B, for the result is the same, namely mutual Cooperation throughout the supergame. Thus, if these four are the only equilibria besides (D^∞, D^∞), the outcome is mutual Cooperation throughout the supergame.

If the discount rates are sufficiently great, then it may be that the only equilibria besides (D^∞, D^∞) are the three in which one player chooses B' and the other chooses B' or D^∞. Again, it does not matter whether each player chooses B' or D^∞, for the result (mutual Defection throughout the supergame) is the same in all four cases.

It is possible that (i.e. there are some values of x, y, z, w and the discount rates for which) these four mutual Defection equilibria coexist with the four mutual Cooperation equilibria mentioned above. In this case, one of the latter will be the outcome, since each of them is preferred by both players to each of the mutual Defection equilibria.

The analysis of outcomes is less straightforward than this when the alternation strategy pairs (B, B') and (B', B) are among the equilibria. In the first place, it can be shown that if (B, B') or (B', B) is an equilibrium, then it is Pareto-preferred to (D^∞, D^∞). Thus, it can certainly be said that if (B, B') and (B', B) are the only equilibria besides (D^∞, D^∞), the latter will not be the outcome.

Now, if (A_k, A_k) is an equilibrium as well as these three alternation strategy pairs, then again (D^∞, D^∞) will not be the outcome, since of course (A_k, A_k) is preferred by both players to (D^∞, D^∞). Whether (A_k, A_k) is Pareto-preferred to (B, B') and (B', B), or *vice-versa*, depends upon the values of the ordinary game payoffs: both are possible. If the former, then the conclusion is straightforward: (A_k, A_k) will be the outcome. But if the latter, then it does not follow that one of the two alternation strategy pairs will be the outcome, because, on the one hand, these two do not yield the same payoff to each player (player 1 prefers (B', B), in which *he* Defects in the first ordinary game, whereas player 2 has the opposite preference) and, on the other hand, neither (B, B) nor (B', B') is necessarily an equilibrium. The alternation outcomes are both preferred by both players to (B, B), since they are preferred to (A_k, A_k), and therefore also to (B', B'). I argued in Section 3.2 that the likely outcome here is (B, B).

Finally, it is possible, though unlikely, that (B, B') and (B', B) are equilibria as well as (B, B) and (B', B'). This may occur only under the most restrictive and unlikely conditions, and under these conditions both players are indifferent between strategies B and B'.

To summarize: apart from the alternation outcomes, which are unlikely, there are two possible outcomes to this two-person Prisoners' Dilemma supergame: mutual Cooperation in every ordinary game or mutual Defection in every ordinary game. Just as long as one of the four strategy pairs in which each player chooses one of A_k and B is an equilibrium, mutual Cooperation throughout the supergame is the outcome. Now, the necessary and sufficient conditions for each of these four strategy pairs to be an equilibrium require that each player's discount rate be no greater than some function of the ordinary game payoffs; and when these conditions are compared, it is seen that if a certain one of them is not satisfied, then *none* of these four will be equilibria and hence the outcome will be mutual Defection throughout the supergame. This condition (inequality (3) in Section 3.2) is:

$$a_i \geqslant \frac{y - x}{y - w}$$

(which must hold for each player *i*), and, when rearranged, it says that each player's discount rate $(1 - a_i)$ should not be so great that his payoff from unilateral Defection in the first ordinary game and his payoff from mutual Defection in all succeeding games (which is what would result from his Defection in the first game, since the other player is using a conditionally Cooperative strategy) together exceed his payoff from mutual Cooperation throughout the supergame. In other words, if this condition fails for any player, it means that his discount rate is so great (that is, he values future payoffs so little) that it pays him to 'grab' y in the first game (by Defecting) even though this results in him getting only w (the payoff from mutual Defection) in all succeeding games. The expression on the right-hand side of the inequality above is called player *i*'s *temptation* to Defect from mutual Cooperation in the ordinary game.

Mutual Cooperation, then, is the outcome of this Prisoners' Dilemma supergame, just as long as both players have sufficiently low discount rates. Just how low is 'sufficient' in this respect is a function of the ordinary game payoffs. This Cooperative outcome, it should be emphasized, results from both players using a *conditional* strategy; it is never rational for a player to use the unconditionally Cooperative strategy C^∞.

The N-person Supergame

The supergame examined here consists of an indefinite number of iterations of the same two-strategy Prisoners' Dilemma ordinary game with any finite number (N) of players. The N-person Prisoners' Dilemma ordinary game is defined as it was in Section 1.2: for each player, one of the strategies (D) dominates the other (C), that is, each player obtains a higher payoff if he chooses D than if he chooses C, no matter what strategies are chosen by the other players; but every player prefers the outcome $(C, C, ..., C)$ in which everybody Cooperates to the outcome $(D, D, ..., D)$ in which everybody Defects. The form of the payoffs is simplified by assuming that each player's payoffs in each ordinary game depend upon only two things: his own strategy choice (C or D) in that ordinary game and the *number* of other players choosing C in that game. This assumption is in fact very weak; it simply makes payoffs independent of *which* other players choose C. It is also assumed that, if a player Defects, his payoff when *some* others Cooperate is always greater than his payoff when nobody Cooperates. This too is quite a weak assumption; in fact, in problems of public goods provision, a much stronger assumption would normally hold, namely that the payoff to a Defector (a non-contributor) increases monotonically as the number of Cooperators (contributors) increases.

As in the two-person supergame, five strategies are considered.

(i) C^∞, as before.

(ii) D^∞, as before.

(iii) $A_{k,n}$, a generalization of A_k. Here, C is chosen in the first ordinary game; it continues to be chosen as long as *at least n other players* also chose C (in the preceding game); if the number of other Cooperators falls below n, then D is chosen for the next k games; C is then chosen in the next game no matter what the other players chose in the preceding game; it continues to be chosen as long as at least n other players chose C in the preceding game; when the number of other Cooperating players next falls below n, D is chosen for $k + 1$ games; and so on, as with A_k.

(iv) B_n, a generalization of B. C is chosen in the first ordinary game; thereafter, if the number of other players choosing C in the preceding game is at least n, C is chosen; otherwise D is chosen.

(v) B'_n, a similar generalization of B'.

Of special interest are the strategies obtained when n is set equal to $N - 1$ in $A_{k,n}$, B_n and B'_n. In this case, Cooperation is conditional upon the Cooperation of *all* the other players.

If some of the players use one or more of these conditional strategies, the possible patterns of sequences of ordinary game choices are exceedingly diverse. A complete analysis of all these possibilities is not attempted, but the sorts of conclusions which such an analysis would yield are indicated, I think, in the results of an analysis of two interesting special cases. These results will now be summarized.

First, the set of strategies $A_{k,n}$, B_n, C^∞ and D^∞ was examined; necessary and sufficient conditions were derived for all possible strategy vectors involving these four strategies, on the assumption that only these strategies were available to each player and that the same value of n appeared in all the conditional strategies. Two special cases were first dealt with (i) the strategy vector in which every player chooses D^∞ is of course *always* an equilibrium; (ii) strategy vectors in which some players choose C^∞ and the others choose D^∞ are *never* equilibria, because a player using C^∞ can obtain a higher payoff by unilaterally switching to D^∞. However, when there are some players who choose conditionally Cooperative strategies ($A_{k,n}$ and B_n) and possibly also some players using C^∞ and some using D^∞, then the strategy vector is an equilibrium if the following two conditions are satisfied. First, we must have $m - 1 = n$, where m is the number of players using conditionally or unconditionally Cooperative strategies, that is, the Cooperation of each of the conditional Cooperators must depend on the Cooperation of *all* the other players who are not using D^∞. Any strategy vector of which this is not true is *never* an equilibrium. Second, an inequality (inequality (7) in Section 3.3), relating the discount rate to the ordinary game payoffs, must hold for each of the m players who choose conditionally or unconditionally Cooperative strategies.

Thus, even when some players choose D^∞, Cooperation may still be rational for all the rest, though their mutual Cooperation, it has to be admitted, is rather precarious. I do not think this conclusion would be substantially modified if the strategies available to the players were unrestricted.

The reason why these strategy vectors are equilibria only if $m - 1 = n$ can be explained as follows. If $m - 1 = n$ does *not* hold, then either $m - 1 > n$ or $m - 1 < n$. If $m - 1 > n$, then of course there are more than enough Cooperators (conditional and unconditional) to maintain the Cooperation of the conditional Cooperators throughout the supergame; thus if one of the Cooperators unilaterally changes his strategy to D^∞ ('defects'), this will have no effect on the remaining conditional Cooperators—they will continue to Cooperate; the defector's payoff therefore increases (for the number of other Cooperators is unchanged, and it has been assumed that D dominates C for every player in each ordinary game); therefore, the original strategy vector (with $m - 1 > n$) is not an equilibrium. If, on the other hand, $m - 1 < n$, then there are not enough Cooperators to maintain the Cooperation of the conditional Cooperators after the first ordinary game, even if no player changes his strategy (or, equivalently, the Cooperation of the conditional Cooperators depends upon the Cooperation of too many other players); thus, again, if one of the Cooperators changes his strategy to D^∞, this has no effect on the choices of the remaining players, and it is easily shown that the defector increases his payoff, so that the original strategy vector is not an equilibrium. However, if $m - 1 = n$, then there are exactly enough players (m) choosing C in each ordinary game to maintain throughout the supergame the Cooperation of the conditional Cooperators—to maintain their 'compact'. Here, unlike the two previous cases when $m - 1 \neq n$, if one of the Cooperators changes his strategy by Defecting in any ordinary game, this 'compact' would collapse immediately and the erstwhile conditional Cooperators would choose D for the rest of the supergame; and whereas before, his change of strategy brought him an increased payoff because he could rely on the continued Cooperation of all the remaining Cooperators or because their Cooperation would not have endured beyond the first ordinary game anyway, now (when $m - 1 = n$) his change of strategy *may or may not* bring him an increased payoff: this depends, as in the two-person supergame, on the value of his discount rate (and this is the second condition for equilibrium mentioned above).

This analysis for strategy vectors containing $A_{k,n}$, B_n, C^∞ and D^∞ includes the cases when there are no players using either or both of C^∞ and D^∞. In the case of the absence of D^∞ players, the results show that the Cooperation of all N players is possible; the Cooperation of each of the conditional Cooperators must be conditional upon the Cooperation of *all* the $(N - 1)$ remaining players.

However, it has also been shown that even when some players use D^∞, Cooperation may still be rational for all the rest; again, for this to be so, the Cooperation of all the conditional Cooperators must be conditional upon the Cooperation of all the players who are not using D^∞, In addition, each Cooperator's discount rate must not exceed a certain number which is a function of the ordinary game payoffs. This number of course depends upon the number of players using the unconditionally non-Cooperative strategy D^∞ (since this affects the actual values of the ordinary game payoffs); generally speaking, the greater the number of players using D^∞, the smaller must be the discount rate if this second condition for equilibrium is to be satisfied.

The second class of strategy vectors considered in Section 3.3 were those containing only B_n and B'_n. Equilibrium conditions were derived, on the assumption that the available strategies were B_n, B'_n and D^∞ (in other words, a player could defect from B_n or B'_n to D^∞) and the same value of n appeared in all the conditional strategies. These strategy vectors were found to be equilibria only under very restrictive conditions: in the first place, equilibrium here can occur only when the two blocs of players using B_n and B'_n are of equal size (N, the total number of players, being even) or when the B'_n bloc has one more player than the B_n bloc (N being odd); and in addition to this stringent requirement, certain conditions relating the ordinary game payoffs to the discount rates must, as usual, be met.

In the analysis of the classes of strategy vectors just considered, it was assumed that the same value of n appeared in all the conditional strategies, that is, the choices of all those using conditional strategies were contingent on the choices of the same number of other players. A brief analysis was also made in Chapter 3 of the first class of strategy vectors ($A_{k,n}$, B_n, C^∞, D^∞) in the more general case when n is permitted to vary amongst the players. Only a partial analysis was made; however, it was carried far enough to show that some of the strategy vectors in which there are conditional Cooperators are equilibria under certain conditions, but these conditions are much more stringent than the conditions in the earlier case when n was not variable.

It plainly cannot be concluded from these results that the 'dilemma' in the Prisoners' Dilemma game is 'resolved' upon the introduction of time: that people will Cooperate voluntarily in Prisoners' Dilemma supergames. Nevertheless, it has been shown that, *no matter how many players there are*, it is rational for some or all of the players to Cooperate throughout the supergame *under certain conditions*. The question arises, whether these conditions are likely to be met in practice. In this connection, it is clear that Cooperation amongst a relatively large number of players is 'less likely' to occur than Cooperation amongst a small number. This is for two reasons. In the first place, we have seen that if mutual Cooperation amongst some of the players throughout the supergame is to occur at all, it will occur only when some players adopt conditionally Cooperative strategies which in every case are such that Cooperation is conditional upon the Cooperation of *all* the other Cooperators (conditional and unconditional). Thus, this mutual Cooperation becomes more precarious the more other Cooperative players there are. In the second place, we have seen that Cooperation depends additionally on certain conditions which relate discount rates to the ordinary game payoffs. At least one such condition must hold for each of the (conditionally and unconditionally) Cooperating players. This requirement clearly becomes more demanding as the number of Cooperators increases: the chances for it to fail are multiplied.

Now, if some players are to adopt conditionally Cooperative strategies (as is required for equilibrium), they must obviously have knowledge, at the start of every ordinary game, of the strategies chosen by the other players in the preceding ordinary game. More precisely, these conditional Cooperators must know whether *at least* a certain number of other players Cooperated in the previous game; they do not need to know *which* other players Cooperated or even exactly how many Cooperated. (This is guaranteed, of course, by the assumption, which was made at the outset, that at every stage of the supergame all players have knowledge of all other players' previous choices. This assumption is in fact stronger than is required, but simplifies the analysis considerably.) This requirement of a high degree of awareness on the part of the conditional Cooperators is itself 'more likely' to be met in a small group of players than in a large group—and even more likely in the sort of small community in which people have contact with and can observe the behaviour of many of their fellows and which is fairly static, in the sense that there is little mobility in or out. This is the sort of community which is the ideal of many anarchist writers, and I shall have more to say about it in Chapter 7.

5.2. ALTRUISM IN THE PRISONERS' DILEMMA

In the analysis of the Prisoners' Dilemma game which I have just summarized, each player is assumed to be a 'pure egoist', in the sense that he seeks to maximize only his own payoff. It was shown that even pure egoists might find it rational to Cooperate throughout the supergame. Now it is reasonable to suppose that the prospects for voluntary Cooperation are even brighter if the players are not pure egoists but rather are possessed of some degree of 'positive altruism' or benevolence. And indeed it is easily shown that if they are sufficiently benevolent, then it is rational for them to Cooperate in the Prisoners' Dilemma *ordinary* game (and *a fortiori* throughout the supergame). On the other hand, it might be expected that mutual Cooperation is even harder to achieve if players are in some degree 'negative altruists', that is to say, if they derive some satisfaction from *decreases* in other players' payoffs.

The effect of various forms of altruism on behaviour in the Prisoners' Dilemma is the subject of Chapter 4. I give here a brief summary of the ideas and results of that chapter which will be of some use in the next two chapters. Before doing so, it is necessary to recall (from the Introduction to Chapter 3) that a payoff is to be thought of as a quantity of some basic private good, or amounts of several private goods reduced to a single quantity of some *numeraire*, such as money. In Chapter 3, every individual was assumed to maximize only his own payoff (*pure egoism*); hence, in that chapter, 'utility' and 'payoff' could be equated.

Suppose now that a player seeks to maximize a utility which depends both on his own payoff and on the payoffs of the other players. Then he is said to act *altruistically*. Consider first the two-person game. In this game, the altruist's utility function is assumed to take the form of a *weighted sum* of his own payoff and the other player's payoff. If this utility function increases when the other player's payoff increases, the player's altruism is said to be *positive*; if his utility decreases, it is *negative*. If his utility depends *only* on the other player's payoff, he is called a *pure altruist*. (If a player's utility is a function of the other player's *utility*, he is said to be a *sophisticated altruist*. The effects of this sort of altruism on behaviour in the Prisoners' Dilemma are only briefly illustrated in Chapter 4.)

If the entries in the payoff matrix of the two-person Prisoners' Dilemma ordinary game are replaced by the corresponding utilities (in the general weighted sum form specified above), the resulting game is called the *transformed game*. The necessary and sufficient conditions for this transformed game to be a Prisoners' Dilemma (with D being the dominant strategy for each player and (C, C) being preferred to (D, D) by both players) are easily stated, and it is immediately seen that, for given values of the ordinary game payoffs (x, y, z, w), the conditions for D to dominate C are 'more readily' satisfied as the player's 'egoism' increases relative to his (positive) 'altruism', that is, as the ratio of the weight attached to his own payoff (in his utility function) to the weight attached to the other player's payoff increases. Conversely, if the two players are sufficiently positively altruistic, then (C, C) will be the outcome of the (transformed) game.

Of special interest here is the case when each player's utility increases both with his own payoff and with the *difference* between his and the other player's payoff. (This is a case of egoism combined with negative altruism.) The resulting (transformed) game is called a *Game of Difference*. It is easily shown that, just as long as each player attaches *some* positive weight to his own payoff, the Game of Difference is a Prisoners' Dilemma with (D, D) the only equilibrium; and that, furthermore, each player's *temptation* to Defect from mutual Cooperation in the Game of Difference is always greater than it was in the original Prisoners' Dilemma. (In this sense, we say that the Game of Difference is a 'more severe' Prisoners' Dilemma than the original game.)

The Game of Difference is of special interest in this book because (as I shall argue in the next chapter) it is the sort of game which Hobbes assumes people to be playing in the 'state of nature'. It is the only game involving egoism and altruism which is considered in Chapter 4 in a generalized N-person form. This N-person version is defined as follows.

In the two-person Game of Difference, each individual sought to maximize a combination of his own payoff and the difference between his payoff and the other player's. Call this difference his *eminence* over the other player. In the N-person Game of Difference, each individual is assumed to seek to maximize a combination of his own payoff and the *average* of his eminence over each other player.

Now if it can be established that an N-person Prisoners' Dilemma game, when transformed in this way into a Game of Difference, is still a Prisoners' Dilemma, then we can use the general results obtained earlier for the N-person Prisoners' Dilemma supergame. (We can, for example, immediately obtain the conditions for mutual Cooperation throughout the super-Game of Difference to be an equilibrium, simply by replacing the payoffs in the earlier conditions by the utilities, combinations of own payoff and average eminence, specified above.) In fact, it turns out that this Game of Difference is an N-person Prisoners' Dilemma (satisfying the assumption made at the beginning of the N-person Prisoners' Dilemma analysis that, if a player Defects, his payoff when some others Cooperate is always greater than when nobody Cooperates) *if* (i) the game is not one of *pure* eminence, that is to say, each individual attaches *some* weight to his own payoff *per se* as well as to his average eminence, and (ii) the payoff to a Defector in the original (untransformed) game increases monotonically as the number of Cooperators increases. Neither of these conditions is very demanding. The second one, as I remarked earlier, would normally be satisfied in public goods interaction, for it requires only that a non-Cooperating individual's payoff increases as more of the others contribute to the provision of the public good.

5.3. EXTENSIONS

My aim in this book is to criticize what I believe is the strongest and most popular argument for the desirability of the state. I make no attempt to provide a positive theory of anarchy or even an indication of how people might best provide themselves with public goods. I am therefore not concerned with developing a detailed dynamic model of public goods provision. I have merely tried to show that, even if we accept the pessimistic assumption (an assumption unfavourable to the case I am making out) that individual preferences have the structure of a Prisoners' Dilemma at any point in time, mutual Cooperation over time may nevertheless take place. However, the scope of the application of this part of my critical argument would be increased if the broad conclusions of the analysis in Chapters 3 and 4 could be shown to apply to a more detailed, more realistic model of the dynamic process of public goods provision than the Prisoners' Dilemma supergame model (with or without some form of altruism) considered in those two chapters. In this section, I want briefly to indicate, then, some ways in which this supergame model might be extended or revised so as to provide a more realistic picture of public goods interaction. I shall not give any analysis of the alternative models or even specify them fully; to do so would require another book.

In the Prisoners' Dilemma supergame considered above, it is assumed that the time taken for a player to change from one strategy to another is zero. There is no time lag between the decision to change and the actual change. Each player is perfectly 'flexible' in this respect, and therefore, in particular, his strategy choice in any ordinary game can be contingent upon the other player's choice in the immediately preceding game. In the real world, this sort of flexibility may exist in decisions such as those to commit or refrain from committing anti-social acts (a decision can be translated immediately into 'action', with instantaneous production of the public good or bad, social order or disorder), but with respect to most kinds of public goods, flexibility is less than perfect. People must be trained, equipment obtained, public works constructed, and so on, before there is any benefit to anybody.

Intuitively, it would seem that the presence of time-lags of this sort would tend to increase the 'likelihood' of non-Cooperation in the Prisoners' Dilemma supergame; for a player (A) contemplating Defection from mutual Cooperation knows that it will take the other player (B) several time periods to change his strategy after observing A's Defection, and can expect the unilateral Defection payoff during this interval; this will offer A a greater compensation for the mutual Defection payoffs which will be his lot after B's eventual Defection than it would in the model in Chapter 3 where A can 'exploit' B (receive the unilateral Defection payoff) for only one ordinary game. Thus, the conditions for Cooperation to be rational are likely to require a progressively smaller discount rate as this flexibility decreases (that is, as the time-lag between decision and effect increases). This conclusion finds some support in Nicholson's study of the Prisoners' Dilemma supergame (although his analysis cannot be compared directly with the one in Chapter 3).[1]

A second kind of inflexibility which may be present in individual decisions in public goods interaction is the limitation on the *frequency* with which strategy choices may be changed. If every strategy of every individual could be changed equally regularly, no matter how infrequently, the supergame models of Chapter 3 and 4 would not have to be modified, since the durations of the time periods specified there are essentially arbitrary. However, if only *some* strategy changes could be made at any time (in any time period) while others could be changed less frequently (for example, a decision to contribute to the provision of a public good for the first time could perhaps be made at any time, but a decision to cease contributing—to switch from Cooperation to Defection—might be possible less often, because, for example, resources have been committed), then the model would have to be modified. Again, I suspect that the result of the modification would be to render more restrictive the conditions for mutual Cooperation to be the outcome of the supergame.

Perhaps the most important shortcoming of the Prisoners' Dilemma supergame as a model of the process of public goods provision is that it takes place in a static environment: the supergame consists of iterations of the same ordinary game. In some of the public goods problems of interest here, a more realistic description of reality would require a *changing* payoff matrix, possibly a changing set of available strategies, and even a changing set of players. These changes, especially the first, might be the result of influences external to the game or of the history of strategy choices of the players themselves. Where, for example, a 'commons' (of the kind discussed in Chapter 1) is being exploited, the payoffs might decrease steadily as more and more non-Cooperative ('exploitative') choices are made over time; they might radically change quite suddenly with the ecological collapse of the 'commons' following a long succession of non-Cooperative choices; and, for the same reasons, the set of available strategies might become restricted and some of the players might be obliged to withdraw from the game.

The possibilities here are very numerous, and it is impossible to make any general statements about the effects of extensions of this sort on the conclusions of the analysis in Chapters 3 and 4.[2] These effects would very much depend on the particular manner in which the game changed over time. Perhaps the most important class of changes is the one suggested above: all payoffs decline as a result of non-Cooperative choices (the greater the number of players Defecting, the greater the decline), and all payoffs increase, or at least do not decrease, as a result of Cooperative choices. It seems very probable that an analysis of this sort of dynamic game would show that mutual Cooperation is a more likely outcome here than in the 'static' supergame of Chapter 3; that is to say, a lower discount rate than in the earlier model would suffice to make Cooperation rational, for the gains from unilateral Defection from the mutual Cooperation position (assuming that conditional strategies are being used so that this unilateral Defection would cause other players to Defect also) would clearly be smaller, other things being equal.

5.4. NOTES

1. Michael Nicholson, *Oligopoly and Conflict* (Liverpool: Liverpool University Press, 1972), Section 3.2; see also his discussion of this type of flexibility in Chapter 6.

2. A beginning is made on models of this sort in Nicholson, *Oligopoly and Conflict*, Section 5.3.

CHAPTER 6

Government

In the Introduction to this book, a sketch was made of an argument for the desirability of government. The first part of this argument is that the static preferences of individuals amongst alternative courses of action with respect to the provision of public goods (in particular, domestic peace and security and environmental public goods) are those of a Prisoners' Dilemma game, at least where relatively large numbers of individuals are involved. I examined this part of the argument in Chapter 2 and found that it is not necessarily true and needs to be qualified. Accepting the first part of the argument, I considered in Chapter 3 the second part of the argument: that individuals would not voluntarily Cooperate in such situations. If the problem is properly specified as a Prisoners' Dilemma (ordinary) game, this conclusion is obviously correct; but to treat the problem, as it is usually treated (tacitly or explicitly), in terms of a Prisoners' Dilemma *ordinary* game, is clearly inadequate. I therefore treated it in terms of a Prisoners' Dilemma supergame in which the players discount future payoffs. Formulated in this way, the second part of the argument is not necessarily true: under certain conditions, it is rational to Cooperate in the supergame. It remains to examine the third part of the argument, that the failure of individuals, at least in large groups, to Cooperate voluntarily (to provide themselves with certain public goods) makes government desirable.

This part of the argument will be examined in the present chapter in the forms in which it appears in the political theories of Hobbes and Hume, and more generally in the final chapter.

In this chapter, I consider two versions, those of Hobbes and Hume, of the *whole* of the argument about the desirability of government. My reasons for doing so, and in particular for choosing Hobbes and Hume as exemplars of the general argument, were given earlier (in Section 1.4) and I shall not repeat them here. I shall give an account of the two theories in such a way that they can be compared at certain points with some of the ideas in the earlier chapters. A large part of my account of Hobbes's theory is devoted to showing (what at first sight may appear almost obvious) that men, in what Hobbes calls the 'state of nature', find themselves in a Prisoners' Dilemma game.

My treatment of Hobbes's theory is based entirely on his *Leviathan*. I have resisted the temptation to buttress my argument at any point with selective quotation from his other works. *Leviathan* contains the clearest and most coherent version of the argument which is of interest here, and I have thought it unjustified to refer to a passage from another version which, taken as a whole, is different, less coherent and generally less satisfactory than the one in *Leviathan*. My treatment of Hume's theory is based chiefly on *A Treatise of Human Nature*, which I think gives a clearer and more complete account than the one in *An Enquiry Concerning the Principles of Morals*. The second differs in places from, but is not inconsistent with the first, and I have referred to it once or twice.

6.1. HOBBES'S *LEVIATHAN*

I begin with Hobbes's description of those parts of the structure of individual preferences on which his political theory is based. His conclusions on this subject are presented here as assumptions, whereas in *Leviathan* Hobbes claims to deduce them from more fundamental, physical premises. His political theory is unaffected by this shift in the point of logical departure.

A. Individual Preferences

All men, says Hobbes, *desire* certain things (*Lev* 31).[1] He derives this proposition from his assumptions about 'motion' and these lead him to speak of man's *ceaseless* striving for the things he desires: 'Life it self is but Motion, and can never be without Desire' (*Lev* 48); and 'Nor can a man any more live, whose Desires are at an end, than he whose Senses and Imagination are at a stand. Felicity is a continuall progresse of the desire from one object to another; the attaining of the former, being still but the way to the later' (*Lev* 75). But this adds nothing to the original statement that all men desire certain things. For this statement, in which there is no reference to time, is to apply at each point in time. The same is true of man's 'perpetuall and restlesse desire of Power'.

Hobbes defines power as follows. 'The POWER *of a Man*, (to take it Universally), is his present means, to obtain some future apparent Good. And is either *Originall*, or *Instrumentall*' (*Lev* 66). Later he concludes that he puts '... for a general inclination of all mankind, a perpetuall and restelesse desire of Power after power, that ceaseth only in Death' (*Lev* 75). This can be viewed either as a part of the initial proposition that men desire certain things (one of them, then, being power) or, better, as derivative from it: for if a man desires something, he desires also the means to obtain it in the future ('... anything that is a pleasure in the sense, the same also is pleasure in the imagination' (*Lev* 76)—although Hobbes is never explicit about *how* men presently value future expected goods).

Thus power-seeking (which has been so much emphasized in discussions of Hobbes) does not play an independent role in Hobbes's theory and will not appear in my restatement of it.

Now Hobbes seems to say that men do not simply desire certain primary goods, but rather they desire to have them to an 'eminent' degree. 'Vertue generally, in all sorts of subjects, is somewhat that is valued for eminence; and consisteth in comparison. For if all things were equally in all men, nothing would be prized' (*Lev* 52). Thus '… man, whose Joy consisteth in comparing himself with other men, can relish nothing but what is eminent' (*Lev* 130). Power, which all men seek and which is a means to other desirable things, is divided by Hobbes into 'natural' and 'instrumental' power, the first being defined as 'the eminence of the Faculties of Body, or Mind: as extraordinary Strength, Forme, Prudence, Arts, Eloquence, Liberality, Nobility', while 'Instrumentall are those Powers, which acquired by these, or by fortune, are means and Instruments to acquire more: as Riches, Reputation, Friends, and the secret working of God, which men call Good Luck' (*Lev* 66). A desire for power, then, entails by definition a desire for 'eminence'.

In my restatement of Hobbes's main argument, there will be just one assumption about individual preferences, to the effect that each person seeks to maximize a convex combination of his own payoff and his eminence (to use the language of Chapter 4). But the desire for eminence needs to be specified more carefully than Hobbes does, in the passages referred to above. No problems arise if there are only two individuals who both desire the same object and nothing else. For then the assumption is that each individual seeks to maximize the excess of his amount of the object over the other individual's amount.

Yet, in the first place, Hobbes has said that not all men desire the same things (*Lev* 40). Perhaps, in the two-person case, each man seeks to have more of the things he wants than the other man has of those same things, even though the latter has no desire for them. Or, more plausibly, he seeks to have more of the things he wants than the other man has of the things *he* wants: in this case, he must presumably have some means of comparing his and the other individual's amounts of the different objects. However, neither of these is terribly plausible unless there is an acknowledged scheme for comparing the extents to which the two men desire their different objects. Yet it can be argued that Hobbes has in mind *particular* objects of desire and assumes that *all* men desire at least these objects. For example, all men desire their own preservation. All men (he seems to say in Chapter 8) desire to be eminent in the 'intellectual virtues'. All men desire to be eminent in 'Strength, Forme ,Prudence, Arts, Eloquence, Liberality, Nobility', for eminence in these things gives one 'Natural Power', which all men desire, and all men desire 'Riches, Reputation, Friends, and the secret working of God, which men call Good Luck' for these are 'Instrumentall powers', which all men desire (*Lev* 66).

It is not necessary here to resolve this problem in *Leviathan* (if it is a problem). In whatever way it is resolved, the following assumption (or something very like it) must in any case be made: corresponding to every possible state of affairs which is the outcome of individual choices, there is for each individual a *payoff* ; each individual's payoff scale is unique at least up to a linear transformation, and each individual is able to compare other individuals' payoffs with his own (he is able to place any other player's payoff scale in a one-to-one-correspondence with his own). Then, in the two-person case, if the payoff to the ith individual is p_i, I define the *eminence* of the ith over the jth individual as $p_i - p_j$.

In the second place, there are of course more than two people in the societies Hobbes is writing about. In this case, there are a number of ways of specifying the assumption that men seek 'eminence'. (I mentioned a few in Section 4.3.) In Hobbes's theory, several of these alternative definitions of 'eminence' would suffice as part of the logical basis for the rest of his argument. For the sake of concreteness, in my restatement of his argument I shall adopt the definition given in Section 4.3 ('An N-person Game of Difference'), where an individual's *eminence* is defined as the average of his eminences over each other individual. Also I shall assume that each individual seeks to maximize a convex combination (as defined in the same section) of his own payoff and his eminence. This convex combination is referred to as his *utility*. It should be noted that 'pure egoism' (that is, maximizing one's own payoff only) is a special case of maximizing this convex combination; in this case, 'utility' and 'payoff' can be viewed as the same thing.

In *Leviathan* (but not in all his earlier works), Hobbes clearly believes that 'benevolence', 'pity' and other manifestations of *positive* altruism are possible, that in some degree they are found in some individuals, and that they are not reducible to or mediated by self-interest. Nevertheless, it is true that the assumption on which his political theory is based is that in the state of nature (that is, in society without government) a man seeks only to maximize a convex combination of his own payoff and his eminence; that is to say, his preferences contain a mixture of egoism and *negative* altruism only.

B. A Prisoners' Dilemma

In this section I argue that in what Hobbes calls the 'state of nature' men find themselves in a Prisoners' Dilemma; that is to say, Hobbes is assuming that the choices available to each man (or 'player') and the players' preferences amongst the possible outcomes are such that the game is a Prisoners' Dilemma; and the Prisoners' Dilemma is the *only* structure of utilities (out of a very large number of possibilities) which Hobbes *must* have assumed to obtain in the state of nature.

I shall present two versions of this argument and evaluate their relative merits. The first version argues that Hobbes's theory is essentially static, being an analysis of the Prisoners' Dilemma *ordinary* game. The second version is more dynamic: although, in this version, time does not play an explicit role and there is no talk of the present valuation of future benefits, *conditional* Cooperation is thought to be sometimes rational (and conditional Cooperation is of course not possible in a game played only once).[2]

I assume (as Hobbes does in effect) that each individual is confronted with a number of alternative courses of action, which I call *strategies*. The number of strategies available to each player is assumed to be just two. I shall show later that nothing essential in Hobbes's argument is affected if this assumption is relaxed. Call these two strategies C and D. (It need not be assumed that C and D denote the same two courses of action for every individual; but no confusion will arise if the same two labels are used for all individuals.) There are thus four possible states of affairs or *outcomes*. A *strategy vector* is defined as a list (an ordered N-tuple, if there are N individuals in the society) of strategies, one for each player.

One of the outcomes is called 'the state of War' or simply 'War' (*Lev* 96). This is the state of affairs which obtains when every individual seeks, in the absence of restraint, to maximize his utility (as Hobbes assumes he does). If the state of War is to be a determinate, unique outcome, then it must be assumed that 'maximizing utility' has a clear meaning and entails the choice by each individual of a single strategy. Let us suppose that this strategy is D. (For the time being, strategy C is simply 'not acting without restraint so as to maximize one's utility'.) Now, when men are under no restraint, when they 'live without a common power to keep them all in awe', they are said to be in the 'state of nature' (*Lev* Chapter 8).

When men are not in the state of War, then there is 'Peace', says Hobbes. There are of course *three* outcomes other than War (assuming that there are only two strategies available to each player), but it is clear that Hobbes means that Peace corresponds to only one of these outcomes: it obtains only when *no* individual chooses strategy D. (For he later argues that *everybody* must behave differently if society is to move out of the state of War into that of Peace.) Thus, Peace obtains when every individual chooses strategy C.

Now the state of War is Pareto-inferior: every man prefers Peace to War. For in War, 'men live without ... security' and there is 'continuall feare, and danger of violent death; And the life of man, solitary, poore, nasty, brutish, and short' (*Lev* 96–97). Despite this rhetorical flourish, Hobbes makes it clear that 'the nature of War, consisteth not in actuall fighting; but in the known disposition thereto, during all the time there is no assurance to the contrary' (*Lev* 96). Nevertheless, in this condition, a man cannot expect to obtain what he desires; whereas in the state of Peace, life and security are guaranteed to each man and he can reasonably expect to obtain some of the things he desires; so that 'all men agree ... that Peace is good' (*Lev* 122).

In the state of nature, then, each man will so act that the outcome is War, which is Pareto-inferior. The only way, in Hobbes's view, to prevent this outcome occurring and to ensure Peace instead is for men to erect a 'common power' which will maintain conditions in which each individual will not wish to choose D; and the only way to erect such a common power is to 'authorize', by 'convenanting' amongst themselves, one man or assembly of men to do whatever is necessary to maintain such conditions. The man or assembly of men so authorized is called the 'Sovereign' (*Lev* Chapter 17).

This needs explanation. For this, several definitions are required. The 'right of nature', says Hobbes, is 'the Liberty each man hath, to use his own power, as he will himselfe, for the preservation of his own Nature; that is to say, of his own Life; and consequently, of doing any thing, which in his own Judgement, and Reason, hee shall conceive to be the aptest means thereunto' (*Lev* 99). In the state of nature, therefore, 'every man has a Right to every thing; even to one anothers body' (*Lev* 99); so there is no security of life; 'and consequently, it is a precept, or generall rule of Reason, *That every man, ought to endeavour Peace, as farre forth as he has hope of obtaining it; and when he cannot obtain it, that he may seek, and use, all helps, and advantages of Warre*' (*Lev* 100). Notice that the second part of this statement is just the Right of Nature and that this is part of 'a precept, or generall rule of Reason'. Hobbes is saying, in effect, that it is rational for a man to choose *D* if he thinks he cannot obtain Peace, that is, if he thinks that some other people will choose *D*. Hobbes calls the first part of this statement the Fundamental or First Law of Nature, a 'law of nature' having been defined earlier as 'a Precept, or generall Rule, found out by Reason, by which a man is forbidden to do, that, which is destructive of his life, or taketh away the means of preserving the same; and to omit, that, by which he thinketh it may be best preserved' (*Lev* 99).

We may now say that strategy *C* is 'laying aside one's Right of Nature'. This only restates our earlier definition of *C* as not acting without restraint so as to maximize one's utility.

This statement of the first Law of Nature will be clarified after we have seen Hobbes's discussion of obligation and covenanting.

The definition of obligation given in *Leviathan* is straightforward. The second Law of Nature requires a man under certain conditions to lay down his right to all things. He may do this by simply 'renouncing' it ('when he cares not to whom the benefit thereof redoundeth') or by 'transferring' it to another (when he does so care). 'And when a man hath in either manner abandoned, or granted away his Right, then he is said to be OBLIGED, or BOUND, not to hinder those, to whom such Right is granted, or abandoned, from the benefit of it' (*Lev* 101). A man will of course only transfer or renounce his Right in exchange for some good to himself, in particular 'for some Right reciprocally transferred to himselfe' (*Lev* 101). This mutual transferring of right is called 'contract', and a contract in which at least one of the parties promises to perform his part in the future is called a 'covenant' (*Lev* 102), a 'covenant of mutual trust' being one in which both parties so promise (*Lev* 105, 110).

Now contracts would not serve their end of securing Peace if they were not kept. Thus, the third Law of Nature is that 'men performe their Covenants made' (*Lev* 110). Yet, by performing unilaterally his part of a covenant of mutual trust, a man may expose himself, and this he is forbidden to do by all the Laws of Nature. Thus, a man should not do his part unless he is sure that the other party will do his. A covenant of mutual trust made *in the state of nature* is therefore void 'upon any reasonable suspicion': 'For he that performeth first, has no assurance that the other will performe after ... And therefore ... does but betray himselfe to his enemy; contrary to the Right (he can never abandon) of defending his life, and means of living'. But 'if there be a common Power set over them both, with right and force sufficient to compell performance', then 'that feare is no more reasonable' and so the covenant is not void (*Lev* 105).

Thus Hobbes comes to the last stage of his main argument. The central point (leaving aside the details of 'authorization' and of acquisition of sovereignty by conquest) is that the only way for men to obtain Peace is for every man to make with every other man a covenant of mutual trust instituting a Sovereign with the power to do whatever is necessary to secure Peace (*Lev* 131–2). The Sovereign will maintain Peace by compelling men 'equally to the performance of their Covenants, by the terrour of some punishment, greater than the benefit they expect by the breach of their Covenant' (*Lev* 110); in other words, by creating appropriate laws and punishing transgressors.

I will return later to this point in Hobbes's argument to discuss his account of *why* men obey the Sovereign, and again in part E to present his description of the Sovereign's powers.

We are now in a position to develop the argument that in the state of nature men find themselves in a Prisoners' Dilemma game.

The 'game' which Hobbesian men in the state of nature are 'playing' is certainly *non-cooperative* (in the game theorists' sense, as I defined it in Chapter 1), for although agreements are possible, they are not binding: the state of nature, by definition, is precisely the absence of any constraint which would keep men to their agreements.

It has been assumed that each man has a choice between two strategies, *C* and *D*. We have already seen that in the state of nature it is rational for each man to choose *D*, and thus the outcome in the state of nature is War. Since, as we have seen, the state of Peace is preferred by every individual to the state of War, we can conclude that the game is a Prisoners' Dilemma if *D* is the 'rational' strategy for each man, in the sense that it *dominates* all other strategies, that is, it yields a more preferred outcome than any other strategy no matter what strategies the other individuals choose. (There are of course other and more controversial ways in which a strategy can be said to be the 'rational' one to use; but dominance is required for the game to be a Prisoners' Dilemma.)

Now first, it is clear that in the state of nature no individual has an incentive *unilaterally* to change his strategy from *D* to *C*, if the other players are choosing *D*. For, as we have seen already, 'if other men will not lay down their Right, as well as he; then there is no Reason for any one, to devest himselfe of his: For that were to expose himselfe to Prey ...' (*Lev* 100). If this were not the case, there would be no need for him to enter into a covenant. Thus the state of War, (*D*, *D*, ..., *D*), is certainly an equilibrium.

Consider next any two individuals who have made a covenant of mutual trust to lay down their Right of Nature, that is, to choose *C*. Hobbes says that it does not pay a man to perform his part of the covenant (to choose *D*) if he believes the other man will not. On each of the occasions in *Leviathan* where he argues this, there is no mention of what all the other members of the society are doing. Yet, clearly, the payoffs to the two individuals, each of whom is choosing between keeping and not keeping the agreement, depend on what the rest of the society is doing (on how many others are choosing D, for example). We must infer that Hobbes is assuming that his argument holds no matter what others are doing. It follows that, just as long as one other individual (the one with whom I am covenanting) chooses D, it pays me to choose D also.

This establishes that D dominates C for each individual in every contingency (i.e. for every combination of strategy choices by the $N - 1$ other individuals) *except* where all other individuals choose C. This contingency remains to be considered. And it is here that I believe Hobbes's argument is not wholly satisfactory; it is this contingency which gives rise to the two interpretations I mentioned earlier. The first interpretation is the static one, that Hobbes treats only a Prisoners' Dilemma *ordinary* game, a game played only once. The second interpretation is more dynamic, at least to the extent that it admits *sequences* of choices and the possibility of using *conditional* strategies (which are of course ruled out in an ordinary game).

Now if, as I believe, individual preferences in Hobbes's state of nature have the structure of a Prisoners' Dilemma game *at any point in time*, then (i) if the first interpretation is the correct one, it will never be rational (in the state of nature) for any individual to choose C, even if (indeed, especially if) every other individual chooses C; it will never be rational for a party to a covenant to keep his promise if the other party has performed his part already (and it makes no difference, in the state of nature, whether the two players make their choices simultaneously or one player's choice *follows* the other's in full knowledge of it); but (ii) if the second, dynamic interpretation is the correct one, it *may* be rational for an individual to Cooperate when the other individuals Cooperate; more precisely, we have seen (in Chapters 3 and 5) that conditional Cooperation is rational under certain conditions in a (two-person or N-person) Prisoners' Dilemma supergame with future payoffs exponentially discounted. With this in mind, let us examine the relative merits of the two interpretations.

Hobbes does in fact assert that if one of the parties to a covenant has *already* performed his part, then it is rational (and obligatory) for the other to perform his, even in the state of nature: '... where one of the parties has performed already; or where there is a Power to make him performe; there is the question whether it be against reason, that is, against the benefit of the other to performe, or not. And I say it is not against reason' (*Lev* 112). This statement would seem to preclude the first, static interpretation, or at least to render it less plausible. In the continuation of this passage, Hobbes explains why it is 'not against Reason' to Cooperative when others do:

'First, that when a man doth a thing, which notwithstanding any thing can be foreseen, and reckoned on, tendeth to his own destruction, howsoever some accident which he could not expect, arriving may turne it to his benefit; yet such events do not make it reasonably or wisely done. Secondly, that in a condition of Warre, wherein every man to every man, for want of a common Power to keep them all in awe, is an Enemy, there is no man can hope by his own strength, or wit, to defend himselfe from destruction, without the help of Confederates; ... and therefore he which declares he thinks it reason to deceive those that help him, can in reason expect no other means of safety, than what can be had from his own single Power. He therefore that breaketh his Covenant, ... cannot be received into any Society, that unite themselves for Peace and Defence, but by the errour of them that receive him; nor when he is received, be retayned in it, without seeing the danger of their errour; which errours a man cannot reasonably reckon on as the means of his security ...' (*Lev* 112).

In this passage, Hobbes clearly suggests that a man should perform his part of a covenant after the other has done so, out of a fear of the future consequences to himself should he not do so; in other words, it is suggested that the behaviour of each of the two parties to the covenant is conditional upon the behaviour of the other. The same idea appears in an earlier passage (*Lev* 108–9) where Hobbes mentions two other possible motives for not breaking any sort of covenant (not merely one in which the other party has already performed). These are fear of the consequences of breaking one's word and pride in appearing not to need to break it. The latter is a 'generosity too rarely found to be presumed upon'. The former is of two kinds: fear of the power of those one might offend and fear of God. The first of these is too limited to be effective, because of the approximate equality (to be discussed shortly) of men in the state of nature. This leaves only the fear of God; but Hobbes sets little store by this and clearly thinks it will not be effective enough to keep men to their covenants.

This idea of conditional cooperation is expressed more generally in the Fundamental Law of Nature, 'That every man, ought to endeavour Peace, *as farre as he has hope of obtaining it;* and *when he cannot obtain it*, that he may seek, and use, all helps, and advantages of Warre', and in the Second Law of Nature which follows from it, 'That a man be willing, *when others are so too*, as farre-forth, as for Peace, and defence of himself he shall think it necessary, to lay down this right to all things; and be contented with so much liberty against other men, as he would allow other men against himselfe' (*Lev* 100; emphasis supplied—the originals are italicized throughout). Hobbes seems to be saying here, and in the passages quoted earlier, that every man ought always to do what is conducive to Peace just as long as he can do so safely and this means that, in the state of nature, he should Cooperate *if* others do, but otherwise he should not Cooperate. This sounds like the 'tit-for-tat' strategy B or its N-person generalization B_n which were considered in Chapter 3, though it obviously cannot be said that this is precisely what Hobbes had in mind.

Earlier, we saw that the Sovereign, which men institute by convenants of mutual trust, will maintain Peace by compelling men 'equally to the performance of their Covenants, by the terrour of some punishment, greater than the benefit they expect by the breach of their Covenant' (*Lev* 110). Yet it is clear that Hobbes is not simply asserting that the Sovereign will be effective in maintaining Peace because each man will obey him only from fear of his sanctions. He believes that because men want Peace (or at least prefer Peace to War), each of them will obey because the Sovereign has removed the only reason for not keeping one's covenants, which is a 'reasonable suspicion' that other men will not keep theirs.

Hobbes's position here is widely misunderstood. A standard view of Hobbes is that 'he has such a limited view of human motives that he cannot provide any other explanation for acceptance of authority than the fear of ... sanctions'.[3] Exceptions to this distortion of what Hobbes actually said in *Leviathan* are rare. H. L. A. Hart, in his discussion of the 'minimal content of natural law', based on *Leviathan* and on Hume's *Treatise*, concludes that centrally organized sanctions are required 'not as the normal motive for obedience, but as a *guarantee* that those who would voluntarily obey should not be sacrificed to those who would not';[4] and Brian Barry writes that 'It is not so much that the Sovereign makes it pay to keep your covenant by punishing you if you don't, but that it always pays anyway to keep covenants provided you can do so without exposing yourself'.[5] The Sovereign is required, then, to ensure that nobody will expose himself.

Let us recall the results of the analysis of N-person Prisoners' Dilemma supergames in Chapter 3. It was found there that Cooperation in these games is rational only under certain conditions: in the first place, only *conditional* Cooperation is ever rational, and it must be contingent upon the Cooperation (in the previous ordinary game) of *all* the other Cooperators (conditional and unconditional); in the second place, the discount rates of each of the Cooperators must not be too high, relative to a certain function of the ordinary game payoffs. (The first condition does not require Cooperation to be conditional upon the Cooperation of all the $N - 1$ other players; it can be rational for each of a subset of the N players to Cooperate conditionally while the remaining players use unconditionally Cooperative or non-Cooperative strategies.) Now, we obviously cannot make a precise comparison of Hobbes's argument with these results. Hobbes does not clearly specify the form of the conditional Cooperation which he says is rational in the state of nature (is it, for example, contingent upon other players' behaviour in only the immediately preceding time period?); there is no talk of discounting of future benefits; and so on. Nevertheless, it is clear from these results that, even if the requirement concerning the discount rates is ignored, voluntary Cooperation in the N-person Prisoners' Dilemma supergame is somewhat precarious (see the discussion at the end of Section 5.1), and it can be argued that it was just this precariousness which in Hobbes's view made a Sovereign necessary: the Sovereign would provide the conditions in which it was rational for a man to Cooperate conditionally, by ensuring that he could rely on a sufficient number of other individuals to Cooperate.

This, then, is the case for the second, dynamic interpretation of what I take to be the core of Hobbes's political theory. According to this interpretation, individual preferences at any point in time are those of a Prisoners' Dilemma; nevertheless it is rational to Cooperate *conditionally*. The problem with this interpretation, however, is that, although the idea of conditional Cooperation is in *Leviathan* (and therefore Hobbes's analysis cannot be entirely static, for conditional Cooperation is not possible in a game played only once), Hobbes has virtually nothing explicit to say about any sort of dynamics. *Time* plays no explicit role in his political theory. It is true that Hobbes sometimes speaks of 'anticipation' and 'foresight' and of how men are in 'a perpetuall solicitude of the time to come', but on these occasions he is not speaking of the present valuation of future benefits and the effect of discounting on the prospects for voluntary Cooperation. Nor do his few explicit statements on the subject of discounting play an essential role in his theory. The most explicit statement of this kind is where, speaking of the unwillingness of the Sovereign's subjects to pay their taxes so that he may be enabled to defend them at any time in the future, Hobbes says: 'For all men are by nature provided of notable magnifying glasses, (that is their Passions and Selfe-love), through which, every little payment appeareth a great grievance; but are destitute of those prosepective glasses (namely Morall and Civill Science,) to see a farre off the miseries that hang over them, and cannot without such payment be avoyded' (*Lev* 141). This preference of man for a near to a remote good plays an important role in Hume's justification of government, as we shall see later, but nothing is made of the idea in Hobbes's *Leviathan*.

It is for this reason that it is tempting to fall back on the first, static interpretation: that Hobbes is in effect treating only a Prisoners' Dilemma ordinary game, with no dynamic elements at all. Yet on this view Hobbes's theory is not entirely coherent. Most of what he says is certainly consistent with the view that individual preferences are those of a Prisoners' Dilemma; but, as we have seen, Hobbes argues that it is rational for an individual to choose C if the other players do, whereas, of course, it is not rational in a Prisoners' Dilemma game to choose C in any contingency, if that game is played only once. It seems to me, then, that the more dynamic interpretation, in which conditional Cooperation is rational (*always* rational according to Hobbes, though only sometimes rational in the supergame model of Chapter 3) but precarious, is closer to what Hobbes has to say in *Leviathan*, but at the same time it has to be admitted that Hobbes does not give a very full account of any sort of dynamics of interdependent individual choices.

There is a shorter route which might be taken to the conclusion that Hobbes is talking about a Prisoners' Dilemma ordinary game than the one taken at the start of this section, and it does not involve any consideration of the performance of covenants. Hobbes says: 'Feare of oppression, disposeth a man to anticipate, or to seek ayd by society: for there is no other way by which a man can secure his life and liberty' (*Lev* 77); and again, because of the 'diffidence' which every man has, simply by virtue of his knowledge that others, like himself, are seeking to maximize their utility, 'there is no way for any man to secure himselfe, so reasonable, as Anticipation ...' (*Lev* 95). Now Hobbes could be read as asserting here that a man should choose D because he can be fairly sure that the others will choose D, and even if they don't, D is still his best strategy. (And it makes no difference whether the others choose at the same time as he does, or at a later time with or without knowledge of his choice.) However, this is perhaps reading too much into too little. In any case it would still have to be shown that the remainder of the core of Hobbes's argument was consistent with the assumption that the game is a Prisoners' Dilemma played only once.

It is worth noting here that if it were accepted that in the state of nature men find themselves in a Prisoners' Dilemma ordinary game, then it would not make sense to argue that the Sovereign's sanctions are required, not so much to compel everybody to obey, but rather to provide a guarantee that those who would obey voluntarily can do so without exposing themselves. Clearly, if the 'game' in the state of nature is a Prisoners' Dilemma, then it follows that if a player is certain that the other players will choose C (because they fear the Sovereign's punishments), then he would not consider it in his interest to choose C himself—*unless he fears the Sovereign's punishments*. In other words, although his expectation that the Sovereign would punish others for their disobedience may reassure him that he will not be 'double-crossed', this alone does not give him reason to obey. Rather, it gives him a greater incentive to disobey: unless the Sovereign's presence changes *his* (subjective, perceived) utilities as well as his perception of the other players' utilities.

If it is still insisted that Hobbes is analysing a game played only once, but this game is not a Prisoners' Dilemma, then there are, I think, only two plausible alternatives. In both of them, as in the Prisoners' Dilemma game, each player prefers Peace to War and it pays each player to choose D if the other players do, for there is no question about these two items in *Leviathan*. But in the first alternative game, each player prefers to Cooperate rather than Defect as long as all other players Cooperate. In the two-person case, then, the preferences take the following form:

	C	D
C	x, x	z, y
D	y, z	w, w

with $x > y > w > z$; whereas in the two-person Prisoners' Dilemma the utilities satisfied the inequalities $y > x > w > z$. In this new game, there is not a dominating strategy for either player and there are now two equilibria, (C, C) and (D, D). Yet since (C, C) is preferred by both players to (D, D), neither player will expect (D, D) to be the outcome, so it will not be the outcome (cf. the discussion of equilibria and outcomes in Chapter 3). In this game there is no need for coercion to prevent a Pareto-inferior equilibrium occurring; mutual Cooperation will occur without it.

The second alternative game is the one which Hart might have in mind if he is not thinking of a more dynamic model. Some players' preferences amongst the possible outcomes are as in the Prisoners' Dilemma game; those of the others are as in the first alternative game which I have just defined. In its simplest version, the two-person game in which there is one player with each of these types of preferences, the preferences take the following form:

	C	D
C	x, x'	z, y'
D	y, z'	w, w'

with $y > x > w > z$ and $x' > y' > w' > z'$. Player 1 (the row chooser) is the sort of person who would Cooperate only if coerced, that is, only through fear of punishment. Player 2 is the sort of person who would Cooperate as long as the other does too; he would not take advantage of the other player. (D, D) is the only equilibrium in this game, and it will therefore be the outcome. Strategy D is of course dominant for player 1; player 2, seeing this, would also choose D. Thus, it appears that coercion is necessary to achieve (C, C); the Sovereign will protect player 2 against player 1; he will directly coerce player 1 by threatening sanctions, and he will thereby provide player 2, who would *voluntarily* Cooperate if he could only be sure that others would too, with a guarantee that he will not expose himself by choosing C.

I think that the assumptions made in this second alternative to the Prisoners' Dilemma game have some plausibility, but they do not fit very well with most of what Hobbes says in *Leviathan*, since they require that some players have a different sort of preference than the others; whereas there is very little in *Leviathan* which does not ascribe the same 'nature' to all men. Hobbes says, it is true, that some men take 'pleasure in contemplating their own power in the acts of conquests, which they pursue farther than their security requires', while others 'would be glad to be at ease within modest bounds' (*Lev* 95). But even if this and similar remarks could be interpreted as meaning that some men would choose C provided only that others would do likewise, there remains the fact that in those statements in *Leviathan* which I have used to support my contention that individual preferences at any point in time in the state of nature are those of a Prisoners' Dilemma game, Hobbes is not speaking of *some* people. And if *all* men would Cooperate as long as others do, as in the first alternative to the Prisoners' Dilemma, then Hobbes's problem disappears.

In my discussion of Hobbes's political theory I have not so far mentioned his assumption of 'equality'. This assumption is that:

'NATURE hath made men so equall, in the faculties of body, and mind; as that though there bee found one man sometimes manifestly stronger in body, or of quicker mind than another; yet when all is reckoned together, the difference between man, and man, is not so considerable, as that one man can thereupon claim to himselfe any benefit, to which another may not pretend, as well as he. For as to the strength of body, the weakest has strength enough to kill the strongest, either by secret machination, or by confederacy with others, that are in the same danger with himselfe' (*Lev* 94).

If the assumption is made that the outcomes of the game and the individuals' preferences amongst them are such that the game at any point in time is a Prisoners' Dilemma, then the assumption of equality is superfluous. For it is, in effect, an assertion of strategic interdependence: that no man alone controls the outcome of the game. No man is safe in the state of nature; he must fear every other man. The outcome of the game and therefore his own payoff depend on the actions of all other men as well as his own. This is the case in a Prisoners' Dilemma game.

Hobbes is not, of course, asserting that the payoffs for each outcome are the same for all players; this can never be the case in a Prisoners' Dilemma. Nor is he asserting (as I assumed in Chapters 3 and 4 to simplify my analysis) that the payoff matrix is necessarily symmetric. It is of course possible in a Prisoners' Dilemma that the players have very unequal payoffs for those outcomes in which they all choose C or all choose D. Hobbes himself clearly did not expect all men to be equally successful in obtaining what they wanted either in the state of nature, which is a state of War, or when at Peace under a Sovereign.[6]

It remains for me to show that nothing essential in Hobbes's argument is altered if the number of strategies available to each player is greater than two. Hobbes himself seems to assume only two strategies; he speaks only of 'laying aside one's natural right to all things' or not doing so. But of course there are *degrees* to which one may lay aside this right, or degrees of cooperation. Thus, to use an example of the kind discussed in Chapter 1, if unrestricted pollution of a lake is strategy D, there are presumably numerous alternatives to D, corresponding to the possible levels of individual pollution less than D. As before, in the state of nature, every player chooses D; the resulting outcome is $(D, D, ..., D)$ which is Pareto-inferior. The Hobbesian problem remains the same: to get the players from this 'miserable condition' to an outcome preferred by every player. If there is only one such outcome this is presumably the only outcome which the players would covenant to have enforced. Hobbes's analysis of covenanting applies unchanged to this covenant. Usually, however, there will be a set (S, say) of outcomes preferred by every player to $(D, D, ..., D)$. The players would presumably only consider covenanting to enforce one of those which are Pareto-optimal with respect to the set S. A covenant to enforce any one of these would be necessary and Hobbes's argument applies to each of the possible covenants. The only new element introduced here is the problem of agreeing on one of the Pareto-optimal outcomes: of agreeing, for example, on a particular level of permissible individual pollution. Hobbes does not of course consider this; but his own analysis, as far as it goes, applies with full force to this multi-strategy case: men will not voluntarily act so as to obtain any one of the Pareto-superior outcomes; they will not keep covenants to refrain from choosing D and use some other strategy; they must erect a 'common power' with sufficient power to enforce one of the Pareto-superior outcomes.

C. A Game of Difference

I argued in part A that the *utility* which a Hobbesian man seeks to maximize is a convex combination of his own payoff and his eminence. *Eminence* was defined there as the average of his eminence with respect to each other individual, and his eminence with respect to another individual was defined as the excess of his payoff over that of the other individual's.

In part B I argued that in Hobbes's state of nature the individual preferences are such that at any point in time the players are in a Prisoners' Dilemma. The argument was entirely in terms of *ordinal* preferences; that is to say, it was independent of any considerations of the relative degree to which one outcome is preferred to another. In particular, it did not rest on the assumption that the *utility* of an outcome to a player takes the form assumed in part A (and is thus a cardinal utility).

If the game defined in terms of the basic *payoffs* (the 'basic game') is a Prisoners' Dilemma (ordinary game), then we know from Section 4.3 that the game defined in terms of the derived utilities (the 'transformed game') is also a Prisoners' Dilemma, if two conditions are met: (i) λ_i is non-zero; that is, the game is not one of *Pure* Difference; and (ii) the payoff $g(v)$ to a player who chooses D is strictly increasing with the number of other individuals (v) who choose C.

However, if the transformed game is a Prisoners' Dilemma, it does not follow that the basic game is a Prisoners' Dilemma. A simple two-person example shows this: if the payoff matrix is

$$\begin{bmatrix} 2, 2 & -2, 1 \\ 1, -2 & 1, 1 \end{bmatrix}$$

which is not a Prisoners' Dilemma, then the utility matrix for the Game of Difference (with $\lambda_i = \frac{1}{2}$ for $i = 1, 2$) is

$$\begin{bmatrix} 1, 1 & -2\frac{1}{2}, 2 \\ 2, -2\frac{1}{2} & \frac{1}{2}, \frac{1}{2} \end{bmatrix}$$

which *is* a Prisoners' Dilemma.

This reveals the possibility that the Hobbesian problem is the result of man's desire for eminence. (The above example illustrates this: there are two equilibria in the basic game, but neither player would expect (1, 1) to be the outcome, since both players prefer (2, 2) to it. Thus the outcome is (2, 2) which is Pareto-optimal, and there is no Hobbesian problem.) It would be of some interest to discover which sorts of games, not themselves Prisoners' Dilemmas, become Prisoners' Dilemmas when transformed to Games of Difference.

I shall not pursue this question, for I believe that in the problems of interest here (those of the kind discussed in Chapter 1) the basic ordinary game is itself a Prisoners' Dilemma. If this is the case, then the transformed game is also a Prisoners' Dilemma, and this is true no matter how much 'eminence' relative to 'egoism' we assume (or read into Hobbes), just as long as eminence is not a man's *only* concern (that is, as long as λ_i is non-zero) and $g(v)$ is increasing with v.

D. The theory restated

I can now recapitulate most of the discussion so far by restating briefly Hobbes's central argument in *Leviathan*.

Only three assumptions are necessary. First, that in the state of nature, men find themselves in a Prisoners' Dilemma; that is, the choices confronting them and their preferences amongst the possible outcomes are such that the game which they are playing is *at each point in time* a Prisoners' Dilemma. The Prisoners' Dilemma is defined in the usual way; in particular, it is a non-cooperative game, so that there is nothing to keep men to any agreements they might make.

There are two versions of the second assumption, corresponding to the two interpretations of Hobbes's argument put forward in part B above in connection with what Hobbes has to say about the rationality of Cooperating when others do. The first version is that the Prisoners' Dilemma game mentioned in the first assumption is not iterated; the whole theory is restricted to the Prisoners' Dilemma ordinary game. The second version is that the Prisoners' Dilemma is iterated; we need not (and on the basis of what Hobbes actually says, we cannot) go further than this and say, for example, that the Prisoners' Dilemma game mentioned in the first assumption is a constituent game of a supergame with future benefits discounted.

The third assumption is that each individual seeks to obtain an outcome which is as high as possible in his preference ranking of outcomes. Equivalently, we may say that each individual seeks to maximize his utility. In particular, if (as in the Prisoners' Dilemma) he has a single dominant strategy, he uses it.

In this third assumption, it does not matter what is the basis of a man's preferences or how 'utility' is defined (as long as the resulting game is a Prisoners' Dilemma). However, I have argued that Hobbes assumes that a man's utility is some convex combination of his own payoff and his eminence.

If the first (static) version of the second assumption is accepted, then it follows from the three assumptions that the outcome of the game is $(D, D, ..., D)$; that is, the condition of men in the state of nature is War. This outcome is Pareto-inferior. There is one (and only one) outcome which every player prefers to it, namely $(C, C, ..., C)$, which is the state of Peace. But if the players agreed that each of them should choose C, there would be no incentive in the state of nature for any of them to carry out his part of the agreement. Clearly, if Peace is to be achieved, every man must be *coerced*, by which I mean simply that he must be made somehow to behave differently than he otherwise would (that is to say, than he would 'voluntarily' in the state of nature).

If the second (dynamic) version of the second assumption is accepted, then what follows from the three assumptions depends on the precise form of the dynamic model specified. Hobbes is not sufficiently specific here, but it is reasonable to conclude (on the basis of the analysis in Chapter 3) that *conditional* Cooperation is *sometimes* rational (even though not all the other players Cooperate) but rather precarious, since the Cooperation of each of the conditional Cooperators must be contingent upon the Cooperation of all the other Cooperators and the discount rates of every one of the Cooperators must not be too high. It can be argued that it is this precariousness which in Hobbes's view makes coercion necessary if Peace is to be achieved, though the necessity of coercion is clearly less apparent here than in the case when the Prisoners' Dilemma is assumed not to be iterated.

But Hobbes goes further than this of course. For he specifies in some detail the particular form that the coercion must take and how it is to be created. Each man must make a covenant with every other man in which he promises, on the condition that the other party to the covenant does likewise, to relinquish the right to all things which he has in the state of nature in order that a 'Sovereign' may enjoy without restraint his natural right to all things and thereby be enabled to ensure 'Peace at home, and mutual ayd against enemies abroad' (*Lev* Chapter 17). The Sovereign must be either one man or an assembly of men, though the former is preferable (*Lev* 143–7).

Hobbes gives two accounts of how a particular man or assembly of men is to be made Sovereign. In the first, the Sovereign is specified in the covenants of each man with every other man and is thus unanimously agreed on (*Lev* 132). In the second, there is in effect a unanimous agreement, in the form of the covenants between every pair of men, to abide by a majority choice of a parti-cular Sovereign (*Lev* 133). My argument is unaffected by this discrepancy; either version may be chosen.

This, in bare outline (for I have omitted, in particular, any reference to 'authorization') is the 'Generation of that great LEVIATHAN' (*Lev* 132). But this Leviathan (whose powers will be described in the next part) is not the only possible form which the necessary coercion can assume. One alternative, which does in fact seem to be sufficient to maintain Peace (in Hobbes's sense) in many so-called primitive societies, is a system of internalized restraints on the indi-vidual backed by the pressure of public opinion, sometimes ritualized in conventional methods of public ridiculing and shaming. Hobbes did not dis-count such possibilities; he believed that by themselves they would be in-adequate. However, if the core of Hobbes's theory is based, as I have argued, on the assumptions that men in the state of nature are players in a Prisoners' Dilemma game and that men are utility maximizers, then, whether the game is iterated or not, Hobbes cannot legitimately deduce the necessity of any *particular* form of coercion, but can only deduce the necessity of *any* form of coercion which has the ability, and is seen to have the ability, to deter men from breaking their covenants.

E. The Sovereign's Powers

Whether Sovereignty has been instituted, in the manner I have just described, or has been acquired by force, the most important of the Sovereign's rights and powers are as follows. His subjects cannot change the form of government or transfer their allegiance to another man or assembly, without the Sovereign's permission; disagreement with the majority's choice of a particular Sovereign does not exempt a man from his obligation to obey the Sovereign; the Sovereign's subjects can neither 'justly' complain of his actions nor 'justly' punish him (this is a trivial consequence of Hobbes's definitions of justice and authority);

the Sovereign has the right to do whatever he thinks is necessary to maintain Peace at home and defence against foreign enemies; he has the right to judge which opinions and doctrines are to be permitted in public speeches and publications, as being not detrimental to Peace; he has the 'whole Power of prescribing the Rules, whereby a man may know, what Goods he may enjoy, and what actions he may do, without being molested by any of his fellow subjects'; he has the 'Right of Judicature', that is to say, 'of deciding all controversies'; he has the right of making war and peace with other nations and commonwealths, when he thinks it is 'for the public good', of maintaining an army and taxing his subjects to pay for it, and (of course) of being in command of it; he has the right to choose 'all Counsellours, and Ministers, both of Peace and War'; he has the right to reward and punish his subjects according to the laws he has already made, or, in the absence of a law, as he thinks will most conduce 'to the encouraging of men to serve the Commonwealth, or deterring them from doing dis-service to the same' (*Lev* Chapter 18); and finally, the Sovereign has the right to choose his successor (*Lev* 149). These rights, says Hobbes, are indivisible, for control of the judicature is of no use without control of a militia to execute the laws, and control of the militia is of no avail without the right to legislate taxes to support it, and so on (*Lev* 139).

This makes the Sovereign very powerful. Hobbes himself sometimes describes the Sovereign's power as being 'absolute' and 'unlimited' and 'as great, as possibly men can be imagined to make it' (*Lev* 160). Nevertheless, it has to be emphasized that Hobbes consistently makes it clear that the Great Leviathan exists *only* to maintain Peace amongst his subjects and to defend them against foreign enemies and that his powers are only those which are required to perform this role. Thus, in their covenants with each other to institute a Sovereign, men authorize the Sovereign to 'Act, or cause to be Acted, in those things which concern the Common Peace and Safetie' (*Lev* 131), and by this authority 'he hath the use of so much Power and Strength conferred on him, that by terror thereof, he is inabled to forme the wills of them all, to Peace at home, and mutuall ayd against their enemies abroad' (*Lev* 132). Again, 'the OFFICE of the Soveraign ... consisteth in the end, for which he was trusted with the Soveraign Power, namely the procuration of *the safety of the people*' (*Lev* 258). To this end, he must make 'good laws', a good law being one 'which is *Needful, for the Good of the People* ...'; and Hobbes adds that 'Unnecessary Lawes are not good Lawes; but trapps for Mony ...' (*Lev* 268). In the few places where he speaks of the Sovereign's 'absolute power', he seems to be equating it only with that power which is 'necessarily required' for 'the Peace, and defence of the Commonwealth' (*Lev* 247). Above all, he asserts that obedience to the Sovereign is obligatory only as long as he is doing what he was established for, namely, maintaining Peace and defence (*Lev* 170).

I have argued in the preceding section that Hobbes may not legitimately deduce from his own assumptions the conclusion that the coercion which is necessary to get men out of the condition of War must take the particular form which he specifies. However, if the coercion must be in the form of a Sovereign

which is either one man or an assembly of men, then Hobbes *is* quite correct
to give the Sovereign just those powers which are required by him to maintain
Peace. I have argued in this part that this is what Hobbes does.

F. Possessive Market Society

C. B. Macpherson, in his widely read book, *The Political Theory of Possessive
Individualism,* has put forward a reconstruction of Hobbes's political theory
which seriously restricts the scope of its application.[7] He argues that the theory
can be made coherent only if Hobbes is assumed to be speaking of a society
which resembles our modern, bourgeois, market societies. I believe that
Hobbes's theory has a much greater range of application than this. More
specifically, I have argued that the situations analysed by Hobbes are Prisoners'
Dilemmas (possibly iterated). These are neither identical with, nor are they
only to be found in market societies. In this section, then, I must show how
Macpherson's argument fails.

There are two steps in the argument: (i) Macpherson claims that after
defining a man's 'power' as his means to obtain what he desires, Hobbes
proceeds to *redefine* power and that a 'new postulate is implied in this redefinition of power, namely that the capacity of every man to get what he wants is
opposed by the capacity of every other man' (Macpherson, p. 36); (ii) 'the
postulate that the power of every man is opposed to the power of every other
man requires the assumption of a model of society which permits and requires
the continual invasion of every man by every other' (Macpherson, p. 42), and
that the only such model of society is the 'possessive market society, which
corresponds in essentials to modern market society' (Macpherson, p. 68).

Each of these assertions is incorrect. Consider (i): first, Macpherson believes
that Hobbes speaks for the first time of the relations between men, of man in
society, only when he comes to discuss power. Yet Hobbes has said earlier that
all men desire eminence. Now clearly, desire for eminence brings men into
opposition with one another, for they cannot all be eminent over others simultaneously. (And the greater the ratio of 'eminence' to 'own payoff' in each man's
utility function, the more nearly the game approximates to a zero-sum game,
or one of 'pure opposition'.) Second, given that every man seeks to obtain what
he desires and given Hobbes's definition of power as the means to obtain what
one desires, it follows (as we have seen) that every man desires power; given
further that man desires to be eminent, it follows that he desires to have more
power than others. No 'redefinition' of power, from 'absolute' to 'comparative'
power, is involved here.

Macpherson seems to be aware that, if these two points are granted, this
first step in his argument is unnecessary (Macpherson, p. 45), and we can pass
immediately to the second and more important step.

If, as I have argued earlier, Hobbes's propositions about power seeking can
be derived from his definition of power and his proposition that men seek to
obtain the things they desire, so that 'power' plays no logically essential role

in Hobbes's political theory, then Macpherson's assertion in the second part of his argument is clearly incorrect. But let us see how he defends it.

Possessive market society is an ideal type to which modern capitalist societies approximate. Its distinctive feature, as far as Macpherson's argument is concerned, is that every individual owns his capacity to labour and may sell it or otherwise transfer it as he wishes. The consequence of this (and other assumptions) is that there is a market in labour as well as in other commodities. It is this labour market which provides the means by which 'the continual invasion of every man by every other' is carried on. Labour markets may of course have this property, but Macpherson is asserting that *only* societies with (amongst other things) labour markets can provide such means. This is plainly false, for there are many societies (and many more that have perished or have been transformed) in which there is no market in labour (and in some cases there are no markets in anything) and yet there is 'continual invasion of every man by every other'. This 'invasion' may take several forms. The primary objects of a man's desire may be the possession of physical strength, skill in hunting, cattle and wives and good crops (if there is individual ownership of these things), peace of mind, ceremonial rank, and so on; his means to obtain these things, his 'power', may include all of these things and others besides; and he may suffer continual invasion and transfers of his power, simply because people steal his women, cattle and foodstocks, hunt more skilfully, spread rumours that he is a sorcerer, or whatever. None of this requires a market in labour (or in anything else for that matter).

Macpherson's only defence against this would be to *define* power as 'access to the means of labour' or 'control of labour'. This would make the second part of his argument about possessive market society trivial. At one point (p. 49) he seems to do just this, but then later (p. 56) he says only that power must 'by definition include access to the means of labour', which leaves room for power also to depend upon cattle and ceremonial rank and all the rest.

I have argued that *Leviathan* is about Prisoners' Dilemmas, and this means that Hobbes's argument, in the form in which I restated it, is not confined to situations of the sort that Hobbes himself was obviously most concerned about. If I am right, and if Prisoners' Dilemmas are to be found outside possessive market societies, then Macpherson's argument collapses. I believe that the problem Hobbes treats *is* to be found in one form or another in most, if not all societies, including so-called primitive societies with no markets in labour. In 'primitive' and other societies, stealing one another's cattle, stealing corn from the communally owned fields, or disturbing the tribe's tranquillity by excessive display, are simple examples of behaviour which may lead to the problem Hobbes was concerned with.

Although Macpherson's thesis is unacceptable, there is an interesting proposition about possessive market society and the argument in *Leviathan*, which I think has some plausibility. Very roughly, it is that the more a society approximates to the possessive market type, the more numerous are the sites and occasions for Prisoners' Dilemmas and the greater is the severity of the Prisoners' Dilemmas, where by 'greater severity' I mean a greater 'temptation' unilaterally to Defect from mutual Cooperation (see Section 4.2). I could not, of course, begin to prove this.

I should add finally that while I disagree with Macpherson's view that Hobbes's political theory is coherent only if society is assumed to be of the possessive market variety, I nevertheless agree with him that Hobbes seems to have been conscious of the possessive market nature of the society in which he lived and that in *Leviathan* he sometimes speaks of characteristic features of possessive market societies.

6.2. HUME'S LEVIATHAN

Hume's explanation of the necessity and desirability of government is not very different from Hobbes's. But he begins with assumptions about human nature which seem much less gloomy than those of Hobbes; his explanation of the origin of government appears to be more plausible than Hobbes's contractarian account; and in place of the great Leviathan that Hobbes sometimes made to sound so terrifying he describes a government resembling the sort of governments that 'large and civilis'd societies' in fact possess. Nevertheless, his assumptions about human nature (which I shall discuss in part A) are *effectively* the same as those of Hobbes; his account of the origin of government (part D below) rests on an analysis of the evolution of property 'conventions' (part B below) which is itself not entirely plausible (for reasons which I discuss in part C); and as for the government which Hume concludes to be necessary, its function is similar to that of Hobbes's Leviathan and it must therefore be given as much power. (Hence the title of this section.)

For all its essential similarity to Hobbes's theory, Hume's political theory warrants a brief discussion here. First, because there are in fact two new elements in Hume's account, which, though they have not been given much attention by students of Hume, are important in the analysis of voluntary cooperation and played an important role in my discussion in Chapter 3. Second, because it is Hume's version of the theory rather than the stark account of Hobbes which was more acceptable to later writers and to which many modern justifications of government still largely correspond.

A. Individual Preferences

I begin with a discussion of those elements of 'the passions' which are incorporated in the assumptions on which Hume's political theory is based.

(i) While Hobbes does not deny (in *Leviathan* at least) the existence in some men of a positive altruism which is not reducible to egoism, he has very little to say about it, and the effective assumption in his political theory is that men's preferences reflect a combination of egoism and the negative altruism which is involved in a desire for eminence. For Hume, positive altruism, or 'benevolence', is more important. He distinguishes two kinds of benevolence, 'private' and 'extensive'. Private benevolence is a desire for the happiness of those we love, our family and friends. It is not the same thing as love, but rather is a result of it; love is always 'follow'd by, or rather conjoin'd with benevolence ...' (*Tr* 367).[8] This private benevolence is an 'original instinct implanted in our nature', like love of life, resentment, kindness to children, hunger and 'lust' (*Tr* 368, 417, 439).

Extensive benevolence or 'pity' is 'a concern for ... others, without any friendship ... to occasion this concern or joy. We pity even strangers, and such as are perfectly indifferent to us' (*Tr* 369). This kind of benevolence is not instinctive; it is due to *sympathy*. Hume defines 'sympathy' with others as our propensity 'to receive by communication their inclinations and sentiments, however different or even contrary to our own' (*Tr* 316); it is 'the conversion of an idea into an impression by the force of imagination' (*Tr* 427). This is not to say that sympathy is a form of altruism. Nor is it to say, for example, that we suffer for ourselves when we contemplate others suffering: we do not fear for our own lives when we see, and sympathize with, others in danger of death and fearing for their lives. Sympathy is simply the name for what makes it possible for us to experience, to have an impression of, the feelings of others.

Sympathy, then, makes extensive benevolence possible. 'Tis true, there is no human, and indeed no sensible, creature, whose happiness or misery does not, in some measure, affect us, when brought near to us, and represented in lively colours: ... this proceeds merely from sympathy ...' (*Tr* 481). Again: 'We have no such extensive concern for society but from sympathy' (*Tr* 579).

The important role played by sympathy in the *Treatise* is somewhat reduced in the *Enquiry*. In particular, extensive benevolence, which was due only to sympathy in the *Treatise*, now seems to be included with private benevolence as one of the instincts. This view is given in the Appendix on 'Self-Love' together with the argument (taken from Bishop Butler's *Fifteen Sermons*, especially the first) that self-love is not our only motivation—that there are 'instincts' (such as benevolence) which motivate us directly and are not reducible to a species of self-love. It is worth quoting Hume's argument at length:

'There are bodily wants or appetites acknowledged by every one, which necessarily precede all sensual enjoyment, and carry us directly to seek possession of the object. Thus, hunger and thirst have eating and drinking for their end; and from the gratification of these primary appetites arises a pleasure, which may become the object of another species of desire or inclination that is secondary and interested. In the same manner there are mental passions by which we are impelled immediately to seek particular objects, such as fame or power, or vengeance without any regard to interest; and when these objects are attained a pleasing enjoyment ensues, as the consequence of our indulged affections. Nature must, by the internal frame and constitution of the mind, give an original propensity to fame, ere we can reap any pleasure from that acquisition, or pursue it from motives of self-love, and desire of happiness. ... Were there no appetite of any kind antecedent to self-love, that propensity could scarcely ever exert itself; because we should, in that case, have felt few and slender pains or pleasures, and have little misery or happiness to avoid or to pursue.

Now where is the difficulty in conceiving, that this may likewise be the case with benevolence and friendship, and that, from the original frame of our temper, we may feel a desire of another's happiness or good, which, by means of that affection, becomes our own good, and is afterwards pursued, from the combined motives of benevolence and self-enjoyments?' (*Enquiry*, pp. 301–2).

(ii) The operation of sympathy and the extent of benevolence are limited by our manner of comparing ourselves with others. 'We seldom judge of objects from their intrinsic value', says Hume, 'but form our notions of them from a comparison with other objects; it follows that, according as we observe a greater or less share of happiness or misery in others, we must make an estimate of our own, and feel a consequent pain or pleasure' (*Tr* 375). 'This kind of comparison is directly contrary to sympathy in its operation ...' (*Tr* 593), and accounts for the origin of malice and envy (*Tr* 377). It is itself limited, inasmuch as men tend to compare themselves with, and are envious of, only those who are similar to them in relevant respects (*Tr* 377–8).

Negative altruism is real enough for Hume; but in his political theory it does not assume the importance that it does in Hobbes's theory (as part of the desire for eminence). Hume shrinks from making any general statement, in the form of a simplifying assumption, about the predominance of positive or negative altruism. He allows that in some situations positive altruism may dominate negative altruism, and *vice versa* in other situations. But in the statement of his political theory, the effective assumptions about individual preferences contain no reference to negative altruism; as we shall see shortly, they refer only to egoism, limited positive altruism and 'shortsightedness'.

(iii) Although Hume argues for the existence of an independent motive of private benevolence and that extensive benevolence or pity is found in all men, since they are all capable of sympathy (*Tr* 317, 481), nevertheless it is clear that, when he comes to explaining the origins of justice, property and government, he assumes that benevolence is very limited. In one place, he suggests that each individual loves himself more than any other single person, but the aggregate of his benevolent concerns for all others exceeds his self-love (*Tr* 487). But more generally, he says that some men are concerned only for themselves, and that, as for the others, their benevolence extends only or chiefly to their family and friends, with only a very weak concern for strangers and indifferent persons (*Tr* 481, 489, 534).

Hume is not very precise about the relative weights of benevolence and self-interest. All we can say is that, in his political theory, his assumption is effectively that men are self-interested and benevolent, but that the benevolence is not so great that there is no need for 'conventions' about property (*Tr* 486, 492, 494–5). These will be explained below.

(iv) There is another element in the structure of individual preferences, to which Hume (in the *Treatise*) attaches great importance: we *discount* future benefits, their present value to us diminishing as the future time at which we expect to receive them recedes farther from the present. What is close to us in time or space, says Hume, affects our imagination with greater force than what is remote, the effect of time being greater than that of space (*Tr* 427–9). The consequence of this is that men 'are always much inclin'd to prefer present interest to distant and remote; nor is it easy for them to resist the temptation of any advantage, that they may immediately enjoy, in apprehension of an evil, that lies at a distance from them' (*Tr* 539, 535).

B. Property

Hume distinguishes 'three different species of goods' which we may possess: mental satisfactions, our natural bodily endowments, and 'such possessions as we have acquir'd by our industry and good fortune'. Only the third species, *external possessions*, may be transferred unaltered to others and used by them (*Tr* 487–8).

These external possessions are the source of 'the principal disturbance in society' and this is because (i) they are scarce and easily transferred between people (*Tr* 488–9); (ii) everyone wants them: 'This avidity alone, of acquiring goods and possessions for ourselves and our nearest friends, is insatiable, perpetual, universal, and directly destructive of society. There scarce is any one, who is not actuated by it; and there is no one, who has not reason to fear from it, when it acts without any restraint ...' (*Tr* 491–2); and (iii) man's selfishness in the pursuit of them is insufficiently counteracted by his benevolence towards others to make him abstain from their possessions (*Tr* 492, 486–8).

The resulting situation is essentially the same as Hobbes's 'state of nature', though Hume has described it in less dramatic terms. The only remedy for it is a 'convention enter'd into by all the members of the society to bestow stability on the possession of those external goods, and leave every one in the peaceable enjoyment of what he may acquire by his fortune and industry' (*Tr* 489). However, a permanent 'stability' of possession would itself be 'a grand inconvenience', for 'mutual exchange and commerce' is necessary and desirable. Therefore there must also be a 'convention' facilitating the transfer of possessions by consent (*Tr* 514). This in turn would be of little use without a 'convention' to keep one's promises, since it is usually impracticable for the parties to an exchange to transfer possessions simultaneously (*Tr* 516–22).

There are thus three 'conventions' which men must make to obtain 'peace and security': 'that of the stability of possession, of its transference by consent, and of the performance of promises'. These are the 'laws of justice' or 'the three fundamental laws of nature' (*Tr* 526). 'Property' can now be defined as 'nothing but those goods, whose constant possession is establish'd ... by the laws of justice' (*Tr* 491); and we can say that 'justice' consists in the observation of the current laws fixing the distribution of property and protecting the parties to exchanges of property.

C. Conventions

A convention, says Hume, is not like a promise; for promises themselves arise from human conventions (*Tr* 490). Conventions, he means to tell us, are not like the covenants which, according to Hobbes, are the only means of escape from the state of nature. A convention is rather

'a general sense of common interest; which sense all the members of the society express to one another, and which induces them to regulate their conduct by certain rules. I observe, that it will be for my interest to leave another in the possession of his goods, *provided* he will act in the same manner with regard to me. He is sensible of a like interest in the regulation of his conduct. When this common sense of interest is mutually express'd, and is known to both, it produces a suitable resolution and behaviour. And this may properly enough be call'd a convention or agreement betwixt us, tho' without the interposition of a promise; since the actions of each of us have a reference to those of the other, and are perform'd upon the supposition, that something is to be perform'd on the other part' (*Tr* 490).

Now this is a perfectly reasonable definition of convention; it is roughly what we still typically mean by convention. But then, it seems to me, the laws of justice are not conventions. If they were, there would be no need for a government to constrain people to conform to them, as Hume goes on to argue.

Since this point is rather important, it is worth giving here a more precise definition of convention. We can use the one constructed by David Lewis in his *Convention: A Philosophical Study*.

Conventions are solutions to *coordination problems*. The most clear-cut case of a coordination problem (to which we may confine our attention) is the situation facing the players in a *game of pure coordination*. This is a game, having two or more proper coordination equilibria, and in which the players' interests coincide, so that their payoffs at each outcome are equal. A *coordination equilibrium* is a strategy vector such that no player can obtain a larger payoff if he *or any other player* unilaterally uses a different strategy (so that a coordination equilibrium is an equilibrium, as defined in Chapter 3, but not conversely); and a coordination equilibrium is *proper* if each player *strictly* prefers it to any other outcome he could obtain, given the other strategy choices. Thus the two-person game with the payoffs shown in Matrix 1 below is a pure coordination game; strategy vectors (r_1, c_1) and (r_2, c_2) are proper coordination equilibria, while (r_3, c_3) is improper.

	c_1	c_2	c_3	
r_1	2, 2	0, 0	0, 0	
r_2	0, 0	2, 2	0, 0	(Matrix 1)
r_3	0, 0	1, 1	1, 1	

A simple example of a coordination problem is the situation facing two people who are not in communication and who wish to meet but are indifferent between several alternative meeting places. Suppose there are just three possible meeting places. Then the payoff matrix is that shown as Matrix 2 (the payoffs there being merely ordinal).

$$
\begin{bmatrix}
1,1 & 0,0 & 0,0 \\
0,0 & 1,1 & 0,0 \\
0,0 & 0,0 & 1,1
\end{bmatrix}
\qquad \text{(Matrix 2)}
$$

Another simple example is that of several drivers on the same road; nobody cares which side of the road he drives on, as long as everybody else drives on the same side as he does. This is an example of an iterated or *recurrent* co-ordination problem.

The definition of a coordination problem requires that there be at least two coordination equilibria. If there is only one, the problem is trivial, for the players will have no difficulty in coordinating their choices.

We are now in a position to define convention.

'A regularity R in the behaviour of members of a population P when they are agents in a recurrent situation S is a *convention* if and only if, in any instance of S among members of P,
(1) everyone conforms to R;
(2) everyone expects everyone else to conform to R;
(3) everyone prefers to conform to R on condition that the others do, since S is a coordination problem and uniform conformity to R is a coordination equilibrium in S'.[9]

Players in a coordination game will achieve coordination if they have what Lewis calls 'suitably concordant mutual expectations'. If a player is sufficiently confident that the others will do their parts of a particular coordination equilibrium, then he will do his part. Where communication is possible, *agreement* is the simplest means of producing concordant mutual expectations and hence coordination, but a convention need not be started by an agreement. In a recurrent coordination problem, concordant mutual expectations may be built up gradually, as more and more people conform to a regularity, until a convention is established. Thus, without an explicit agreement and without any coercion, a convention to drive on a particular side of the road could be expected to grow up: each man prefers to drive on the side of the road on which most others are driving; at some stage of the process, more or less by chance, a majority will be driving on the left, say; this produces or strengthens an expectation in each driver that a majority will in the future drive on the left; and in this way, a convention to drive on the left is very quickly established.

Lewis's definition of convention is (as he himself recognizes) essentially the same as the one given by Hume. Hume, too, recognizes that conventions will emerge 'spontaneously', without agreements or governments. Speaking of the conventions on property, he says that when a 'common sense of interest is mutually express'd, and is known to both, it produces a suitable resolution and behaviour'; and: 'Nor is the rule concerning the stability of possession the less deriv'd from human conventions' that it arises gradually, and acquires force by a slow progression, and by our repeated experiences of the inconveniences of transgressing it. On the contrary, this experience assures us still more, that the sense of interest has become common to all our fellows, and gives us a confidence of the future regularity of their conduct: And 'tis only on the expectation of this, that our moderation and abstinence are founded' (*Tr* 490).

Conventions not only emerge but also *persist* spontaneously; for a convention is an equilibrium, from which no individual has an incentive unilaterally to deviate. It follows that everyone will conform to a convention without being coerced by a government or by any other agency.[10] Yet Hume goes on to argue that men will not voluntarily observe the conventions they make about property and government is necessary to constrain them to conform. The reason he gives for this, as I shall argue in the next part, is essentially that men find themselves, not in a recurrent coordination game, but in a recurrent or iterated Prisoners' Dilemma game (with future payoffs discounted). If this is the case, then the laws of justice cannot be conventions. And for precisely the same reason that men will not voluntarily observe their property conventions, these conventions would not emerge spontaneously in the first place.

It would be proper to call the laws of justice 'conventions' only if all men preferred *any* system of such laws (and therefore any distribution of possessions) to no laws at all and were indifferent (or nearly so) between all possible systems. The first condition is accepted by Hume, for, like Hobbes, he believes that 'without justice, society must immediately dissolve and fall into that savage and solitary condition, which is infinitely worse than can possibly be suppos'd in society', so that, upon the introduction of the laws of justice 'every individual person must find himself a gainer ...' (*Tr* 497). As for the second condition, it is true that in the *Enquiry* Hume remarks that 'What possessions are assigned to particular persons; this is, generally speaking, pretty indifferent ...' (*Enquiry*, p. 309 note). But this remark is quite contrary to the assumption, which is essential to his whole theory, that men have an 'insatiable, perpetual, universal' avidity for acquiring external possessions. Men are certainly not indifferent between different distributions of property and therefore are not indifferent between different laws of justice, which determine the distributions.

D. The Necessity of Government

According to Hume, government is necessary *in large societies* because without it men will not observe the laws of justice; and it is on the observance of these laws alone that 'the peace and security of human society entirely depend' (*Tr* 526; see also 491). His argument that men will not keep the laws of justice in large societies has two threads. The first is essentially the argument given by Olson in *The Logic of Collective Action*, which we considered in Chapter 1. The second concerns the discounting of future benefits, which played such an important role in Chapter 3. Hume does not maintain a clear distinction between these two elements. Nevertheless, the spirit of this part of his theory is that men will not voluntarily cooperate (abstain from each other's possessions; observe the laws of justice) because they are players in a Prisoners' Dilemma supergame and their discount rates are too great.

The 'size' argument appears clearly in the following passage.

'Two neighbours may agree to drain a meadow, which they possess in common; because 'tis easy for them to know each others mind; and each must perceive, that the immediate consequence of his failing in his part, is the abandoning the whole project. But 'tis very difficult, and indeed impossible, that a thousand persons shou'd agree in any such action; it being difficult for them to concert so complicated a design, and still more difficult for them to execute it; while each seeks a pretext to free himself of the trouble and expence, and wou'd lay the whole burden on others' (Tr 538).

Hume gives here both of the reasons why, according to Olson, large groups do not provide themselves with public goods, such as a drained meadow shared by the group: first, each individual member has no incentive to make his contribution because it is a *public* good which is being provided and he therefore benefits from it, if it is provided at all, whether he contributes or not; second, and less important, the larger the group the greater are the costs of organization.

Hume makes it quite clear that this part of his argument applies only to *large* societies, and several times proclaims his belief that the members of small societies may voluntarily conform to the property 'conventions' and may therefore live without government (Tr 499, 539–41, 543, 546, 553–4). But this is partly because small societies tend to be 'uncultivated', that is, they do not have very many possessions to quarrel about.

In the meadow-drainage example which I have quoted from the *Treatise*, Hume deals only with the 'static' part of his argument. But elsewhere, whenever he presents the 'logic of collective action', it is bound up with the proposition (which I discussed earlier) that men discount future benefits. Men '... prefer any trivial advantage, that is present, to the maintenance of order in society, which so much depends on the observance of justice. The consequences of every breach of equity seem to lie very remote, and are not able to counter-balance any immediate advantage, that may be reap'd from it' (Tr 535; see also 499, 537–9, 545).

In the continuation of this passage, Hume in effect speaks of behaviour in a sequence of Prisoners' Dilemmas: when you commit acts of injustice as well as me, 'Your example both pushes me forward in this way by imitation, and also affords me a new reason for any breach of equity, by shewing me, that I should be the cully of my integrity, if I alone should impose on myself a severe restraint amidst the licentiousness of others' (Tr 535).

The only remedy for this situation is to establish government. The only way men can obtain security and peace is to induce a few men, 'whom we call civil magistrates, kings and their ministers', to constrain every member of the society to observe the laws of justice (*Tr* 537).

Thus, Hume's case for government rests on the alleged inability of men to cooperate voluntarily in the provision of peace and security. However, he goes on to add that 'government extends farther its beneficial influence' by forcing men to cooperate in the provision of other public goods. Thus, he says, 'bridges are built; harbours open'd; ramparts rais'd; canals form'd; fleets equipp'd; and armies disciplin'd; every where, by the care of government ...' (*Tr* 538–9).

E. Hume and Hobbes

The assumptions about the structure of static individual preferences on which Hume bases his political theory are not quite the same as those made by Hobbes. To use the language of Chapter 4, Hobbes assumes that each man's preferences are a combination of egoism and negative altruism, reflecting a desire to maximize his own payoff and his eminence, whereas Hume assumes that they are a combination of egoism and positive altruism, with egoism predominant. However, the effect is the same in both cases: the resulting game at any point in time is a Prisoners' Dilemma. If in both cases the payoffs are such that the game is a Prisoners' Dilemma when only pure egoism is assumed on the part of each player, then we can say that the 'transformed game' (the game which results when altruism is introduced) is a more severe Prisoners' Dilemma under Hobbes's assumptions than under Hume's.

This assumption of Hume's about preferences applies only to men in *large* societies. Hume is aware that in sufficiently small societies the game may not be a Prisoners' Dilemma, and here he largely anticipates the ideas which form the core of Olson's argument. Hobbes, on the other hand, does not discuss these ideas; but we cannot say that he was unaware of them, for in *Leviathan* he apparently has in mind only large societies (especially the one in which he lived) and accordingly *assumes* in effect that the game is a Prisoners' Dilemma.

There is another important element in Hume's argument which is largely absent from Hobbes's, namely *time*. I have already commented (in Section 6.1) on the fact that, although Hobbes's argument is not entirely static, there is no reference to intertemporal preferences in his assumptions; no account is taken of the discounting of future benefits, which, as we saw in Chapter 3, plays such a crucial role in determining whether voluntary Cooperation will occur in sequences of Prisoners' Dilemma games. Hume's treatment is in this respect more realistic than Hobbes's. Time appears in his assumptions about individual preferences: future payoffs are to be discounted in calculating their present value. This fact plays an important role in his argument, for the discount rate is a principal reason why men do not voluntarily cooperate in observing the laws of justice.

Hume is not so specific in his detailed assumptions and arguments that one can make precise comparisons of his theory with that of Hobbes or with the analysis of the Prisoners' Dilemma supergame given in Chapter 3 and 4. We certainly cannot say, for example, that Hume understood (what is shown in Chapter 3) that Cooperation is rational throughout an N-person Prisoners' Dilemma supergame only if the players adopt conditional strategies of a certain form and a certain inequality relating the discount rate and the payoff functions is satisfied for each player. We cannot even say that the *Treatise* contains an analysis of the Prisoners' Dilemma supergame. Nevertheless, the general outline of Hume's theory is quite clear and we can say that there is an approximate similarity between his ideas and parts of the analysis in Chapter 3. If this comparison is legitimate, then we can say that Hume failed to appreciate that even when the society is so large that the ordinary game is a Prisoners' Dilemma, Cooperation in the supergame may yet be rational if the individual discount rates are not too great.

Despite his more 'dynamic' treatment of the problem, Hume comes to essentially the same conclusion as Hobbes: governments, powerful enough to enforce 'justice' and maintain Peace, are necessary and desirable. The comment made earlier on Hobbes's conclusion applies to Hume also: from their assumptions (including, in Hume's case, the assumption of a 'high' discount rate), one can deduce only that *some* form of coercion is necessary to establish or maintain Peace; one cannot, strictly speaking, conclude that this coercion must take the form of government.

My final comment on Hobbes and Hume, before I turn in the next chapter to consider more fundamental criticisms of their approach, concerns the assumption, which is absolutely essential to their arguments, that 'the greatest, that in any forme of Government can possibly happen to the people in generall, is scarce sensible, in respect of the miseries, and horrible calamities, that accompany a Civill Warre; or that dissolute condition of masterlesse men ...' (*Lev* 141; for an almost identical statement by Hume, see *Tr* 497). In other words, it is assumed that government-enforced Peace is preferred by every individual to the state of War no matter how great are the costs of government.

Now the only kinds of costs which Hobbes and Hume appear to have in mind in this connection are those which are to be merely *subtracted*, so to speak, from the benefits of mutual Cooperation (the resulting utility for the mutual Cooperation outcome being for every individual diminished but still greater than that of the mutual non-Cooperation outcome). Yet a government powerful enough to enforce Cooperation may impose costs of other kinds. In the first place, it may diminish the desirability of the state of Peace *per se* (in addition, that is, to imposing costs merely in order to ensure this outcome). This is because people tend to derive more satisfaction from doing things which are initiated and carried out spontaneously and voluntarily than from doing the same things at the suggestion and command of others, including the government.

Secondly, a government may have cumulative effects on the very conditions which, according to Hobbes and Hume, make government necessary. In particular, it may over a period of time cause a Prisoners' Dilemma to appear where none existed before or cause an already existing Prisoners' Dilemma to become more severe. Dynamical effects of this sort are of a wholly different order from those mentioned earlier, and I believe that the entire approach to the justification of government which has been considered in this chapter is undermined if they are taken seriously. I shall try to take them seriously in the next chapter.

6.3. NOTES

1. References to *Leviathan* (abbreviated *Lev*) are to the pages of the edition by W. G. Pogson Smith (Oxford: The Clarendon Press, 1909).

2. I must thank Brian Barry for helping me to see *Leviathan* in a more 'dynamic' light.

3. Alasdair MacIntyre, *A Short History of Ethics* (London: Routledge and Kegan Paul, 1967), p. 138.

4. H. L. A. Hart, *The Concept of Law* (Oxford: The Clarendon Press, 1961), p. 193.

5. Brian Barry, 'Warrender and His Critics', *Philosophy*, **48**, 117–37 (1968), p. 125.

6. On symmetry, see Chapter 3, note 3.

7. C. B. Macpherson, *The Political Theory of Possessive Individualism: Hobbes to Locke* (Oxford: The Clarendon Press, 1962).

8. The citations of Hume give the page numbers of the Selby-Bigge editions: L. A. Selby-Bigge, (Ed.), *A Treatise of Human Nature* (Oxford: The Clarendon Press, 1888) and *Enquiries Concerning the Understanding and Concerning the Principles of Morals* (Oxford: The Clarendon Press, second edition, 1902). The *Treatise* is abbreviated to *Tr* and *Enquiry* refers to *An Enquiry Concerning the Principles of Morals*.

9. David Lewis, *Convention: A Philosophical Study* (Cambridge, Mass.: Harvard University Press, 1969), p. 42. Lewis later refines this definition by adding the condition that it is 'common knowledge' in *p* that (1), (2) and (3) obtain. He also considers *degrees* of convention. But this 'first, rough definition' will suffice for my purposes.

10. Governments are in fact very active in establishing and modifying conventions and in many cases they make laws of them and punish nonconformists. If they are pure conventions, this is not necessary. For example, driving on the 'right' side of the road is almost a pure convention, and once it is established, there is almost no need for government enforcement: very few individuals will want to drive on the 'wrong' side. Of course, a central coordinating agency may be useful in *establishing* a convention more quickly and less painfully than it would establish itself 'spontaneously'. But this is not an argument in favour of government; for such an agency need have no *power*, and it need only be *ad hoc* and temporary: there is no need, in this connection, for a single agency to take charge of all conventions, and once a convention is established, the agency in question can be disbanded.

CHAPTER 7

Anarchy

'By his entry into any society the individual ... offers up a portion of (his) liberty so that society will vouchsafe him the rest. Anybody who asks for an explanation is usually presented with a further saying: "*The liberty of each human being should have no limits other than that of every other.*" At first glance, this seems utterly fair, does it not? And yet this theory holds the germ of the whole theory of despotism.'[1]

Bakunin, *L'Empire Knouto-Germanique*

'Therefore we can only repeat what we have so often said concerning authority in general: "To avoid a possible evil you have recourse to means which in themselves are a greater evil, and become the source of those same abuses that you wish to remedy ..." '

Kropotkin, *The Conquest of Bread*

The treatment of the problem of voluntary cooperation in the first four chapters and the political theories of Hobbes and Hume as I presented them in Chapter 6 rest solely on assumptions about individuals. These assumptions embody a conception of the individual as being endowed with a *given* and *unchanging* 'human nature'. More specifically, it is assumed that each individual is characterized by a certain combination of egoism and some form of altruism, and it is further assumed that this characterization does not change with time. His preferences are treated as exogenous to what has to be explained (or justified) by the theories in question. They are independent of, and do not change in response to, his social situation. He is an example of what Marx called the 'abstract man'.

This means, in particular, that no account is taken of the effect on individual preferences of the activities of the state or of the activities of the individuals themselves. If the activities of the state may result in changes in individual preferences, then clearly it cannot be deduced from the structure of preferences in the absence of the state that the state is desirable. More generally, if individual preferences change (not necessarily as a result of state activity), the question of the desirability (or 'preferability') of the state becomes much more complex than it is in the static theories we have been considering; and if preferences change as a result of the state itself, then it is not even clear what is *meant* by the desirability of the state.

The effects of the state on individual preferences and the ways in which preferences may change in the absence of the state are the subjects of the main section of this final chapter (Section 7.3). I shall argue there (and in other ways in the first two sections) that the effect of the state is to exacerbate the very conditions which are claimed to provide its justification and for which it is supposed to provide a partial remedy.

I have been speaking here of 'state' rather than 'government', and of 'the activities of the state', as if the state were a single actor. It is time to explain what I mean by 'the state'. This term (as it will be defined shortly) is more appropriate than 'government' in the theories of Hobbes and Hume. In the last chapter, I used the expressions which these two writers themselves use. But when they speak of the 'Sovereign' or 'common power' or 'government' of a society, they refer to something with sufficient control over all the members of the society to be able at least to coerce them to Cooperate in Prisoners' Dilemma situations. Governments, in the sense of the term as we use it now, do not have such control. Rather, they must work *with* or *through* (and sometimes even at the command of) a number of other institutions: police, security, military and para-military forces; a judiciary; a legislative assembly; an 'administrative' service (now extending, as Ralph Miliband notes in *The State in Capitalist Society*, far beyond the traditional bureaucracy to include corporations, central banks, regulatory commissions, and so on); and various units of sub-central government. I shall follow Miliband and call the government, together with these other institutions, 'the state' or 'the state system'.

Some of the components of this system may be relatively independent of each other. The bureaucracy does not in practice simply 'administer'; the military, though it is usually supposed to serve the government, often does not, and indeed may itself effectively rule through the government; the judiciary, though it may be constitutionally independent, cooperates with other elements of the state system, especially the government and the legislature; the work of the government, the assembly and the bureaucracy is modified in its practical application by the judiciary and the police; and so on.

If 'the state' is a complex system of interacting, partially independent components, then expressions like 'the activities of the state' are to be taken as referring to the aggregate of the activities of the components, and the activities of a component are in turn the aggregate of the activities of its individual members. Thus, statements of the kind, 'states build nations', will be shorthand for something like the following: the individual members of the component institutions of the state system act in such a way that the outcome or resultant of their actions is such as to further the building of the nation. (This particular statement is discussed in Section 7.2.)

7.1. INTERNATIONAL INSECURITY

In Hobbes's political theory the Sovereign is instituted to ensure defence against foreign enemies as well as to maintain domestic Peace. In Hume's version of the theory, government is established to keep men to the 'conventions' of property, and the need for external defence plays no part; nevertheless, as I noted earlier, Hume adds that the government, once established, will ensure that armies and navies are maintained. In both cases, then, although more importance is attached to the provision of domestic security, the government is to provide for the defence of the nation.

Now Hobbes believes that, when several governments take steps to 'defend' their respective nations, these nations, in the absence of 'a common power to keep them all in awe', are in a 'state of nature':

> 'But though there had never been any time, wherein particular men were in a condition of warre one against another; yet in all times, Kings, and Persons of Sovereigne authority, because of their Independency, are in continuall jealousies, and in the state and posture of Gladiators; having their weapons pointing, and their eyes fixed upon one another; that is, their Forts, Garrisons, and Guns upon the Frontiers of their Kingdoms; and continuall Spyes upon their neighbours; which is a posture of War' (*Lev* 98).

War, it should be recalled, 'consisteth not in actuall fighting; but in the known disposition thereto during all the time there is no assurance to the contrary' (*Lev* 96). Nevertheless, neither Hobbes nor Hume applies to the international 'state of nature' the analysis which they make of the domestic one. There are, indeed, difficulties in making such an application of their analysis (and even greater difficulties in applying at the international level the criticisms of that analysis which are the subject of the other sections of this chapter). These difficulties arise, in particular, because states are not individual persons and because a state's behaviour *vis-a-vis* other states is not determined solely by the behaviour of the other states (but also, and some would say predominantly, by domestic factors).

Despite these difficulties, certain aspects of international relations have often been treated explicitly in terms of a Prisoners' Dilemma game.[2] In particular, this game has been said to characterize the structure of the choices involved in arms races and disarmament. In such characterizations, the strategies *C* and *D* are, for example, to acquire or not to acquire a certain type of weapons system, to reduce or not to reduce one's armaments, and so on.

If arms races and disarmament are properly described as a Prisoners' Dilemma game, then we can say that states, established at one level (the national level) to rescue people in a Prisoners' Dilemma from the state of War, may cause a Prisoners' Dilemma to emerge at another level (the international level) or exacerbate an already existing one.

However, even if the Prisoners' Dilemma is not a good description of the structure of choices involved in arms races and disarmament, I think it can still be said that defensive preparations on the part of some states tend to result in defensive preparations on the part of others, and that increases in such preparations by some tend to result in increases by others.

It is possible to take the view that when two or more enemy nations are highly but equally armed, actual fighting is less likely to occur than when they are less armed, because the consequences of fighting would probably be more disastrous. But the other possibility (which I happen to find more plausible for any level and type of arms, and which, in any case, is supported by the evidence of the history of most previous arms races in non-nuclear weapons) is that increased military preparations, whether or not they are matched by other nations, are more likely to lead eventually to actual fighting, and therefore tend to increase the insecurity of the individual members of the nation initiating the increase.

7.2. THE DESTRUCTION OF SMALL COMMUNITIES

Hume argues that in large societies life without government is appalling, but that in small societies this need not be the case. Therefore, he says, people in a large society need, and will in fact ˙establish, a government. When the argument is put this way, however, a radically different conclusion suggests itself: that large societies should be (or will be) disaggregated into smaller societies, and the enlargement of societies and the destruction of small ones should be (or will be) resisted. This conclusion does not follow logically from Hume's premises any more than does his own conclusion. Given these premises (or those of Hobbes), the most that we can assert in this connection is that the larger the society, the less likely it is that there will be voluntary Cooperation in the provision of public goods—because, as we have seen, the more numerous the players, the more likely it is that the problem of the provision of public goods will take the form of a Prisoners' Dilemma (but see the last part of Section 2.3) and, if the problem is treated in terms of a Prisoners' Dilemma supergame, then voluntary Cooperation amongst a large number of players is less likely to occur than Cooperation amongst a small number of players (see Section 5.1).

Of course, there are other (and probably more important) reasons why cooperation might occur more readily in small societies without government than in large ones. For example, smallness facilitates (and may even be a necessary condition for) an effective use of the sanctions of public censure and shame. These play an important role in the maintenance of internal Peace and Security (and in the provision of other public goods) in many 'primitive' societies whose members live in small communities without governments, police forces or judiciaries.

That the state should be presented as the saviour of men caught in the Prisoners' Dilemmas of a large society might appear somewhat ironical when we consider the important part that states historically have played in providing the conditions in which societies (and nations in particular) could grow and indeed in systematically *building* large societies and destroying small ones. The state has in this way acted so as to make itself even more 'necessary'.

Now a 'nation' is a species of 'community' in the sense of Carl Friedrich, who defines a community as a 'togetherness of persons who are united by having in common some of their values, interests, ideas (including ideologies), myths, Utopias and their symbols, as well as religion and its rituals ...' with the qualification (in recognition of the impossibility of separating the 'organic' and the 'purposive' aspects of community) that the uniting is 'partly by emotional attachment and partly by subjection to common rules, responding partly to organic need and partly to conscious purpose, expressing what already exists or what is consciously willed.'[3]

It is clear from this definition that 'community' is a matter of degree (or, more precisely, of degrees), the degree to which a set of people is a 'community' (or the 'strength' of the community) depending upon how many values, interests, etc. are shared and with how much agreement, the extent of emotional attachment to each of these, and so on. It also follows from the definition that a man may be a member of several communities, and that a community may *contain* other communities. Thus, a 'nation' (a species of community) may contain several 'national communities' or 'nationalities'.

We can say now that a nation 'grows' in two ways: when its present members become more of a community, and when other people (or peoples) become part of the community. Thus, when several communities increasingly share values, interests, etc. we have a growing nation. The causes of such growth are numerous: migration or expansion of communities into greater geographical proximity with one another; increasing trade between communities; the exposure of the separate communities to common mass communication sources; subjection to a common invader; cooperation for common defence; and so on.

Now part of this growth is due to the state. If the nation over which a state exercises *de jure* control is only a weak community, or hardly a community at all, then the state usually tries to strengthen this national community. It will do this in order to turn its *de jure* control (which might merely be exercised over scattered populations some of whom remain unaware of the state's very existence) into *de facto* control; to facilitate common defence and the waging of War; to extend its tax basis (for various purposes, including its own maintenance and enlargement); to expand domestic markets; and so on.

Systematic state activity of this kind has been especially important in the growth of nations made independent since the War. In some of these countries, a state has begun life, at the moment of independence, without a nation under its control but rather with jurisdiction over a territory inhabited by literally hundreds of separate communities, each of them commanding intense loyalty from its members and most of them having little or nothing to do with each other (and speaking, in the case of Nigeria, for example, hundreds of distinct languages). Thus we read, in numerous accounts of the 'modernization' of new nations (and also of some of the older but still 'developing' nations), of 'the problem of tribalism'. For example, Rupert Emerson, writing on the new nations of Africa in a volume on *Nation-Building*, has this to say: 'At the extremes, tribalism can be dealt with in two fashions—either use of the tribes as the building blocks of the nation or eradication of them by a single national solidarity. It is the latter course which is more generally followed.'[4] And William Foltz, speaking generally of the new nations in his conclusion to this volume, writes: 'The old argument over the priority of state or nation is being resolved by these countries' leaders in favour of first building the state as an instrument to bring about the nation'.

Throughout the world at the present time this process of nation-building is still going on. The states of 'underdeveloped' countries are still unifying their subject peoples; a European nation is being created by a proto-state; and in old and new nations alike, demands for the secession or greater autonomy of subject nationalities, ethnic groups and regions are in most cases being resisted. When it is seen how much of the growth of nations is the work of states, and is therefore the conscious work of man, it is not at all Utopian to propose that this process be reversed.

In promoting this process—in providing a framework in which nations can grow at the expense of smaller communities within the nation, in systematically destroying these smaller communities or hastening their assimilation into the larger nation, and in expanding the nation's territory—the state makes itself even more necessary, according to the theories of Hobbes and Hume. For in the growing nation, voluntary cooperation in the provision of public goods will become far more difficult than it was in the smaller communities. In this way, the state exacerbates the conditions which are claimed to provide its justification and for which it is supposed to be the remedy.

7.3. THE STATE AND THE DECAY OF VOLUNTARY COOPERATION

The arguments for the necessity of the state which I am criticizing in this book are founded on the supposed inability of individuals to cooperate voluntarily to provide themselves with public goods, and especially, in the theories of Hobbes and Hume, with security of person and property. The intervention of the state is necessary, according to these arguments, in order to secure for the people a Pareto-optimal provision of public goods, or at least to ensure that *some* provision is made of the most important public goods.

In this section I argue that the more the state intervenes in such situations, the more 'necessary' (on this view) it becomes, because positive altruism and voluntary cooperative behaviour *atrophy* in the presence of the state and *grow* in its absence. Thus, again, the state exacerbates the conditions which are supposed to make it necessary. We might say that the state is like an addictive drug: the more of it we have, the more we 'need' it and the more we come to 'depend' on it.

Men who live for long under government and its bureaucracy, courts and police, come to rely upon them. They find it easier (and in some cases are legally bound) to use the state for the settlement of their disputes and for the provision of public goods, instead of arranging these things for themselves, even where the disputes, and the publics for which the goods are to be provided, are quite local. In this way, the state *mediates* between individuals; they come to deal with each other through the courts, through the tax collector and the bureaucracies which spend the taxes. In the presence of a strong state, the individual may cease to care for, or even think about, those in his community who need help; he may cease to have any desire to make a direct contribution to the resolution of local problems, whether or not he is affected by them; he may come to feel that his 'responsibility' to society has been discharged as soon as he has paid his taxes (which are taken coercively from him by the state), for these taxes will be used by the state to care for the old, sick and unemployed, to keep his streets clean, to maintain 'order', to provide and maintain schools, libraries, parks, and so on. The state releases the individual from the 'responsibility' or 'need' to cooperate with others directly; it guarantees him a 'secure' environment in which he may safely pursue his private goals, unhampered by all those collective concerns which it is supposed to take care of itself. This is a part of what Marx meant when he wrote (in 'On the Jewish Question') of state-enforced security as 'the assurance of egoism'.

The effects of government on altruism and voluntary cooperation can be seen as part of the general process of the destruction of small societies by the state which was described earlier. The state, as we have seen, in order to expand domestic markets, facilitate common defence, and so on, encourages the weakening of local communities in favour of the national community. In doing so, it relieves individuals of the necessity to cooperate voluntarily amongst themselves on a local basis, making them more dependent upon the state. The result is that altruism and cooperative behaviour gradually decay. The state is thereby strengthened and made more effective in its work of weakening the local community. Kropotkin has described this process in his *Mutual Aid*. All over Europe, in a period of three centuries beginning in the late fifteenth century, states or proto-states 'systematically weeded out' from village and city all the 'mutual-aid institutions', and the result, says Kropotkin, was that

> 'The State alone ... must take care of matters of general interest, while the subjects must represent loose aggregations of individuals, connected by no particular bonds, bound to appeal to the Government each time that they feel a common need. ...
>
> The absorption of all social functions by the State necessarily favoured the development of an unbridled, narrowminded individualism. In proportion as the obligations towards the State grew in numbers the citizens were evidently relieved from their obligations towards each other'.[5]

Under the state, there is no *practice* of cooperation and no growth of a sense of the interdependence on which cooperation depends; there are fewer opportunities for the spontaneous expression of direct altruism and there are therefore fewer altruistic acts to be observed, with the result that there is no growth of the feeling of assurance that others around one are altruistic or at least willing to behave cooperatively—an assurance that one will not be let down if one tries unilaterally to cooperate.

A part of this argument has recently been made by Richard Sennett. Sennett's interest is in reversing the trend towards 'purified' urban and suburban communities through the creation of cities in which people would learn to cope with diversity and 'disorder' through the necessity of having to deal with each other directly rather than relying on the police and courts and bureaucracies. The problem, he says, is 'how to plug people into each others' lives without making everyone feel the same'. This will not be achieved by merely devolving the city government's power onto local groups:

> 'Really decentralized power, so that the individual has to deal with those around him, in a milieu of diversity, involves a change in the essence of communal control, that is, in the refusal to regulate conflict. For example, police control of much civil disorder ought to be sharply curbed; the responsibility for making peace in neighbourhood affairs ought to fall to the people involved. Because men are now so innocent and unskilled in the expression of conflict, they can only view these disorders as spiralling into violence. Until they learn through experience that the handling of conflict is something that cannot be passed on to the police, this polarization and escalation of conflict into violence will be the only end they can frame for themselves'.[6]

In his remarkable study of blood donorship, *The Gift Relationship*, Richard Titmuss has given us an example of how altruism *generates* altruism—of how a man is more likely to be altruistic if he experiences or observes the altruism of others or if he is aware that the community depends (for the provision of some public good) on altruistic acts.[7] The availability of blood for transfusion is of course a public good. In England and Wales, all donations are purely voluntary (with the partial exception of a very small amount collected under pressure from prison inmates). In the United States, only 9% of donations were purely voluntary in 1967 (and the percentage was falling). Of the rest, most are paid for or are given 'contractually' (to replace blood received instead of paying for it, or as a 'premium' in a family blood insurance scheme). As Titmuss recognizes, even the donors he calls 'voluntary' (those who do not receive payment, do not give contractually, and are not threatened directly with tangible sanctions or promised tangible rewards) must have 'some sense of obligation, approval and interest'. Nevertheless, the voluntary donation of blood does seem to approximate as closely as is perhaps possible to the ideal of pure, spontaneous altruism: for it is given impersonally and sometimes with discomfort, without expectation of gratitude, reward or reciprocation (for the recipient is usually not known to the donor), and without imposing an obligation on the recipient or anyone else; and 'there are no personal, predictable penalties for not giving; no socially enforced sanctions of remorse, shame or guilt'.[8]

It is, then, an example of the kind of altruism which Hume specifically declared to be very limited or absent; it is precisely not the 'private benevolence' towards family and friends which he thought was common.

Now, if there is any truth in the general argument about the growth and decay of altruism which was put forward above, we should at least expect that the *growth* of voluntary donations should be greater in a country in which non-voluntary donations are absent than in one where they are present, and even that voluntary donations should *decline* with time in a country where a very large proportion of donors were non-voluntary. This is precisely what has happened in the countries which Titmuss examines. In the developed countries the demand for blood has risen very steeply in recent years, much more steeply than the population. Yet in England and Wales, from 1948 to 1968, supply has kept pace with demand, and there have never been serious shortages. On the other hand, in the United States, in the period 1961–1967 for which figures are available, supply has not kept pace with demand and there have been serious shortages; even more significantly, those blood banks which paid more than half of their suppliers collected an increasing quantity of blood in this period, while the supply to other banks *decreased*. In Japan, where the proportion of blood which is bought and sold has risen since 1951 from zero to the present 98%, shortages are even more severe than in the United States.

These differences, between England and Wales on the one hand and America and Japan on the other, are consistent with the hypothesis that altruism fosters altruism (though of course they do not confirm it). Support (also inconclusive) for this explanation of the growth of blood donations in England comes from some of the responses to a question included in Titmuss's 1967 survey of blood donors in England: 'Could you say why you *first* decided to become a blood donor?'. Many people, it appears, became blood donors as a result of *experiencing* altruism: they or their friends or relatives had received transfusions. For example:

> 'To try and repay in some small way some unknown person whose blood helped me recover from two operations and enable me to be with my family, that's why I bring them along also as they become old enough' (married woman, age 44, three children, farmer's wife). 'Some unknown person gave blood to save my wife's life' (married man, age 43, two children, self-employed windowcleaner).

Some responses hint at an altruism resulting from an appreciation of the *dependence* of the system on altruism and of people's dependence on each other:

> 'You cant get blood from supermarkets and chaine stores. People themselves must come forward, sick people cant get out of bed to ask you for a pint to save thier life so I came forward in hope to help somebody who needs blood' (married woman, aged 23, machine operator).[9]

Peter Singer, in his discussion of Titmuss's book, has drawn attention to some experiments which also support the hypothesis that altruism is encouraged by the observation of altruism.[10] He mentions an experiment in which a car with a flat tyre was parked at the side of the road with a helpless-looking woman standing beside it. Drivers who had just passed a woman in a similar plight but with a man who had stopped to change her wheel for her (this scene having of course been arranged by the experimenters) were significantly more likely to help than those who had not witnessed this altruistic behaviour.[11] Singer himself writes: 'I find it hardest to act with consideration for others when the norm in the circle of people I move in is to act egotistically. When altruism is expected of me, however, I find it much easier to be genuinely altruistic'.

The argument I have made in this section is not of course new. A similar (though not identical) argument is familiar to us from the writings of the classical liberals, and especially of John Stuart Mill. With the partial exception of Kropotkin, the only anarchist writer who makes full and explicit use of something like this argument is William Godwin. (Though Godwin is not wholly an anarchist. His case against government in the *Enquiry Concerning Political Justice* represents in most respects a more extensive and more through-going application of Mill's argument than Mill himself makes.)

For Godwin, government is an evil which is necessary only as long as people behave in the way in which they have come to behave as a result of living for a long time under government. If governments were dissolved, he says 'arguments and addresses' would not at first suffice to persuade people to 'cooperate for the common advantage' and 'some degree of authority and violence would be necessary. But this necessity does not appear to arise out of the nature of man, but out of the institutions by which he has been corrupted.'[12] Later, government would not be necessary at all: there would be a transition to anarchy during which people would learn to cooperate voluntarily (or, at least, to cooperate in order to avoid the disapprobation of neighbours: 'a species of coercion' which would presumably be effective in the *small* 'parishes' of Godwin's ideal social order[13]). The growth of cooperation would in part result from the growth of benevolence. Benevolence is 'a resource which is never exhausted' but becomes stronger the more it is exercised; and if there is no opportunity for its exercise, it decays. The idea permeates much of Godwin's *Enquiry*; we see it, for example, in his criticism of punishment by imprisonment:

> 'Shall we be most effectually formed to justice, benevolence and prudence in our intercourse with each other, in a state of solitude? Will not our selfish and unsocial dispositions be perpetually increased? What temptation has he to think of benevolence or justice, who has no opportunity to exercise it'?[14]

At the same time as Godwin wrote the *Enquiry Concerning Political Justice*, Wilhelm von Humboldt was composing *The Limits of State Action*, a book which contains many of the ideas to be found in the *Enquiry*, especially those which are of interest here.[15] Humboldt was certainly not an anarchist; but he did argue that the scope of state activity should be strictly limited to the provision of 'mutual security and protection against foreign enemies', and his case against the further interference of the state rested on arguments similar to Godwin's and more fundamentally on the axiom (on which Mill's *On Liberty* was also to be based) that '… the chief point to be kept in view by the State is the development of the powers of its citizens in their full individuality.'[16]

By *security*, Humboldt meant 'the assurance of legal freedom': freedom, that is, to enjoy one's legal rights of person and property undisturbed by the encroachments of others.[17] The state must therefore investigate and settle disputes about such encroachments and punish transgressions of its laws, since these threaten security.[18] Humboldt never considers the possibility that disputes could be settled and crimes punished directly by the people themselves without the help of the state. Indeed, his only argument in support of the thesis that security must be provided by the state is that 'it is a condition which man is wholly unable to realize by his own individual efforts.'[19] Yet, if this is true of security, why is it not also true of other public goods (and perhaps some other goods too)? A case can of course be made for the special status of security. One can argue, with Hobbes, that it is fundamental, being a prerequisite to the attainment of other goods. Humboldt does in fact take this line: 'Now, without security', he writes, 'it is impossible for man either to develop his powers, or to enjoy the fruits of so doing.'[20] However, in the first place, it still remains to be shown that security cannot be realized without the help of the state, and secondly, it can be argued that if the state *is* required to provide security, then for the same reasons it will be required to provide other public goods; in other words, even when they enjoy state-enforced security, citizens will not necessarily be able to obtain other things which they want without the further intervention of the state, which Humboldt expressly forbids.

Nevertheless, the arguments which Godwin uses—and Humboldt refrains from using—against *any* sort of state intervention are eloquently set out by Humboldt in his case against the intervention of the state in matters not involving security or defence. Here, in particular, is Humboldt on the effects of the state on altruism and voluntary cooperation:

'As each individual abandons himself to the solicitous aid of the State, so, and still more, he abandons to it the fate of his fellow-citizens. This weakens sympathy and renders mutual assistance inactive: or, at least, the reciprocal interchange of services and benefits will be most likely to flourish at its liveliest, where the feeling is most acute that such assistance is the only thing to rely upon …'[21]

In Mill's *On Liberty* we do not encounter this argument until, at the end of the essay, he considers cases in which the objections to government interference do not turn upon 'the principle of liberty'. These include cases, he says, in which individuals should be left to act by themselves, without the help of the state, as a means to their own development and of '… accustoming them to the comprehension of their joint interests, the management of joint concerns—habituating them to act from public or semi-public motives, and guide their conduct by aims which unite instead of isolating them.'[22] The argument appears also in the *Principles of Political Economy*, as 'one of the strongest of the reasons against the extension of government agency'.[23] Nevertheless, Mill gives to state interference a considerably wider scope than does Humboldt. In addition to the maintenance of security,[24] he allows a number of other important exceptions to his general rule of non-interference.[25]

One of these exceptions is of peculiar interest here. The exception essentially concerns 'free-rider' situations. Mill gives the example of collective action by workers to reduce their working hours. In such situations, he says, no individual will find it in his interest to cooperate voluntarily, and the more numerous are those others who cooperate the more will he gain by not cooperating; so the assistance of the state is required to 'afford to every individual a guarantee that his competitors will pursue the same course, without which he cannot safely adopt it himself'.[26] Penal laws, he goes on to say, are necessary for just this reason: 'because even an unanimous opinion that a certain line of conduct is for the general interest, does not always make it people's individual interest to adhere to that line of conduct.' This is all Mill has to say on this subject. He is merely providing an argument for an *exception* to the general rule of non-interference. He does not appear to recognize that the same argument would justify state interference in a vast class of situations. Nor, at the same time, does he appear to recognize that his general case against the interference of the state could be applied in all of these situations, including all aspects of the provision of peace and security.

7.4. HUMAN NATURE

In the last chapter, I criticized Hobbes for drawing the conclusion that government is the *only* means whereby men may be coerced to Cooperate and, more fundamentally, for his relatively static treatment of the problem. I went on to note that Hume's political theory, while it also suffers from the first of these failings, to some extent remedies the second: but although his approach is more dynamical, Hume concurs with Hobbes in concluding that Cooperation will not occur voluntarily, neglecting the possibility that the voluntary Cooperation of all individuals may occur in a dynamic game because the adoption of a conditionally Cooperative strategy is rational under certain conditions for each individual. Finally, I questioned the assumption of both Hobbes and Hume that a government-enforced state of Peace is preferred by every individual to the state of War, and in this connection I drew particular attention to the way in which government might not only impose costs on the individual but *in addition* diminish the satisfaction he derives from being in the state of Peace.

This last point refers only to a *static* effect of government—to an effect which operates in the same way at each point in time without causing cumulative changes.

Even when time is explicitly brought into the analysis in the way this is done in Hume's political theory and in the treatment of Chapter 3, the resulting formulation is static in a further sense, namely, that 'human nature' is taken as given and assumed to be constant. More precisely, egoism or some combination of egoism and altruism is assumed once and for all to characterize each individual; it undergoes no modification at any stage during the 'game', no matter how the players have previously behaved; and it remains unaltered upon the introduction of government and by the continued presence of government.

This assumption can be modified, and a further dynamic element injected, by allowing 'human nature' (the combination of egoism and altruism) to change over time, while still assuming that at each point of time an individual can be characterized by a utility function embodying some combination of egoism and altruism. In particular, it could now be assumed that the egoism–altruism combination changes in a way which depends on the history of the players' choices in previous games and on whether these choices were made voluntarily or as a result of the presence of state sanctions.

Modification of this sort would already take us outside the 'abstract man' framework which I mentioned at the start of this chapter, for it introduces an individual whose 'human nature' is no longer given and fixed but is partly determined by his changing social situation (including the effects on him of the state) and is something which to some extent he himself creates.

The effects of the state on individual preferences were the subject of the preceding section. The arguments put forward there were not rigorously demonstrated, and no conclusive evidence was given in their support (I doubt if this is possible). But even if it is conceded only that they *may* be true, it follows that it is not at all clear what can be assumed about 'human nature' at any point in time—what preferences are like in the absence of the state, and so on. The assumptions made by Hobbes and Hume were supposed to characterize human behaviour in the absence of the state; but perhaps they more accurately describe what human behaviour would be like immediately after the state has been removed from a society *whose members had for a long time lived under states.* This is surely the mental experiment which Hobbes and Hume were performing.

It has often been argued that the choice of the scope and form of social institutions (such as the state) must be based on 'pessimistic' assumptions, so that they will be 'robust' against the worst possible conditions (such as a society of egoistic or even negatively altruistic individuals) in which they might be required to operate. It is assumed in such arguments that if an institution can 'work' (or work better, in some sense, than the alternatives) when everyone is, for example, egoistic, then it will certainly do the same when some or all people are positively altruistic. But if the institutions themselves affect individual preferences—affect the content of the assumptions from which their relative desirability has been deduced—then this approach is inappropriate and may be dangerously misleading. This is not to say that the assumption of pure egoism is not an appropriate one to make in certain kinds of theories; but it will be appropriate, I think, only in theories which are in the first place explanatory and in the second place narrowly circumscribed in the scope of their application in time, place and subject. For example, if one wishes to explain the process of bargaining between representatives of trade unions and management who are trying to settle a wage dispute in contemporary Britain, then a theory based on the assumption that each side acts egoistically (for example, maximizes some discounted function of its own future income or profits) will probably do better than one based on the assumption that each side is positively altruistic.

The Hobbesian case for the state rests on assumptions about individual preferences; and although Hobbes spoke in *Leviathan* of many different characteristics of individuals, the core of his political theory makes essential use of only one of these, namely the individual's egoism or some combination of egoism and negative altruism. The same is true of Hume's political theory, except that the negative altruism of Hobbes is replaced by a severely limited positive altruism. I have suggested in this chapter that these assumptions tend to be *self-fulfilling*, in the sense that, if they were not true before the introduction of the state, which they are said to make necessary, they would in time become true as a result of the state's activity, or, if individuals already lacked sufficient positive altruism to make the state unnecessary, they would 'learn', while they lived under the care of the state, to possess even less of it. However, the balance of egoism and altruism in each individual is not the only thing which might be affected by the activity of the state. If it is allowed that other things, and in particular the *relations* between individuals (other than the narrow kind of altruism considered in this book), might be modified by the state, then these too must be incorporated into any evaluation of the desirability of the state. Now it seems to me that the assumption that they can be ignored—the assumption that the individual is characterized only by a combination of egoism and altruism—is itself to some extent self-fulfilling; for the state's activity may tend over time to have the result that the individual himself thinks more and more in these terms: thinks, that is, in terms of his interests *vis-à-vis* the interests of others; and even thinks of himself, as he becomes more isolated from others, as *unrelated* to them (except insofar as he must think in his isolation of their interests in relation to his own).

If we pursue this line of thought, we find that we must question not merely the assumption of a limited amount of positive altruism, not merely the assumption that this is the only characteristic of individuals which must be taken account of, and not merely the assumption that this characteristic is static, but even more fundamentally we must question again the use, in theories of this kind, of the conception of the 'abstract man' according to which human nature is taken as a *given* quality or set of qualities inherent in each individual *in terms of which* social phenomena (including, for example, the origin and growth of the state) are to be explained and the desirability of any social institution (such as the state) is to be evaluated.

This is not to say that such an approach must be rejected out of hand. I have suggested already that it may be appropriate in the development of explanatory theories of social phenomena which are narrowly confined in subject, time and place; but theories which are supposed to provide a justification for the state are clearly not of this kind. To these theories, such a conception of 'human nature' is inappropriate.

7.5. NOTES

1. Arthur Lehning, (Ed.), *Michael Bakunin: Selected Writings* (in *Writings of the Left*, Ralph Miliband, (Ed.), London: Jonathan Cape, 1973; New York: Grove Press, 1973).

2. For an introduction, see Anatol Rapoport, *Strategy and Conscience* (New York: Harper and Row, 1964), or Glenn H. Snyder, '"Prisoner's Dilemma" and "Chicken" Models in International Politics', *International Studies Quarterly*, **15**, 66–103 (1971).

3. Carl J. Friedrich, *Man and His Government* (New York: McGraw-Hill, 1963), p. 144.

4. In Karl W. Deutsch and William J. Foltz, (Eds.), *Nation-Building* (New York: Ahterton Press, 1963).

5. Peter Kropotkin, *Mutual Aid: A Factor of Evolution* (London: Allen Lane The Penguin Press, 1972; reprinted from the edition of 1914), p. 197.

6. Richard Sennett, *The Uses of Disorder: Personal Identity and City Life* (London: Allen Lane The Penguin Press, New York: Alfred A. Knopf, 1971). This quotation is from the Pelican edition (Harmondsworth, Middlesex: Penguin Books, 1973), pp. 132–3, by courtesy of Penguin Books Ltd and Alfred A. Knopf Inc.

7. Richard M. Titmuss, *The Gift Relationship: From Human Blood to Social Policy* (London: George Allen and Unwin, New York: Random House, 1970). References here are to the Pelican edition (Harmondsworth, Middlesex: Penguin Books, 1973), quoted by courtesy of George Allen & Unwin Ltd and Pantheon Books, a Division of Random House, Inc.

8. *The Gift Relationship*, pp. 84–5.

9. *The Gift Relationship*, pp. 256–8.

10. Peter Singer, 'Altruism and Commerce: A defense of Titmuss against Arrow', *Philosophy and Public Affairs*, **2**, 312–20 (1973).

11. This experiment is reported in J. H. Bryant and M. A. Test, 'Models and Helping: Naturalistic Studies in Aiding Behavior', *Journal of Personality and Social Psychology*, **6**, 400–7 (1967). The best source for reports of experiments of this kind is J. Macaulay and L. Berkowitz, (Eds.), *Altruism and Helping Behavior* (New York: Academic Press, 1970), especially the chapters of the first part, 'Situational Determinants of Helping'. Some of the experiments are also surveyed in D. L. Krebs, 'Altruism—an Examination of the Concept and a Review of the Literature', *Psychological Bulletin*, **73**, 258–302 (1970), and in the chapter on altruism in Derek Wright, *The Psychology of Moral Behavior* (Harmondsworth, Middlesex: Penguin Books, 1971).

12. William Godwin, *Enquiry Concerning Political Justice* (abridged and edited by K. Codell Carter, Oxford: the Clarendon Press, 1971; first published in 1793), p. 221.

13. For Godwin on 'size', see especially pp. 249 and 216 of the *Enquiry*.

14. *Enquiry*, p. 271.

15. An English translation of *The Limits of State Action* did not appear until 1854, five years before the publication of Mill's *On Liberty*. I have used here the edition of J. W. Burrow (Cambridge: The University Press, 1969).

144

16. *The Limits*, p. 127.

17. *The Limits*, p. 83.

18. *The Limits*, Chapters XII and XIII.

19. *The Limits*, p. 43.

20. *The Limits*, p. 43.

21. *The Limits*, p. 26.

22. *On Liberty* (Everyman edition, London: Dent, 1962), p. 164.

23. *Principles of Political Economy* (Vols. II and III of *Collected Works*. Toronto: University of Toronto Press, London: Routledge and Kegan Paul, 1965), Book v, Chapter XI, Section 6.

24. In support of the necessity of government to the maintenance of security, Mill contents himself, as Humboldt does, with pointing out that 'Insecurity of person and property, is as much to say, uncertainty of the connection between all human sacrifice, and the attainment of the ends for the sake of which they are undergone'. (*Principles*, Book V, Chapter VIII, Section 1. See also the final paragraph of the *Principles*.) However, later, as we shall see, in treating of *other* exceptions to the rule of non-interference, Mill mentions (without reference to the general problem of security) that penal laws are necessary for 'free-rider' reasons.

25. *Principles*, Book V, Chapter XI.

26. *Principles*, Book V, Chapter XI, Section 12.

Bibliography

Barry, Brian, 'Warrender and His Critics', *Philosophy*, **48**, 117–37 (1968).
Barry, Brian, *Sociologists, Economists and Democracy* (London: Collier-Macmillan, 1970).
Barry, Brian, *The Liberal Theory of Justice* (Oxford: The Clarendon Press, 1973).
Baumol, William J., *Welfare Economics and the Theory of the State*, second edition (London: G. Bell, 1965).
Bookchin, Murray, *Post-Scarcity Anarchism* (Berkeley, Calif.: The Ramparts Press, 1971).
Bray, Jeremy, *The Politics of the Environment* (Fabian Tract no. 412, London, 1972).
Bryant J. H. and M. A. Test, 'Models and Helping: Naturalistic Studies in Aiding Behavior', *Journal of Personality and Social Pscychology*, **6**, 400–7 (1967).
Buchanan, James M., 'An Economic Theory of Clubs', *Economica*, N.S., **32**, 1–14 (1965).
Buchanan, James M., 'Cooperation and Conflict in Public–Goods Interaction', *Western Economic Journal*, **5**, 109–21 (1967).
Buchanan, James M., *The Demand and Supply of Public Goods* (Chicago: Rand McNally, 1968).
Buchanan, James M. and Wm. Craig Stubblebine, 'Externality', *Economica*, N.S., **29**, 371–84 (1962).
Chamberlin, John, 'Provision of Collective Goods as a Function of Group Size', *American Political Science Review*, **68**, 707–16 (1974).
Christy, Frances T. and Anthony Scott, *The Common Wealth in Ocean Fisheries* (Baltimore: Johns Hopkins Press, 1965).
Clark, Colin, 'The Economics of Overexploitation', *Science*, **181**, 630–4, (August 17, 1973).
Crosland, Anthony, *A Social Democratic Britain* (Fabian Tract no. 404, London, 1971).
Deutsch, Karl W. and William J. Foltz (Eds.), *Nation-Building* (New York: Atherton Press, 1963).
Ecologist (edition of), *A Blueprint for Survival* (Harmondsworth, Middlesex: Penguin Books, 1972). Originally published as Vol. 2, No. 1 of *The Ecologist*, 1972.
Ehrlich, Paul R. and Anne H. Ehrlich, *Population, Resources, Environment*, second edition (San Francisco: W. H. Freeman, 1972).
Emshoff, James R., 'A Computer Simulation Model of the Prisoner's Dilemma', *Behavioral Science*, **15**, 304–17 (1970).
Friedman, James W., 'A Non-cooperative Equilibrium for Supergames', *The Review of Economic Studies*, **38**, 1–12 (1971).
Friedrich, Carl J., *Man and His Government* (New York: McGraw-Hill, 1963).

Gallo, P. S., Jr., 'Asymmetry of Payoff Structure and Cooperative Behavior in the Prisoner's Dilemma Game', *Journal of Conflict Resolution*, **17**, 321–33 (1973).

Godwin, William, *Enquiry Concerning Political Justice*, abridged and edited by K. Codell Carter (Oxford: The Clarendon Press, 1971).

Hamburger, Henry, '*N*-Person Prisoner's Dilemma', *Journal of Mathematical Sociology*, **3**, 27–48 (1973).

Hardin, Garrett, 'The Tragedy of the Commons', *Science*, **162**, 1243–8 (1968).

Hardin, Russell, 'Collective Action as an Agreeable *n*-Prisoners' Dilemma', *Behavioral Science*, **16**, 472–81 (1971).

Harris, Richard J., 'Note on "Optimal Policies for the Prisoner's Dilemma"', *Psychological Review*, **76**, 363–75 (1969).

Hart, H. L. A., *The Concept of Law* (Oxford: The Clarendon Press, 1961).

Head, J. G., 'Public Goods and Public Policy', *Public Finance*, **17**, 197–219 (1962).

Heilbroner, Robert L., 'The Human Prospect', *The New York Review of Books*, January 24, 1974.

Hobbes, Thomas, *Leviathan*, W.G. Pogson Smith (Ed.) (Oxford: The Clarendon Press, 1909).

Howard, Nigel, *Paradoxes of Rationality: Theory of Metagames and Political Behavior* (Cambridge, Mass.: The M.I.T. Press, 1971).

Humboldt, Wilhelm von, *The Limits of State Action*, J.W. Burrow (Ed.) (Cambridge: The University Press, 1969).

Hume, David, *A Treatise of Human Nature*, L.A. Selby-Bigge (Ed.) (Oxford: The Clarendon Press, 1888).

Hume, David, *Enquiries Concerning the Understanding and Concerning the Principles of Morals*, L.A. Selby-Bigge (Ed.) (Oxford: The Clarendon Press, second edition, 1902).

Kramer, Gerald H. and Joseph Hertzberg, 'Formal Theory', in volume 7 of *The Handbook of Political Science*, F. Greenstein and N. Polsby (Eds.) (Reading, Mass.: Addison-Wesley, 1975).

Krebs, D.L., 'Altruism—an Examination of the Concept and a Review of the Literature', *Psychological Bulletin*, **73**, 258–302 (1970).

Kropotkin, Peter, *The Conquest of Bread* (London: Allen Lane The Penguin Press, 1972; reprinted from the edition of 1913).

Kropotkin, Peter, *Mutual Aid* (London: Allen Lane The Penguin Press, 1972; reprinted from the edition of 1914).

Lehning, Arthur (Ed.), *Michael Bakunin: Selected Writings* (in *Writings of the Left*, Ralph Miliband (Ed.), London: Jonathan Cape, 1973; New York: Grove Press, 1973).

Lewis, David, *Convention: A Philosophical Study* (Cambridge, Mass.: Harvard University Press, 1969).

Litwak, James M. and Wallace E. Oates, 'Group Size and the Output of Public Goods: Theory and an Application to State–Local Finance in the United States', *Public Affairs*, **25**, 42–58 (1970).

Luce, R. Duncan and Howard Raiffa, *Games and Decisions* (New York: John Wiley, 1957).

Macaulay, J. and L. Berkowitz (Eds.), *Altruism and Helping Behavior* (New York: Academic Press, 1970).

MacIntyre, Alisdair, *A Short History of Ethics* (London: Routledge and Kegan Paul, 1967).

Macpherson, C. B., *The Political Theory of Possessive Individualism: Hobbes to Locke* (Oxford: The Clarendon Press, 1962).

Mill, John Stuart, *On Liberty* (Everyman edition, London: Dent, 1962).

Mill, John Stuart, *Principles of Political Economy* (vols. II and III of *Collective Works*. Toronto: University of Toronto Press; London: Routledge and Kegan Paul, 1965).

Milleron, Jean-Claude, 'Theory of Value with Public Goods: A Survey Article', *Journal of Economic Theory*, **5**, 419–77 (1972).

Mishan, E. J., 'The Relationship between Joint Products, Collective Goods, and External Effects', *Journal of Political Economy*, **77**, 329–48 (1965).

Nicholson, Michael, *Oligopoly and Conflict* (Liverpool: Liverpool University Press, 1972).

Olson, Mancur, *The Logic of Collective Action* (Cambridge, Mass.: Harvard University Press, 1965).

Ophuls, William, 'Leviathan or Oblivion?', in Herman E. Daly (Ed.), *Toward a Steady-State Economy* (San Francisco: W. H. Freeman, 1973).

Rapoport, Amnon, 'Optimal Policies for the Prisoner's Dilemma', *Psychological Review*, **74**, 136–48 (1967).

Rapoport, Anatol, *Strategy and Conscience* (New York: Harper and Row, 1964).

Rapoport, Anatol, 'Escape from Paradox', *Scientific American*, 50–6, July 1967.

Rapoport, Anatol and Albert C. Chammah, *Prisoner's Dilemma* (Ann Arbor: The University of Michigan Press, 1965).

Samuelson, Paul A., 'The Pure Theory of Public Expenditure', *Review of Economics and Statistics*, **36**, 387–9 (1954).

Samuelson, Paul A., 'Diagrammatic Exposition of a Theory of Public Expenditure', *Review of Economics and Statistics*, **37**, 350–6, (1955).

Samuelson, Paul A., 'Pure Theory of Public Expenditure and Taxation', in J. Margolis and H. Guitton (Eds.), *Public Economics* (London: Macmillan, 1969).

Schelling, Thomas C., 'Game Theory and the Study of Ethical Systems', *Journal of Conflict Resolution*, **12**, 34–44 (1968).

Schelling, Thomas C., 'Hockey Helmets, Concealed Weapons, and Daylight Saving: A Study of Binary Choices with Externalities', *Journal of Conflict Resolution*, **17**, 381–428 (1973).

Sennett, Richard, *The Uses of Disorder: Personal Identity and City Life* (London: Allen Lane The Penguin Press, 1971; New York: Alfred A. Knopf, 1970; Harmondsworth, Middlesex: Penguin Books, 1973).

Shubik, Martin, *Strategy and Market Structure: Competition, Oligopoly, and the Theory of Games* (New York, Wiley, 1959).

Shubik, Martin, 'Game Theory, Behavior, and the Paradox of the Prisoner's Dilemma: Three Solutions', *Journal of Conflict Resolution*, **14**, 181–93 (1970).

Shubik, Martin, 'Games of Status', *Behavioral Science*, **16**, 117–29 (1971).

Singer, Peter, 'Altruism and Commerce: A Defence of Titmuss against Arrow', *Philosophy and Public Affairs*, **2**, 312–20 (1973).

Snyder, Glenn H., '"Prisoner's Dilemma" and "Chicken" Models in International Politics', *International Studies Quarterly*, **15**, 66–103 (1971).

Titmuss, Richard M., *The Gift Relationship: From Human Blood to Social Policy* (London: George Allen and Unwin; New York: Random House, 1970; Harmondsworth, Middlesex: Penguin Books, 1973).

Valavanis, Stefan, 'The Resolution of Conflict when Utilities Interact', *Journal of Conflict Resolution*, **2**, 156–69 (1958).

Wright, Derek, *The Psychology of Moral Behaviour* (Harmondsworth, Middlesex: Penguin Books, 1971).

Index